Dazzling Knits

Dazzling

Martingale®
& COMPANY

Building Blocks to Creative Knitting

KNITS

Patricia Werner

Dazzling Knits: Building Blocks to Creative Knitting
© 2004 by Patricia Werner

Martingale®
& C O M P A N Y

Martingale & Company
20205 144th Avenue NE
Woodinville, WA 98072-8478 USA
www.martingale-pub.com

Credits

President . . . . Nancy J. Martin

CEO . . . . Daniel J. Martin

Publisher . . . . Jane Hamada

Editorial Director . . . . Mary V. Green

Managing Editor . . . . Tina Cook

Technical Editor . . . . Ursula Reikes

Copy Editor . . . . Liz McGehee

Design Director . . . . Stan Green

Illustrator . . . . Robin Strobel

Cover and Text Designer . . . . . . Stan Green

Photographer . . . . John Hamel

Photographed in Corrales, New Mexico

Mission Statement

Dedicated to providing quality products
and service to inspire creativity.

The information in this book is presented in good faith, but no warranty is given nor results guaranteed. Since Martingale & Company has no control over choice of materials or procedures, the company assumes no responsibility for the use of this information.

Printed in China
09 08 07 06 05 04   8 7 6 5 4 3 2 1

Library of Congress Cataloging-in-Publication Data

Werner, Patricia.
   Dazzling knits : building blocks to creative knitting / Patricia Werner.
      p. cm.
   ISBN 1-56477-522-4
   1. Knitting—Patterns. I. Title.
   TT825.W46 2004
   746.43'2—dc22

                                        2003027118

Dedication

To my extraordinarily talented students, whose persistence encouraged me to dip my knitting needles into the profound waters of publishing. You have all inspired, guided, and nurtured me.

Acknowledgments

This book would not have been possible without Mark Werner—my rock, my spiritual center, and my greatest teacher; the love and encouragement of my family, especially my incredibly supportive daughter, Monica Cronin; Horst Schulz for truly inspiring workshops; Dana Asbury, my compass, for reading the manuscript and providing invaluable insights; Paula "Rah-Rah" Fowler, who cheered me on every day; Molly Geissman, my knitting muse; the integrity of the entire Martingale staff, including Ursula Reikes, my technical editor, for invaluable guidance; Tina Cook, managing editor, for encouragement; Stan Green, design director, for honoring my vision and making this book sing; John Hamel for exquisite photography and an unmatched aesthetic; Robin Strobel, illustrator, for superb schematics; Rachel Brown, Weaving Southwest, for reproduction of the Autumn in Taos Coat; Diane Bellis and Beverly Clark, Needle's Eye, for reproduction of the Ojo de Dios Vest and support of my classes; the following people who generously shared yarn: Jeannie Duncan for Fiesta Yarns; Sion Elalouf, Knitting Fever Inc., and Mr. Eisaku Noro for the gift of Noro yarns; Patti Subik, Great Adirondack Yarn; Kirstin Muench, Muench Yarns; Till Lindemann, whose poetry and music sustained and nourished me; Jennifer Gear, Cogent Public Relations Inc. and Rowenta Inc. for the Steam Generator; Jill Boland for your friendship and use of your home for photos; Gary Adams for use of your historic hacienda for photos; and Irene and Bill York, The Knitting Basket, for making Herr Schulz's workshops possible. My profound gratitude to you all.

Contents

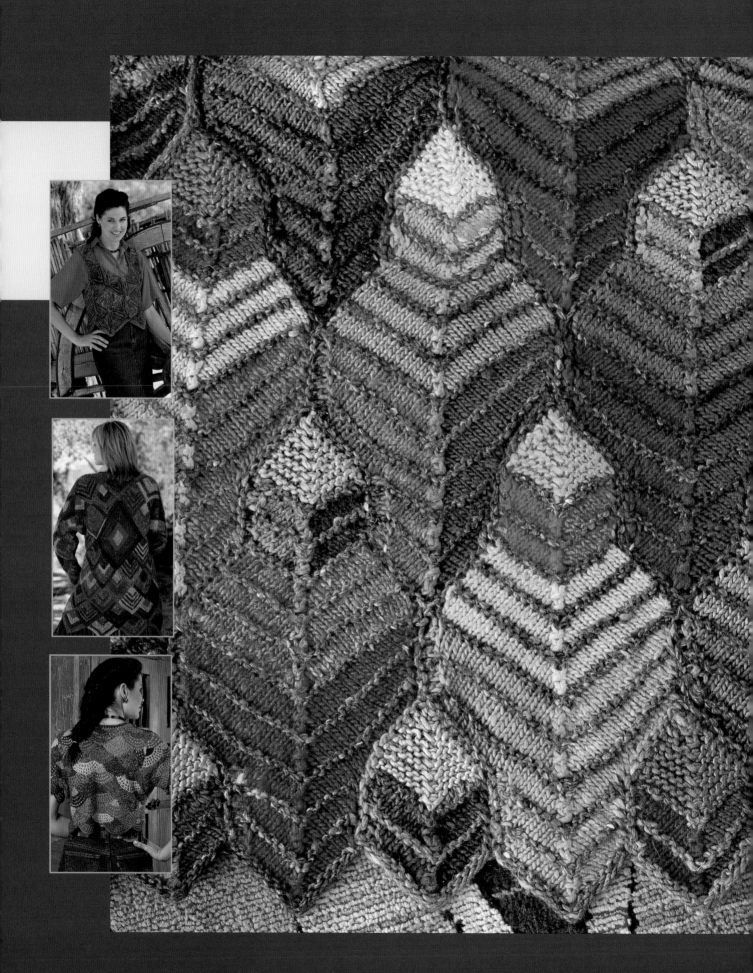

No Limits, No Boundaries Knitting

I truly believe there is nothing new in the universe, simply old ideas in new places and forms. However, I do feel that Horst Schulz—renowned knitter and knitwear designer from Germany—has totally reinvented the concept of modular knitting, elevating it to a glorious new and colorful level. In my opinion, the knitting world owes him a debt of gratitude for his brilliant insights that transformed a previously mundane knitting technique into a sculptural art form.

Knitting with mitered modules opens up an unlimited world of design potential and variations. Once you have learned the basic modules, you can design and knit imaginative garments and distinctive home-decor items. Your designs will incorporate what appear to be very complex shapes and color variations, but you will know how simple it is to achieve traffic-stopping designs. The true beauty of this concept lies in its simplicity. In fact, using my techniques, you have only a few stitches on your needle at a time and rarely more than one color. The modules are knit, not sewn together.

My approach is so intuitive that after knitting only a few modules, most knitters seldom need to refer to the instructions again, freeing them to play with color and design. Modular knitting also eliminates most seams, so you spend more time knitting than sewing elements together. You will learn to "design as you knit" by adding length, width, or shaping as you build your creation, one module at a time.

Since few books on the topic of modular knitting include patterns for knitting the garments, I wanted to produce a book that would fill this void. Seasoned knitters are always looking for stimulating new techniques while those new to knitting are seeking simple yet exciting new methods. I hope this book offers all of you an inspirational journey to creative, colorful knitting without the challenges of intarsia or Fair Isle. With this wonderful method, even a beginner can knit a stunning Kaffe Fassett–type design without the challenge of changing colors multiple times in a single row.

Modular knitting provides instant gratification. You will never again be concerned about having enough yarn, the correct weight, or the right dye lot. At last you can shop for yarn any place in the world, buying only one skein of this or that yarn with no particular project in mind. With my technique, you know you will be able to use it in a future project.

This method of knitting asks you to step beyond your usual habits and comfort zone. It encourages you to exchange familiar habits for a more creative and intuitive approach to knitting. In return, it allows your artistic spirit to soar. Many of my vests can be completed over a long weekend, even by a beginner. My students say they never knew how much fun and totally unrestricted knitting could be. Many vow they will never return to standard knitting again. In addition, they find these styles flattering to any silhouette.

I don't want to teach you to knit and purl. I want to encourage you to trust yourself to design as you knit. I want to inspire you to liberate your creativity by knitting in new directions at every turn, changing your mind and your yarn at a whim without suffering any adverse consequences. I want to awaken in you a new way of seeing.

I want to teach you to take chances with yarn and color and allow your love of knitting to flourish. I encourage you to learn the basics in this book so that you can break through knitting "laws" and discover your own genius. I would much prefer that you

produce a garment that represents your own aesthetic than to know your stitch count is correct. Focus on the end product, and the techniques and methods will take care of themselves.

For me, knitting is an art form not to be approached with scientific or mathematical formulas. You are painting with yarn and sculpting with knitting needles. I hope you will not be bound by preconceived notions, but rather guided by intuition and passion. I encourage you to enter the unknown with joy and confidence. There are no mistakes, only learning opportunities.

So quiet the inner critic. Perfectionism is the voice of the inner oppressor, the enemy of your spirit. It will keep you trapped and inhibit your creativity. The intrinsic beauty of something created by hand lies in its lack of perfection. Perfection is static and inhibits the enchantment of your work of art.

Recently a student told me that knitting was like yoga for her. She had been experiencing many unsettling life changes and found herself immersing deeper into her rhythmic, meditative knitting. It had become a form of contemplative introspection and silent unfolding. I have long understood the comfort and ritual associated with knitting. It has power to revitalize and enrich our spirits and is a vehicle that propels us along our path to personal enlightenment.

Knitting is a powerful art form that can alter consciousness and synthesize what is dearest. There is transformative healing power in knitting. So what are you waiting for? Release your ambitions. Every child is beautiful. Every child is pure. You are a child. Come out and play.

You've Got to Be *Completely* Out of Your Mind to Work with COLOR!

I am very passionate about color and teach my students to approach color fearlessly. Objective reason plays no role in my emotional response to the colors I choose. Nor would I ever assume to guide you in your selection of colors that attract you. Each of us brings with us a diverse view of our world, and we cannot filter our desires through someone else's vision. We want our creations to be an honest representation of our own artistic vision. I encourage you to express this in your knitting and suggest that you refuse to compromise your color choices in deference to the opinion of others. Otherwise, your work will be anemic and devoid of your wonderful personality and color palette.

Color is the language of our feelings—a language that speaks to different people in different ways. Color possesses enormous emotional power and influences most of the decisions we make. Colors have the ability to lift our spirits, make us hungry, agitate, or depress us. So it is very important to tune into those colors that resonate with you and provide you, not others, emotional satisfaction.

If you want to work successfully with color, you must first get completely out of the conscious portion of your mind that is analytical and logical and dive into the ocean of your emotions, instincts, creative spirit, psyche, and soul. Most of our storehouse of genuine knowledge exists at a subconscious level. The subconscious mind works on many levels and can evaluate millions of bits of information simultaneously. The conscious mind can process only one thought at a time. It is exceedingly slow compared to the near instantaneous analysis of information that occurs subconsciously.

Consider driving, running, walking: If we had to stop to think about every element of every movement we make, which neuron to fire, or which muscle to flex before we took even one step, we'd fall down!

You can't be "thinking" about what you are doing. The subconscious mind will automatically make the right decisions. It is immensely rich and intuitively wise compared to our conscious mind.

Intuition and feelings are the repertoire of the subconscious. You feel before you think. Feelings occur before you realize why you react in a particular way. Color is similar to music in this respect. They both speak directly to your soul.

Our feelings and intuition make each of us uniquely different. They are derived from the totality of all our life experiences and the genetic predisposition of our species. Trust your intuition and first impressions. They are hard wired in your psyche. On the other hand, our conscious, analytical, logical mind is a product of training and education. It consists of what others have told us is right and wrong. Logic is just conformity in a nice suit. It is the enemy of creativity.

Your color palette is unique to you. It projects your personality. You will know when it is authentic for you. Trust your intuition, for it is the original, independent source of all knowledge. There are many paths to the unconscious; however, my favorite is to go for simplicity. Here are a few ways of responding to colors before you intellectualize them: Remember, there are no wrong decisions as long as they come from your true feelings. Have no expectations, no preconceived notions, and no particular project in mind. It is important to be exposed to a large variety of colors and determine your immediate emotional response to each of them. When you walk into a yarn store, what colors emotionally attract or distract you? Studies show we have an involuntary psychological response to every color we see. The brain actually secretes chemicals as the eye takes in the color. You have an emotional response before you can logically explain your reaction to it.

Color surrounds us in our homes, our clothes, our gardens, and our world. Look at magazines, billboards, art galleries, and nature. What color combinations are emotionally satisfying to you? Experiment. Don't be afraid of combining colors that might not work. That is the only way you can learn from direct experience what speaks to your soul and what does not. I assure you, I have a lot more "attempts" than successes, but that is how I learn and continue to learn. While attempting to invent the lightbulb, Thomas Edison once said he had not failed; he had simply found 10,000 ways it might not work.

Probably the biggest concern expressed by my students is their anxiety about working with color. Perhaps their reluctance is derived from the realization that colors arouse strong emotions. Goodness knows, no one has ever accused me of being afraid of color. I am not from the knitting school of less is more. In fact, my philosophy is: Too much is never enough!

People frequently ask how I choose my colors. First off, I am driven by the colors that speak to me and my immediate emotional response to them. I put into my garments every color I adore. They simply must learn to get along with one another! I am totally, completely, and entirely seduced by the color and texture of a yarn. Weight of yarn doesn't enter into the equation. Modular knitting is so forgiving that yarn weight is not an issue. Now isn't that just divine?

I joyously embrace color, but I have never followed any color-wheel formulas or fixed rules concerning colors. For me, to reduce creativity to mathematical or scientific tenets would be to compromise the soul of the art. Try the following ideas to discover your own unique palette.

Finding Your Palette

- Trust your instincts.

- Lose yourself in the experience of all the colors. Live dangerously; it is only yarn!

- The eye, using the brain as its vehicle, can distinguish over two million colors, so why limit yourself? There are no wrong choices.

- Choose colors to which you have an immediate, positive emotional response—don't intellectualize.

- Most people want to play it safe when it comes to color. What colors would you use if you thought no one would ever see them or judge you? Fear confines and inhibits our true creativity.

- Keep an album of images clipped from magazines that have color combinations you find appealing. Refer to it for inspiration.

Choosing Your Colors

- Choose yarn colors under daylight conditions. No matter how perfect the artificial lighting, I find I am disappointed with the results if I don't choose yarn in true daylight.

- So you don't know where to start in selecting colors? Choose a variegated yarn you adore and select complementary solid colors that are found in the variegated yarn.

- Choose several colors of yarn that you respond to and hold them tightly together. View them again from a distance. Place them in a basket on your table. Look at them throughout the day, over several days. Eventually, one color may want to leave and another could come to take its place.

- After selecting a variety of colors, lay strands of each side by side or gently twist strands together to give the illusion of how they will appear as knitted fabric.

- Once you have settled upon a few colors, knit a mitered-square swatch. These small units take only minutes to knit and provide volumes of information about color selection without a great investment of time.

Knitting Your Colors

- When changing colors within a module or selecting colors for the next module, don't obsess over the selection. Base choices on your passion. Note how putting two shades together can actually transform them into yet another color.

- Try not to overanalyze one module or one color next to another. Wait until its neighbors are joined around it. Like mixing paint on a palette, the human brain will blend all the dazzling colors into a sublime symphony.

- Use contrasting colors and values to titillate and amuse the brain. Value is the relative lightness or darkness of a color.

- Gently sprinkle a few yellow-based colors throughout the piece to give your garment some pizzazz and sparkling life.

- Don't use a color only once in your work; repeat it elsewhere for balance.

- Remember, you have total creative and artistic control over the visual presentation of your garment. Realizing you have control in one area of your life will nourish you with boundless energy, passion, and power over other aspects of your life. It will heal you and transform your life on many levels forever. It did mine.

And Last, but Not Least

- No one dies; fortunes aren't lost; wars don't spontaneously ignite if you put hot pink next to yellow!

- You learn in the doing, so get the yarn ball rolling. Have fun and don't take colors too seriously.

Becoming One with the Yarn: Let the Creativity Begin

It has been said that in the beginner's mind there are many possibilities, but in the expert's there are few. Because modular knitting and my own approach to it seem to break so many of the traditional knitting laws, I ask you now to become a beginning knitter again where anything is possible. By cultivating a beginner or child's approach, the mind becomes fresh and awakened. Take on a new perspective. Leave all the doors open. Amazing creativity will occur!

Go Play with Your Yarn!

Modular knitting truly is magical. It allows you freedom to create as you knit without having to think or plan ahead. One of the most delightful revelations I discovered about this transformative style of knitting was that yarn weight is not important. When I choose yarns for a project, I am mesmerized by their colors and textures. I never let weight of yarn influence my decision. Since this defies all the old rules about same weight, same dye lot, buying enough yarn ahead of time, and so on, I knew I had to prove it to myself and my hesitant students. Many of the garments in this book are knit with baby-fine to extra-chunky yarns, all combined in the same garment. I do not change needle sizes and I do not double the fine yarn unless I choose to. I know you are not going to believe this until you try it yourself. So challenge old ideas and play! Break all the knitting laws and be astounded by the results.

Reaching Knitting Nirvana: Knitting between the Lines

Enjoy the sheer delight of the knitting experience. It is in the process, not the end result or finishing, that true satisfaction is derived. Your knitting is a form of self-expression, of personal theater. It reveals what you want to say to the world. So let the creativity begin.

- After you knit a module following the directions, strike out on your own. Vary yarn types, colors, and stitch patterns on each module. Try knitting modules in all garter stitch. Seed stitch and slip stitch are also lovely alternatives.

- Use the highest-quality yarn you can afford. You will be spending lots of time with it while knitting your masterpiece. The spirit and soul of your work lie in the materials you use.

- Occasionally, you will have more stitches on your double-pointed needles than they can easily accommodate. Using circular needles for small modules can be cumbersome. So I place point protectors on one end of my double-pointed needles until the stitches are reduced to a manageable number.

- Knitters often feel they must knit in cottons for warmer climates or warm-season wearing. I have found quite the opposite true. First off, I think wool gets a bad rap. Wool is far lighter than cotton and it breathes beautifully. Garments I knit in cotton weigh up to four times more than the same design in wools and silks. I comfortably wear my wool and silk vests and jackets year-round in New Mexico.

- Many knitters wish to plot the outcome of their garment by drawing it on graph paper and coloring in every module. This requires a lot of time that you could spend knitting. I have yet to see a knitter who sticks with the original plan. If it is all planned and colored in, there is no further artistic need to create it! The joy of creating modules as you go is the freedom to change your mind and

mood as you knit without restriction. This is the time when true creativity—knitting from your spirit—comes to fruition.

- While knitting, you are so close to your work that you lose perspective regarding color and proportion. Take breaks and lay your work on a chair. Observe it from a distance and perceive it in an entirely new way, with new eyes.

- I generally have three or more projects going simultaneously. When I lose interest or inspiration in one, there is always another one patiently waiting for me.

- The length of my garments is typically short compared to other designers' work. The longer the garment, the more weight it adds to your appearance. Wherever the hemline falls is where the eye first goes. I personally do not wish my hips to be the focal point of attention! Covering undesirable features of your physique actually draws attention to them.

- Tug the tail of the second or third stitch of each row if it feels a bit loose.

- Use Post-it notes to follow your pattern instructions line by line.

- Place a marker on the front side of your knitting so that you know which side you are on.
  And don't forget . . .

- There are no mistakes, simply learning opportunities.

- To be creative, we must lose our fear of being wrong. Don't plan—*play!*

- Stay curious. Curiosity generates a special

creative energy that causes you to vibrate at a different frequency.

- Abandon logic. Trust your imagination.

- Art and creativity are not about limitations. Break the rules. Push your limits. Step out of your comfort zone.

- Few of us earn our living from knitting. So let your inner child out to frolic.

- Don't take knitting so seriously. Take risks and enjoy the possibilities. Trust me. I'm a knitter!

In the Beginning, There Was Casting On

I use two different cast-on techniques, which I believe create the best edges for modular designs. However, I encourage my students to use any cast on method they wish.

The cast-on row or pick-up row is always row 1 in my patterns. It is best to cast on loosely since most of the patterns require decreases in the very next wrong-side row. It is difficult to decrease if the cast on is tight and unyielding.

Knitted Cast On

(Also known as Knitted-On Cast On*)*

Place a slipknot on the left needle. As with standard knitting, knit into the slipknot and add the new stitch to the left needle rather than dropping it. Continue in this fashion until you have the required number of stitches. The cast-on tail is always on the right-hand edge of your work when viewing the right facing side.

Knit into stitch.   Place new stitch on left needle.

Double Cast On

(Also known as Long-Tail Cast On*)*

Place a slipknot on the right needle, leaving a long tail. Hold the slipknot with your right index finger.

Wrap the tail around your left thumb, front to back. Wrap the working yarn over your left index finger and clasp the ends against your palm. *Insert the needle under the loop on your thumb and over the loop on your index finger, drawing the yarn through the loop. Allow the loop to drop from your thumb and gently tighten the loop on the needle*. Repeat from * to * until all stitches are cast on. The cast-on tail is always on the left-hand edge of your work when viewing the right facing side.

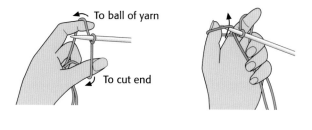

To ball of yarn

To cut end

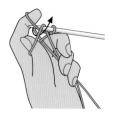

First and Last Stitches

This little tip could mean the success or failure of your future in modular knitting. Like many of you, I do not like to change my old knitting habits. However, once you begin using these recommended first and last stitches on every row of your knitting, you will find how much they can simplify your life in the finishing of both modular and traditional knitting projects. So, give this a try and soon it will be as automatic as reaching for chocolate!

Forming these stitches in the following manner creates a lovely double chain on the sides of your module that serves as your guide for picking up and knitting off of the module to form all future modules.

- **First Stitch: K1tbl:** Unless otherwise indicated, always knit into the back of the first stitch of every row—even on purl rows.

- **Last Stitch: Sl 1F:** Unless otherwise indicated, on the last stitch of every row, with yarn in front, slip as if to purl.

Knitting into the back of the first stitch on the

following row anchors this slipped stitch. A P2tog, if indicated at the end of the row, also maintains the desired chain edge.

Joining Modules As You Go

In modular knitting, the fun and speed associated with the process comes from picking up and knitting from previously formed modules rather than making hundreds of modules and then hoping someday you will sew them all together.

With the right side of your work facing you and always working from right to left, use one double-pointed needle or one end of your circular needles to pick up and knit the required number of stitches. Pick up stitches by placing your needle or hook through both loops of the chain formed on the edge of the knitted module(s) from which you are picking up. Wrap the yarn knitwise around the needle or hook and pull the stitch through both loops of the chain onto the needle. Continue in this fashion until you have picked up the required number of stitches. To ensure that you pick up the correct number of stitches, always start at the extreme right of your work and pick up the last stitch at the extreme left of your work. If you are left-handed and have trouble picking up stitches from right to left with a needle, try picking up stitches from right to left with a crochet hook and transferring them to a needle.

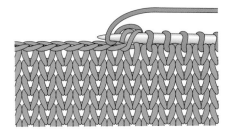

Decreasing: And Then There Were None

The decreases are the magic behind forming mitered modules. The two most-prevalent decreases I use are: sK2po (sl 1, K2tog, pass slipped stitch over) on knit rows and sP2po (sl 1, P2tog, pass slipped stitch over) on purl rows. These double decreases are usually accomplished on the wrong side of the work.

While many knitters can see where the decrease occurs, others prefer to use a ring marker as a reminder. If using a marker, place marker before each sK2po or sP2po on row 2 of the pattern unless otherwise instructed. Starting on row 4 and each succeeding wrong-side row, the following special abbreviations apply:

Knit rows: sK2po = sl 1 wyib, SM, K2tog, pass slipped st over

Purl rows: sP2po = sl 1 wyif, SM, P2tog, pass slipped st over

In general, the modules in this book have an odd number of cast-on stitches. The decreases are worked over the three center stitches, generally on wrong-side rows only, although some decreases may occur on right-side rows as well.

With this concept, an equal number of stitches on either side of the center three stitches are eventually reduced to one stitch during the decrease process. For example, if you have 23 stitches on your needle, you can subtract the three center stitches and divide the remaining 20 stitches by two. This tells you that you should have 10 stitches on either side of the decrease.

Binding Off: Ending It All

Three-needle bind off joins the raw edges (unfinished stitches) of two knitted pieces without sewing them. In your left hand, hold together the two pieces on needles with the right sides facing each other. With a third needle in the right hand, knit together one stitch from each needle in the left hand. Repeat this step again. Each time you have two stitches on the right needle, loosely bind them off. Continue until all stitches are bound off. Cut a 3" tail and pull it through the last stitch.

Knit together one stitch from front needle and one stitch from back needle.

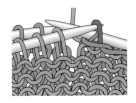

Bind off.

Quick Crocheted Edges

I haven't the patience to pick up and knit hundreds of stitches around a garment to finish it, so most of my pieces are finished with a crocheted edge. Crocheting not only expedites the finishing process, it also offers many beautiful alternatives for framing your knitted garment. Although some pieces require it, I typically do not crochet around the bottom edge. I love seeing the interplay between each module without the distraction of one continuous color edging. While the following describes how I finish my own work, remember that you can add as many rows of crochet as you desire. This is a great way to add width or length to your garment without adding more modules.

Unless otherwise indicated in the finishing section of each pattern, the following is my customary, quick crocheted edging:

Front Trim

Row 1: Starting at lower-right edge of garment with right side facing, hdc up right front, across back neck, and down left front.

Row 2: Buttonhole row: Ch 2, turn work, change yarn colors if desired. Starting at lower-left edge on wrong side of work, hdc in each of the established stitches across left front, back neck, and down right front until reaching point on pattern schematic designated for first buttonhole. Work buttonhole as follows: *Ch 3 or 4, connect with hdc in next stitch, do not skip 3 or 4 stitches unless desired. Continue in established hdc until location of next buttonhole.* Repeat from * to * until reaching bottom of right front side.

Row 3: Ch 1, turn work, change colors if desired. Starting at lower-right edge on right side of work, sc in established stitches up right front, over loop buttonholes, around back neck, and down left front. Cut yarn and fasten off.

Armhole and Cuff Trim

Unless otherwise recommended in the pattern, finish armhole edges and cuffs with two continuous rows of half-double crochet. Each row can vary in color, of course!

The Dreaded Potholder Look

To avoid your modules looking like a bunch of potholders you have randomly sewn together to make a fashion statement, try some of the following tricks:

- Avoid knitting exclusively in garter stitch unless your yarns are very textural and will disguise the pattern anyway.

- Mix stitches, yarns, textures, and colors within and from one motif to another so that the eye can be entertained and bounce from one exciting module to another.

- I have selected two specific decreases that usually occur on the wrong side of the work for a particular reason. These decreases eliminate, in part, that vexing ridge on the right side of the work that other types of decreases actually emphasize. A conspicuous ridge distracts the eye from experiencing the beauty of the colors and textures.

Rules Are Made to Be Broken, but Don't Break These

Anyone who knows me is aware of my dislike for rules or regimentation. But let's start with these basics. Once you have mastered them, you will know how to liberate yourself from the guidelines and engage your own personal aesthetic.

- I highly recommend you knit the Ojo de Dios Vest first to learn the important basics unique to my modular approach.

- Knit every right-side row.

- Change colors on right-side rows only.

- Make double decreases on wrong-side rows.

- Knit in ends as you go so that you don't have hundreds of tails to sew in at the end.

- Do not cut any tails until after blocking.

- Knit the first two to four rows in garter stitch for the modules described in "Squares: The Basics" (pages 28–61).

- Always work the first and last stitches of every row as described in "First and Last Stitches" (page 20).

- Increase or decrease the size of modules by changing needle sizes, weight of yarn, or by adding or subtracting the number of stitches you cast on.

- Cast on somewhat loosely so that you can easily accomplish the double decreases on the next row.

- In all my patterns, row 1 is the cast-on or pick-up-and-knit row. Row 2 is always the wrong side. The wrong side is where most decreases occur.

- When starting a new color or changing colors, bring the new color up under the old color so that there is no hole and yarns link together.

- Carry yarn up the side of your work if you plan to use it later in your module.

- When fastening off the last stitch, cut a tail 3" to 4" long and thread it through the last stitch on your needle. This length is needed for knitting in when joining modules.

Reading the Diagrams

When you look at the diagrams for each project, you'll see wavy lines, dots, dashed diagonal lines, and numbers. These symbols are generally displayed on the first row of the modules to assist you in understanding the order and orientation of the modules as they are constructed. These symbols may also appear in other modules within a diagram as needed.

The wavy lines represent the cast-on and/or picked-up edges of each module. The dots indicate the point at which decreases are made. The dashed diagonal lines represent the direction of the mitered decreases. The numbers represent the order in which each module should be knit.

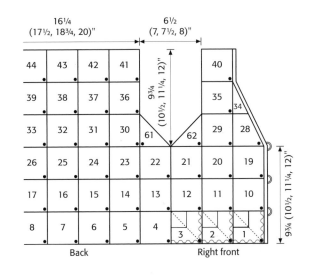

Knitting Niceties

There are two items that will make knitting these modules easier and more enjoyable. Reinforced Pony Pearls double-pointed needles, distributed by Muench Yarns, Inc., are very kind to your fingers. Red Rubber Markers are easy to see and flex effortlessly when you are passing slipped stitches over. Both are available from Patternworks (see "Resources," page 128).

Abbreviations and Definitions

◀	join by slipping next stitch purlwise with yarn in back, knit next stitch on left needle, pass slipped stitch over, turn work, begin next row
approx	approximately
beg	begin(ning)
BG	background
BO	bind off
ch	chain
CO	cast on
col	color
cont	continue
dec(s)	decrease(s)
dpn	double-pointed needles
fasten off	pull tail through last stitch and cut yarn, leaving 3" tail
garter stitch	knit every row
hdc	half-double crochet
K	knit
K1bf	knit 1 in back and knit 1 in front of same stitch
K1fb	knit 1 in front and knit 1 in back of same stitch
K1tbl	knit 1 through back loop of stitch
K2tog tbl	knit 2 stitches together through back loops
kw	knitwise
M1	make 1 stitch: pick up horizontal thread between stitches and knit through back loop
MC	main color
mod	module
P	purl
P1bf	purl 1 in back and purl 1 in front of same stitch
PM	place marker

po	pass over
PU	pick up and knit (see "Joining Modules As You Go," page 21)
pw	purlwise
rem	remaining
RS	right side of work
sc	single crochet
seed stitch	(knit 1, purl 1) across row; on return row, purl the knits and knit the purls unless otherwise indicated
sl 1F	slip 1 stitch as if to purl with yarn in front
sK2po	slip 1 wyib, knit 2 together, pass slipped stitch over
SM	slip marker
sP2po	slip 1 wyif, purl 2 together, pass slipped stitch over
st(s)	stitch(es)
tbl	through back loop
tog	together
WS	wrong side of work
wyib	with yarn in back
wyif	with yarn in front
yds	yards

Yarn Conversion Chart

yds x .91 = m

m x 1.09 = yds

g x 0.035 = oz

oz x 28.35 = g

Achieving a Flawless Fit

One of the greatest advantages of modular design knitting is the infinite number of ways to achieve the perfect fit. This liberating technique allows you to add or subtract components from your garment as you knit. Even after the garment is completed, it is quite simple to insert or delete modules to alter the appearance, shape, or size of the piece as your tastes change. Once you gain confidence in making these changes as a part of the creative process, you will have opened up an entire universe of possibilities that will ensure you will never again be stuck with an ill-fitting garment.

Incorporate one or more of the following techniques to achieve the perfect shape and fit for any size garment you plan to knit.

Method A: Paper Pattern

This technique is quite versatile and works well with any of the designs in the book.

Supplies

Knitted or woven vest or jacket that fits well

Kraft or butcher paper

Pencil

Tape measure

Scissors

Project yarn and needles

Sheet of card stock or other heavy paper

1. On a flat surface, lay a well-fitting garment on top of kraft or butcher paper. Draw around the perimeter of the garment and cut out the paper pattern.

2. With the actual project yarn and needles, knit one each of the different modules.

3. Place the knitted module(s) on card stock, draw around the shape(s), and cut out.

4. This is where the fun begins! Lay out the puzzle pieces on the paper pattern. Repeat the module shape(s) by drawing around them repeatedly over the entire surface of the pattern or just across the bottom row. This tells you how many modules are required to fit the circumference of the garment. If it doesn't come out perfectly but is close, you can fudge by increasing or decreasing the number of crochet rows to finish the button band. Rectangular or chevron side panels (see "Pyramid Vest," page 65) also offer solutions for a flawless fit. Or change needle sizes or the weight of the yarn to increase or decrease the final size of the module.

Since I prefer knitting to drawing around little modules, I rarely ever lay out more than the first row of shapes. Once you knit your first layer of shapes, you'll realize that the fun is in seeing what wonderful shape and color you can incorporate next. You won't want to be confined to a preconceived arrangement of motifs. Laying out the entire design in advance can stifle creativity.

Method B: Graph Paper

This technique works best with square shapes or variations on a square.

Supplies

Knitted or woven vest or jacket that fits well

Standard (not knitting) graph paper

Pencil

Project yarn and needles

Tape measure

1. Measure and record the width, length, armhole opening, sleeve length, and neck opening of a well-fitting garment.

2. With the actual project yarn and needles, knit the module(s). If you achieve the pattern gauge, your module will be the size stated in the pattern. However, it is not critical what the final gauge or module size is. All modules will interlock perfectly with one another. Plus, with modular knitting, you have the luxury of adding or deleting modules as needed for a flawless fit.

3. Measure the modules and note their sizes. Next, go to graph paper. Each square on the graph paper represents one knitted square, no matter what its dimensions. If your module is $3\frac{1}{2}$" square, then each graph-paper square represents $3\frac{1}{2}$". Use this method to represent other shapes on graph paper. Since all shapes interlock perfectly like puzzle pieces, they will all fit correctly on your graph-paper representation of the design layout.

   If you want a vest or jacket that is 43" around and your square is $3\frac{1}{2}$", divide 42" by $3\frac{1}{2}$" = 12 squares plus 1" for the button band. If you want a garment 21" long, divide 21" by $3\frac{1}{2}$" = 6 interlocked squares up the back and each of the fronts.

4. Decide the width and length of your garment and draw an outline of it on graph paper, representing the number of squares across the width and up the length of the front and back. If your math does not work out perfectly, remember that you can adjust with additional rows of crochet on the button band or with the addition of side panels. Also, blocking solves many width and length dilemmas.

5. When the graph paper outline is complete, draw in the desired shapes for the garment. Once you gain confidence, you will likely never draw past the first layer of motifs, since the freedom, fun, and creativity of this form of knitting comes in never having to plan ahead!

Method C: Free-Form Design

This technique is fast, fun, and my favorite, because it provides instant gratification. This evolutionary technique moves beyond traditional knitting and opens up new vistas of creativity.

Supplies

Knitted or woven vest or jacket that fits well

Project yarn and needles

Tape measure

Free-form design is by far the most expeditious, freeing, and artistic approach to fitting. It is also the technique I employ almost exclusively. I start by knitting and connecting modules to one another, thoroughly enjoying the colors and textures as they stimulate my tactile and visual senses. There is no need to be concerned with gauge. Just enjoy the playing! When I have a section of connected modules, say 10" by 10", I lay it on my favorite well-fitting garment. From here, I measure to determine how many more modules I need to achieve the desired width and length. Every time I add a module or two, I lay the work in progress on top of the garment to determine if I am still on target.

Another benefit of this technique is that you can place this beginning "swatch" of knitted fabric anywhere it longs to be in your wearable art. If it is fabulous, it can reside in the center of the back. Then you can pick up and knit off of it in all directions until the back is completed. If it is less than you hoped for, maybe it can inhabit one of the sides where your arm will hide it. If it is totally unacceptable for use in your garment, keep it as one of the best design tools you'll ever have. From it, you will learn what colors and textures do and do not work for you, and you will have a large puzzle piece that you can fit or fold into yet unknitted areas of your garment to determine if you are on track with your proposed shapes.

These liberating approaches to fitting are going to enhance and enrich your knitting life forever! So try one or all of them, or invent your own.

Paper Doll Cutout

As a child, I adored paper dolls, cutting out their divine fashions and layering the dolls in several out-fits at once. When I first started designing in the modular fashion, many students requested vests that were longer, shorter, or wider than the options I offered in the pattern. This reminded me of layering paper doll clothes. Now I suggest that students make two or more photocopies of the design's schematic. Cut along the borders of the copies. Layer the copies on top of each other, shifting them around as needed, to add the desired length and/or width to the design. If your layering leaves a blank area, move modules around or cut out more modules to fill in these voids. Trim any excess modules outside of the design. This solution is especially helpful with more complex shapes, such as the Mola Jacket or the 3-D Cubist Vest. Since all the modules fit perfectly together, this technique makes it more obvious what components go where to lengthen or widen your garment.

If you are like me, you may find it difficult to visualize how some of the elements of these garments fit together. By cutting out the schematic and folding it just as you would the actual knitted garment, it will become apparent how everything fits together.

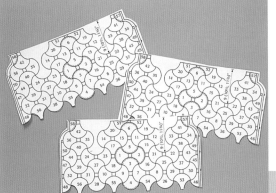

LEFT: PHOTOCOPIES OF THE MOLA JACKET SCHEMATIC.

BELOW: THE PHOTOCOPIES HAVE BEEN LAYERED AND POSITIONED TO EXTEND THE LENGTH OF THE GARMENT. THE SHADED AREAS AT RIGHT AND LEFT SHOW WHICH MODULES ARE NOT NEEDED FOR THE LENGTHENED GARMENT. HOWEVER, THESE SAME SHADED AREAS INDICATE A POTENTIAL STARTING PLACE FOR ADDING WIDTH TO A GARMENT.

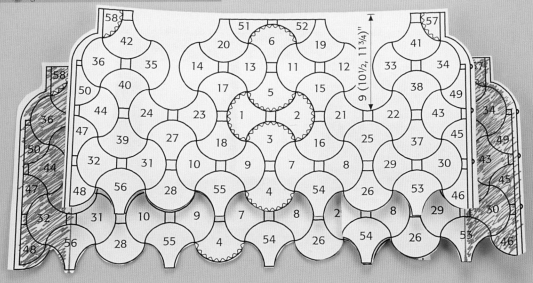

Squares: The Basics

The following five garments are based on the shape of a square and its infinite variations. The four basic modules and their divergent transformations can be joined in endless combinations to achieve the size and shape garment you desire. Once you have mastered the techniques, you can change needle sizes, yarn weights, or the number of cast-on stitches to create smaller or larger design motifs.

Many of the module instructions have been condensed in order to supply more information in the book. However, there are line-by-line instructions for the basic square technique in the Ojo de Dios Vest pattern. If you become confused in other patterns, refer back to this pattern for clarity.

It is quite simple to start knitting at any location on your garment; however, until you become proficient in the modular concept, I highly recommend the following procedure unless the pattern instructs otherwise:

Start knitting your first module at the lower-right front of your garment, connecting modules from right to left across the bottom row. When that row is complete, start again at the far right side of your work, building from right to left on top of the motifs in the row below. Continue in this fashion until you have reached the top row of your garment.

All the modules in this book begin by casting on, picking up and knitting, or a combination of the two to create additional shapes. Carefully review the sections regarding casting on, first and last stitches, joining modules, and decreasing before commencing your pattern (see pages 20–21). Use the "Double Cast On" technique (page 20) for all designs in this section.

Please take a little time to read through all the directions before starting. It is very important to make a swatch square or diamond to determine your gauge. If there are 10 modules worked around the body of the garment, the width of one module multiplied by 10 (plus approximately 1" to 2" of a crocheted band) will determine the finished diameter of your design.

If you are like me, you will want to start by knitting the most complex pattern in the book. However, I highly recommend that you knit the Ojo de Dios Vest first so that you will have a good understanding of the basics.

THE PROJECTS

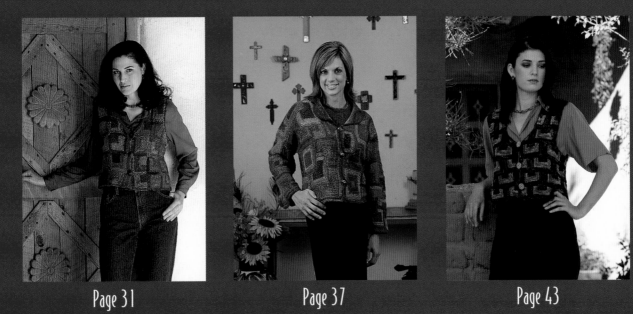

Page 31

Page 37

Page 43

Page 47

Page 53

Ojo de Dios Vest

The inspiration for this vest came from my childhood in the desert Southwest and Mexico. The *Ojo de Dios*, or Eye of God, is a sign of goodwill and fortune or a ritual object entreating divine blessings from the all-seeing God's eye. While the Ojo is prominent in New Mexico and Mexico, it is also found in other ancient cultures from Egypt, Turkey, Greece, Tibet, Peru, Aboriginal Australia, Scandinavia, Thailand, and Burma. Have fun knitting this multicultural vest while learning the basics of modular knitting.

Sizes: Small (Medium, Large, X-Large)

Finished Chest: 40 (43, 46, 49)"

Finished Length: 19½ (21, 22½, 24)"

Materials

Use worsted-weight yarns as listed below or a variety of yarns to achieve gauge.

- 7 (8, 9, 10) skeins Noro Silk Garden (45% silk, 45% kid mohair, 10% lamb's wool; 109 yds [100 m] per skein); color 50 blue variegated

- 2 (2, 2, 3) skeins Noro Cash Iroha (40% silk, 30% lamb's wool, 20% cashmere, 10% nylon; 99 yds [91 m] per skein); colors 21 magenta, 24 purple, 75 turquoise

- Two size 8 double-pointed needles (or size required to obtain gauge)

- Size G crochet hook

- Red Rubber Markers (see "Resources," page 128)

- 3 buttons, ¾" to 1" diameter

Gauge for Basic Square

Small: 25 sts and 24 rows = 3¼"

Medium: 27 sts and 26 rows = 3½"

Large: 29 sts and 28 rows = 3¾"

X-Large: 31 sts and 30 rows = 4"

Body (Right Front and Back)

The following bullet points outline the knitting sequence. For more information, refer to module instructions.

- Knit BS 1. For all rem squares, PU sts from previously knitted squares. See "Joining Modules as You Go" (page 21).

- **BS 2:** PU 13 (14, 15, 16) sts from left side of BS 1, turn work, CO 12 (13, 14, 15) sts. Finish mod beg at row 2 of BS. Rep for squares 3–9.

- **BS 10, 19, 36, 40, 41:** CO 12 (13, 14, 15) sts, PU 13 (14, 15, 16) sts from square below. Finish mod beg at row 2 of BS.

- **BS 11–18, 20–27, 29–33, 35, 37–39, 42–44:** PU 13 (14, 15, 16) sts from left side of square to the right, PU 12 (13, 14, 15) sts from square below. Finish mod beg at row 2 of BS.

Left Front

This section is knit separately and sewn at side and shoulder seams to back of vest. Study photo and schematic closely. Notice that the Ojo squares, or eyes, on the left side of the vest face the opposite direction of all other squares in the vest.

- Knit BS 45 as a single mod.

- **BS 46 and 47:** CO 12 (13, 14, 15) sts, PU 13 (14, 15, 16) sts along right-hand side of square to the left. Finish mod beg at row 2 of BS.

- **BS 48, 51, 58:** PU 13 (14, 15, 16) sts from top of square below, turn work, CO 12 (13, 14, 15) sts. Finish mod beg at row 2 of BS.

- **BS 49, 50, 52, 53, 55, 57:** PU 13 (14, 15, 16) sts from square below, PU 12 (13, 14, 15) sts from right-hand side of square to the left. Finish mod beg at row 2 of BS.

Special Abbreviations after Completing Row 2
Knit rows: sK2po = sl 1, SM, K2tog, pass slipped st over

Purl rows: sP2po = sl 1, SM, P2tog, pass slipped st over

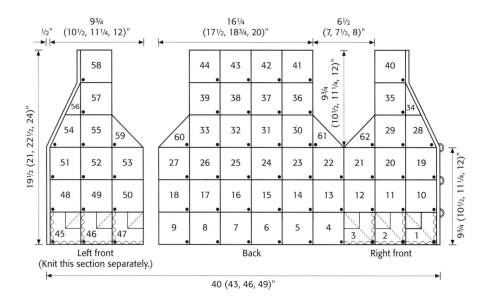

Basic Square (BS)

Change colors on rows 5 and 15. Purl rows 8, 10, and 12.

NOTE: Work 1 st fewer on either side of sK2po or sP2po on every WS row.

Row 1: CO 25 (27, 29, 31) sts.

Row 2 (WS): K1tbl, K10 (11, 12, 13), PM, sK2po, K10 (11, 12, 13), sl 1F—23 (25, 27, 29) sts.

Row 3 and every RS row: K1tbl, knit across, sl 1F.

Row 4: K1tbl, K9 (10, 11, 12), sK2po, K9 (10, 11, 12), sl 1F—21 (23, 25, 27) sts. Change colors on next row.

Row 6: K1tbl, K8 (9, 10, 11), sK2po, K8 (9, 10, 11), sl 1F—19 (21, 23, 25) sts.

Row 8: K1tbl, P7 (8, 9, 10), sP2po, P7 (8, 9, 10), sl 1F—17 (19, 21, 23) sts.

Row 10: K1tbl, P6 (7, 8, 9), sP2po, P6 (7, 8, 9), sl 1F—15 (17, 19, 21) sts.

Row 12: K1tbl, P5 (6, 7, 8), sP2po, P5 (6, 7, 8), sl 1F—13 (15, 17, 19) sts.

Row 14: K1tbl, K4 (5, 6, 7), sK2po, K4 (5, 6, 7), sl 1F—11 (13, 15, 17) sts. Change colors on next row.

Row 16: K1tbl, K3 (4, 5, 6), sK2po, K3 (4, 5, 6), sl 1F—9 (11, 13, 15) sts.

Row 18: K1tbl, K2 (3, 4, 5), sK2po, K2 (3, 4, 5), sl 1F—7 (9, 11, 13) sts.

Row 20: K1tbl, K1 (2, 3, 4), sK2po, K1 (2, 3, 4), sl 1F—5 (7, 9, 11) sts.

Row 22: K1tbl, K0 (1, 2, 3), sK2po, K0 (1, 2, 3), sl 1F—3 (5, 7, 9) sts.

Row 24: Small: sK2po. Fasten off. **All other sizes:** K1tbl, K0 (0, 1, 2), sK2po, K0 (0, 1, 2), sl 1F.

Row 26: Medium: sK2po. Fasten off. **Large and X-Large:** K1tbl, K0 (0, 0, 1), sK2po, K0 (0, 0, 1), sl 1F.

Row 28: Large: sK2po. Fasten off. **X-Large:** K1tbl, sK2po, sl 1F.

Row 30: X-Large: sK2po. Fasten off.

Dazzling Idea!

Silk Garden yarn by Noro or other variegated yarns offer many entertaining possibilities for using color. You can use the color as it dances off the ball of yarn, but often I find that too confining. If I see a yummy color in the center of the skein or near the end of the yarn that calls to me, I simply dig into the yarn, pull out that color, cut it, and start knitting with it. It's *just* yarn! Don't let it boss you around. You are in charge.

Right Neck Edge Triangle (28)

Change colors on rows 5 and 15. Purl rows 8, 10, and 12.

Row 1: CO 5, PU 13 (14, 15, 16) sts from top of BS 19.

Row 2 (WS): K1tbl, K10 (11, 12, 13), PM, sK2po, K3, K1fb.

Row 3 and every RS row: K1tbl, knit across, sl 1F.

Row 4: K1tbl, K9 (10, 11, 12), sK2po, K3, K1fb.

Row 6: K1tbl, K8 (9, 10, 11), sK2po, K3, K1fb.

Row 8: K1tbl, P7 (8, 9, 10), sP2po, P3, P1fb.

Row 10: K1tbl, P6 (7, 8, 9), sP2po, P3, P1fb.

Row 12: K1tbl, P5 (6, 7, 8), sP2po, P3, P1fb.

Row 14: K1tbl, K4 (5, 6, 7), sK2po, K3, K1fb.

Row 16: Small: K1tbl, K3, sK2po, K3, sl 1F. **All other sizes:** K1tbl, K0 (4, 5, 6), sK2po, K3, K1fb.

Row 18: Small, Medium: K1tbl, K2 (3, 0, 0), sK2po, K2 (3, 0, 0), sl 1F. **Large, X-Large:** K1tbl, K0 (0, 4, 5), sK2po, K3, K1fb.

Row 20: Small, Medium, Large: K1tbl, K1 (2, 3, 0), sK2po, K1 (2, 3, 0), sl 1F. **X-Large:** K1tbl, K4, sK2po, K3, K1fb.

Row 22: All sizes: K1tbl, K0 (1, 2, 3) sK2po, K0 (1, 2, 3), sl 1F.

Rep rows 3 and 22 through rows 23 (25, 27, 29) with 3 sts rem.

Next row: sK2po. Fasten off.

Right Neck Edge Triangle (34)

Change colors on rows 5 and 15. Purl rows 8, 10, and 12.

Row 1: PU 8 (8, 8, 9) sts from top of triangle 28.

Rows 2, 6, 14, 18 (WS): K1tbl, knit across, sl 1F.

Row 3 and every RS row: K1tbl, knit across, sl 1F.

Rows 4, 16, 20: K1tbl, knit across, P2tog at neck edge.

Rows 8, 12: K1tbl, purl across, P2tog at neck edge.

Row 10: K1tbl, purl across, sl 1F.

Row 22: Small: sK2po. Fasten off. **All other sizes:** Rep row 2.

Row 24: Medium: sK2po. Fasten off. **Large, X-Large:** Rep row 4.

Row 25: Large: K2tog and fasten off. **X-Large:** sK2po. Fasten off.

Left Neck Edge Triangle (54)

Change colors on rows 5 and 15. Purl rows 8, 10, and 12.

Row 1: PU 13 (14, 15, 16) sts from top of BS 51, CO 5 sts.

Row 2 (WS): K1bf, K3, PM, sK2po, K10 (11, 12, 13), sl 1F.

Row 3 and every RS row: K1tbl, knit across, sl 1F.

Row 4: K1bf, K3, sK2po, K9 (10, 11, 12), sl 1F.

Row 6: K1bf, K3, sK2po, K8 (9, 10, 11), sl 1F.

Row 8: P1bf, P3, sP2po, P7 (8, 9, 10), sl 1F.

Row 10: P1bf, P3, sP2po, P6 (7, 8, 9), sl 1F.

Row 12: P1bf, P3, sP2po, P5 (6, 7, 8), sl 1F.

Row 14: K1bf, K3, sK2po, K4 (5, 6, 7), sl 1F.

Row 16: Small: K1tbl, K3, sK2po, K3, sl 1F. **All other sizes:** K1bf, K3, sK2po, K0 (4, 5, 6), sl 1F.

Row 18: Small, Medium: K1tbl, K2 (3, 0, 0), sK2po, K2 (3, 0, 0), sl 1F. **Large, X-Large:** K1bf, K3, sK2po, K0 (0, 4, 5), sl 1F.

Row 20: Small, Medium, Large: K1tbl, K1 (2, 3, 0), sK2po, K1 (2, 3, 0), sl 1F. **X-Large:** K1bf, K3, sK2po, K4, sl 1F.

Row 22: All sizes: K1tbl, K0 (1, 2, 3), sK2po, K0 (1, 2, 3), sl 1F.

Rep rows 3 and 22 through rows 23 (25, 27, 29) with 3 sts rem.

Next row: sK2po. Fasten off.

Left Neck Edge Triangle (56)

Change colors on rows 5 and 15. Purl rows 8, 10, and 12.

Row 1: PU 8 (8, 8, 9) sts from top of triangle 54.

Rows 2, 6, 14, 18 (WS): K1tbl, knit across, sl 1F.

Row 3 and every RS row: K1tbl, knit across, sl 1F.

Rows 4, 16, 20: K2tog tbl at neck edge, knit across, sl 1F.

Rows 8, 12: K2tog tbl at neck edge, purl across, sl 1F.

Row 10: K1tbl, purl across, sl 1F.

Row 22: Small: sK2po. Fasten off. **All other sizes:** Rep row 2.

Row 24: Medium: sK2po. Fasten off. **Large, X-Large:** Rep row 4.

Row 26: Large: K2tog and fasten off. **X-Large:** sK2po. Fasten off.

Underarm Triangles (59–62)

Change colors on rows 5 and 11. Work 2 fewer sts on either side of dec on WS rows.

Triangle 59: PU half of sts from top of 53, PU rem sts from right side of 55.

Triangle 60: PU half of sts from left side of 33, PU rem sts from top of 27.

Triangle 61: PU half of sts from top of 22, PU rem sts from right side of 30.

Triangle 62: PU half of sts from left side of 29, PU rem sts from top of 21.

Row 1: PU 25 (27, 29, 31) sts.

Row 2 (WS): K1tbl, K10 (11, 12, 13), PM, sK2po, K10 (11, 12, 13), sl 1F.

Row 3: K2tog tbl, knit across, P2tog.

Row 4: K1tbl, K8 (9, 10, 11), sK2po, K8 (9, 10, 11), sl 1F.

Rep rows 3 and 4 through rows 12 (13, 14, 15) with 3 sts rem.

Next row: sK2po. Fasten off.

Finishing

- Sew left front of vest to back at side seam. Sew shoulder seams tog.

- With crochet hook, start at lower-right front edge of vest, hdc approx 13 (14, 15, 16) sts per square up right front, across back neck, and down left front. Refer to "Quick Crocheted Edges" (page 22) for rem 2 rows and armhole trim. Place buttonholes on row 2 at tops of BS 19, 10, 1.

- Sew on 3 fabulous buttons.

OJO DE DIOS VESTS IN FIESTA YARNS LA BOHEME AND LA LUZ.

Conceptual Design Jacket

The following four modules used in this jacket, plus the neck triangles found in Adobe Brick Vest (page 45), can be joined in an endless variety of combinations to achieve the size and shape of the garment you desire. The accompanying schematic is simply one approach to knitting this piece. I encourage you to deviate from it to achieve the desired length and width. While the schematic is depicted flat, it is important to note that this jacket—or vest if you prefer—is knit as one cohesive patchwork unit without side seams. For larger sizes or longer lengths, I recommend that you simply keep adding modules until you achieve the desired fit.

So that I do not stifle your inner creativity, I have not included a detailed pattern. You will learn so much more designing your piece as you knit. For the more cautious among you, there is both a schematic for the jacket and instructions in "Achieving a Flawless Fit" (page 25) for charting your design. Regardless of your approach, you will have so much pride knowing you designed it yourself.

Sizes: Small (Medium, Large, X-Large, XX-Large)
Finished Chest: 39 (43¾, 48½, 53¼, 58)"
Finished Length: 16 (17⅞, 19¾, 21⅝, 23½)"

Materials

Use worsted-weight yarns or a variety of yarns to achieve gauge.

- Approx 1250 (1400, 1600, 1800, 2000) total yds in a variety of yarns and colors*
- Two size 8 double-pointed needles (or size required to obtain gauge)
- Size 8 circular needles (24")
- Size G crochet hook
- Red Rubber Markers (see "Resources," page 128)
- 3 buttons, ¾ to 1" diameter
- Tape measure
- Kraft paper or graph paper
- Knitted or woven garment that fits you well

The size Medium model jacket was knit with 10 skeins Noro Silk Garden (45% silk, 45% kid mohair, 10% lamb's wool; 109 yds [100 m] per skein), color 34; and 1 skein each of Noro Cash Iroha (40% silk, 30% lamb's wool, 20% cashmere, 10% nylon; 99 yds [91 m] per skein) in the following colors: 21 magenta, 24 purple, 62 pink, 14 olive, and 80 dark green.

NOTE: I highly recommend using the listed supplies and simply knitting more or fewer modules as needed to achieve the desired fit. If you do wish to achieve gauge at the larger sizes, you may need to use heavier yarns or 2 strands of worsted-weight yarn. Experiment with several swatches until you are pleased with the resulting fabric.

Gauge

Module	Small	Medium	Large	X-Large	XX-Large
Small Square					
19 sts and 18 rows	2" x 2"	2¼" x 2¼"	2½" x 2½"	2¾" x 2¾"	3" x 3"
Rectangle					
38 sts and 19 rows	2" x 4"	2¼" x 4½"	2½" x 5"	2¾" x 5½"	3" x 6"
L Shape					
57 sts and 19 rows	2" x 4" x 4"	2¼" x 4½" x 4½"	2½" x 5" x 5"	2¾" x 5½" x 5½"	3" x 6" x 6"
Large Square					
72 sts and 20 rows	4" x 4"	4½" x 4½"	5" x 5"	5½" x 5½"	6" x 6"

Learning Swatch Tutorial

- Knit 1 Small Square (SS).

Small Square (SS)

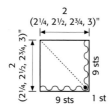

- Holding completed SS with RS facing, follow directions for L shape, working right to left, PU 10 sts from left side of SS, turn work, CO 47 sts (PU 10 + CO 18 + CO 19 + CO 10 sts = 57 sts). Finish mod beg at row 2 of "L."

"L"

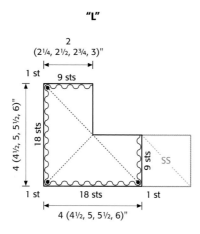

- Holding first 2 joined modules with RS facing, follow directions for rectangle (RT), CO 10 sts, PU 9 sts from top of SS, PU 9 sts from adjacent inside elbow of L shape next to SS, PU 10 sts along other half of inside elbow of L shape (CO 10, PU 9 + PU 9 + PU 10 = 38 sts). Finish mod beg at row 2 of RT.

Rectangle (RT)

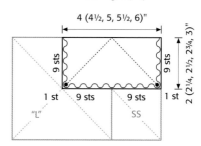

- Holding the 3 joined modules with RS facing, follow directions for Large Square (LS), PU 18 sts from left side of L shape, turn work, CO 54 sts (PU 18 + CO 18 + CO 18 + CO 18 = 72 sts). Finish mod beg at row 2 of LS. Sew up seam of LS.

Large Square (LS)

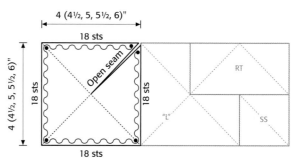

- Continue adding shapes in this general fashion. Any shape can be added any place. They will all fit tog. Sometime PU will occur first, other times CO, sometimes a combo. It will change with each module, depending upon its location.

Special Abbreviations after Completing Row 2

Knit rows: sK2po = sl 1, SM, K2tog, pass slipped st over

Purl rows: sP2po = sl 1, SM, P2tog, pass slipped st over

NOTE: For SS, RT, L, and LS, work 1 less st on either side of every sK2po on WS rows.

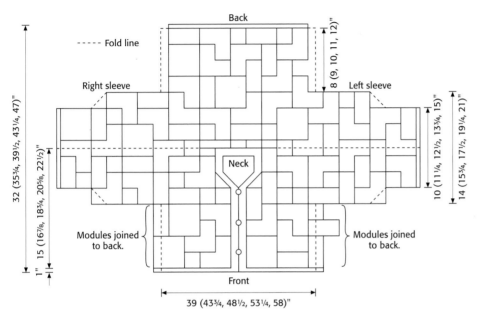

Note: Fold line indicates where garment is folded for sides and shoulder. There are no seams except at sleeve underarms.

CONCEPTUAL DESIGN IN ALTERNATE COLORWAY

Small Square (SS)

Use dpn. Change colors on rows 5 and 11. Purl rows 8 and 10.

Row 1: CO or PU 19 sts (10 + 9).

Row 2 (WS): K1tbl, K7, PM, sK2po, K7, sl 1F—17 sts.

Row 3 and every RS row: K1tbl, knit across, sl 1F.

Row 4: K1tbl, K6, sK2po, K6, sl 1F—15 sts.

Rows 5–17: Rep rows 3 and 4 through row 17 with 3 sts rem.

Row 18: sK2po. Fasten off.

Rectangle (RT)

Use dpn or circular needles. Change colors on rows 5 and 11. Purl rows 8 and 10.

Row 1: CO or PU 38 sts (10 + 18 + 10).

Row 2 (WS): K1tbl, K7, PM, sK2po, K16, PM, sK2po, K7, sl 1F—34 sts.

Row 3 and every RS row: K1tbl, knit across, sl 1F.

Row 4: K1tbl, K6, sK2po, K14, sK2po, K6, sl 1F—30 sts.

Rows 5–17: Rep rows 3 and 4 through row 17 with 6 sts rem.

Row 18: sK2po, sK2po—2 sts.

Row 19: K2tog tbl and fasten off.

L Shape

Use circular needles. Change colors on rows 5, 11, and 17. Purl rows 8, 10, and 12.

Row 1: CO or PU 57 sts (10 + 18 + 19 + 10).

Row 2 (WS): K1tbl, K7, PM, sK2po, K16, PM, sK2po, K16, PM, sK2po, K7, sl 1F—51 sts.

Row 3 and every RS row: K1tbl, knit across, sl 1F.

Row 4: K1tbl, K6, sK2po, K14, sK2po, K14, sK2po, K6, sl 1F—45 sts.

Rows 5–17: Rep rows 3 and 4 through row 17 with 9 sts rem.

Row 18: sK2po, sK2po, sK2po—3 sts.

Row 19: sK2po. Fasten off.

Large Square (LS)

Use circular needles. Change colors on rows 5, 11, and 17. Purl rows 8, 10, and 12.

Row 1: CO or PU 72 sts (18 + 18 + 18 + 18).

Row 2 (WS): K1tbl, K16, PM, K2tog, K16, PM, K2tog, K16, PM, K2tog, K16, sl 1F—69 sts.

Row 3 and every RS row: K2tog tbl, knit across, sl 1F.

Row 4: K2tog tbl, K14, sK2po, K14, sK2po, K14, sK2po, K14, sl 1F—61 sts.

Row 6: K2tog tbl, K12, sK2po, K12, sK2po, K12, sK2po, K12, sl 1F—53 sts.

Rows 7–17: Rep rows 3 and 6 through row 17 with 12 sts rem.

Row 18: K2tog tbl, sK2po, sK2po, sK2po, sl 1F—5 sts.

Row 20: K2tog tbl, K2tog, po. Fasten off. Sew up open seam.

Finishing

- Sew sleeve seams tog.

- With crochet hook, start at middle of back neck. Work 2 rows hdc followed by 1 row sc around entire jacket. Place buttonholes on row 2 where indicated on schematic. See "Quick Crocheted Edges" (page 22) for trim and cuffs.

- Follow instructions for "Maya's Creative Crocheted Collar" (below) if desired.

- Sew on 3 yummy buttons.

Maya's Creative Crocheted Collar

I learned the concept of this wonderful collar from Molly Geissman. I usually change colors at the beginning of each new row.

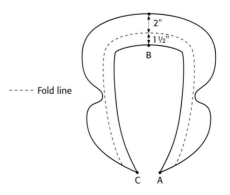

Determine proposed length of collar and place markers at points A and C. Divide total number of sts in half between A and C. Place marker at center point B.

Row 1: With WS facing, beg on left side at point A, hdc first half of sts to point B, hdc rem half of sts to point C.

Row 2: Ch 2, turn work, hdc in established sts to point A.

Row 3: Ch 2, turn work, beg shaping dec by skipping next hdc; then cont in established hdc. When decreasing on one side of collar, dec an equal number at beg of next row.

Row 4: Rep row 3. These 4 rows of hdc = approx 1½" and serve as back inside facing of collar.

Row 5: Rep row 3. This is the fold-over row.

Rows 6–8: Rep row 3.

Row 9: Divided lapel: Rep row 3, stopping 4" to 5" short of point A or C at end of row.

Row 10: Rep row 9.

Rows 11–13: Ch 2, skip 1 hdc, hdc to other side. Cont in this fashion until lapel, not including facing, equals 1½" to 2". Fasten off.

Front small lapels: At point A, hdc approx 3 rows (or number of rows needed to achieve a 2" width), dec 1 st at beg of each row. Finish off. Rep at point C. At this stage, your lapel may look a bit wonky. A complete metamorphosis occurs when you finish with one relaxed row of sc around entire length of collar.

A COLLAGE OF CREATIVE COLLARS

Adobe Brick Vest

This vest is one of many possible design variations presented in the Conceptual Design Jacket. Rather than combining multiple different shapes, an equally beautiful garment can be achieved by simply repeating one or two modules as in this vest.

Everyone's design will vary in size, depending upon the yarn, needle size, width, and length chosen. I am providing the patterns for the shapes, plus a simple schematic to get you started. To create this vest, refer to the Conceptual Design Jacket (pages 37—41).

Sizes: X-Small (Small, Medium, Large, X-Large)

Finished Chest: 33 (37, 41, 45, 49)"

Finished Length: 16 (18, 20, 22, 24)"

Materials

Use worsted-weight yarns or a variety of yarns to achieve gauge.

- Approx 500 (600, 700, 775, 850) total yds in several different colors*
- Two size 8 double-pointed needles (or size needed to obtain gauge)
- Size 8 circular needles
- Size G crochet hook
- Red Rubber Markers (see "Resources," page 128)

Model vest was knit with Great Adirondack Chamois (80% rayon, 20% cotton; 100 yds [91 m] per skein), colors Amethyst and Chili Peppers.

Gauge

Size	Gauge	Square Size	Rectangle Size
X-Small	4.5 sts = 1"	2" x 2"	2" x 4"
Small	4 sts = 1"	2¼" x 2¼"	2¼" x 4½"
Medium	3.6 sts = 1"	2½" x 2½"	2½" x 5"
Large	3.2 sts = 1"	2¾" x 2¾"	2¾" x 5½"
X-Large	3 sts = 1"	3" x 3"	3" x 6"

NOTES:

- Follow directions for Small Square (SS) and Rectangle (RT) in Conceptual Design Jacket (page 39). Refer to "Achieving a Flawless Fit" (page 25), and "Joining Modules As You Go" (page 21).

- To achieve gauge at the larger sizes, you may need to use heavier yarn or 2 strands of worsted-weight yarn. Experiment with several swatches until you are pleased with the resulting fabric. Or, as I prefer, simply knit more modules at a smaller gauge to achieve the desired fit.

Body

- Knit SS 1.

- **RT 2:** PU 10 sts along left side of SS 1, turn work, CO 28 sts (PU 10 + CO 18 + CO 10 = 38 sts). Finish mod beg at row 2 of RT. Set aside.

- **RT 3:** CO 38 sts, finish mod beg at row 2 of RT. Rep for RT 6.

- **RT 4:** PU 10 sts from left side of RT 3, CO 28 sts (PU 10 + CO 18 + CO 10 = 38 sts). Finish mod beg at row 2 of RT. Rep for RT 5. Set aside.

- **SS 7:** PU 10 sts from left side of RT 6, CO 9 sts. Finish mod beg at row 2 of SS.

- **RT 8:** CO 10 sts, PU 9 sts from top of SS 1 and 9 sts from right top half of RT 2, turn work, CO 10 sts. Finish mod beg at row 2 of RT.

- **RT 25, 35, 38, 48, 49, 52:** Work as for RT 8, rep CO and PU sequences.

- **RT 9:** PU 10 sts from left side of RT 8, PU 9 sts from left top half of RT 2, turn work, CO 9, and CO 10 sts—38 sts. Finish mod beg at row 2 of RT. Rep for RT 13.

- **RT 10:** PU 10 sts from left side of RT 9, turn work, CO 9 sts, PU 9 sts from right top half of RT 3, turn work, CO 10. Finish mod beg at row 2 of RT. Rep for RT 14.

- **RT 11:** PU 10 sts from left side of RT 10, PU 9 sts from left top half of RT 3, PU 9 sts from right top half of RT 4, turn work, CO 9 sts. Finish mod beg at row 2 of RT.

- **RT: 12, 15, 17–23, 26–32, 34, 36, 37, 43, 44, 50, 51, 56, 57:** Work as for RT 11, rep CO and PU sequences.

- **SS 16:** PU 10 sts from right top half of RT 8 below, turn work, CO 9 sts. Finish mod beg at row 2 of SS.

- **SS 40, 42, 46, 53, 55, 59:** Work as for SS 16.

- **SS 24:** PU 10 sts from left side of RT 23, PU 9 sts from left top half of RT 15. Finish mod beg at row 2 of SS.

- **SS 41, 45, 47, 54, 58, 60:** Work as for SS 24.

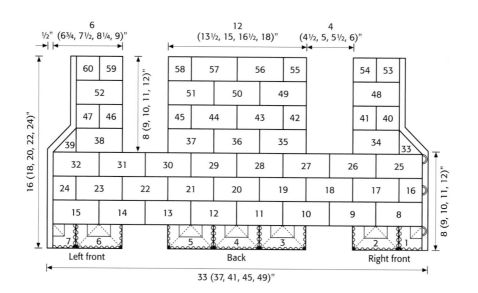

Right and Left Neck Edge Triangles (33, 39)

Triangle 33: PU 10 sts from top right of RT 25, turn work, CO 9 sts. Return to row 2.

Triangle 39: PU 10 sts from left side of RT 38, PU 9 sts from top left of RT 32. Return to row 2.

Row 1: CO or PU 19 sts.

Row 2 (WS): K1tbl, K7, PM, sK2po, K7, sl 1F—17 sts.

Row 3 and every RS row: K2tog tbl, knit across, P2tog—15 sts.

Row 4: K1tbl, K5, sK2po, K5, sl 1F—13 sts.

Rows 5–9: Rep rows 3 and 4 through row 9 with 3 sts rem, working 2 fewer sts on either side of sK2po on WS rows.

Row 10: sK2po. Fasten off.

Finishing

- Work front edge and armhole trims, referring to "Quick Crocheted Edges" (page 22). Place buttonholes at tops of RT 25, middle of SS 16, and top of SS 1.

- Sew on 3 scrumptious buttons.

Autumn in Taos Coat

This glorious three-quarter-length coat is further accentuated by the use of stunning tweed-dyed yarns and a striking back motif. While light in feel, this coat offers substantial warmth for even the snowiest day. It has replaced all my traditional purchased coats.

Sizes: Small (Medium, Large, X-Large)
Finished Chest: 43 (47, 51, 55)"
Finished Length: 29 (32, 35, 38)"

Materials

Use worsted-weight yarns as listed below or a variety of yarns to achieve gauge.

- 10 (11, 12, 13) skeins Weaving Southwest Tweed-Dyed Thick 'n Thin (100% virgin American fine wool; 122 yds [111 m] per skein), colors Mojave Mauve, Winter Plum, Camouflage, and Butterscotch

- 4 (5, 6, 7) skeins Weaving Southwest Solid colors Thick 'n Thin, colors Teal, Sangre, Garnet, and Copper

- Two size 9 double-pointed needles (or size required to obtain gauge)

- Size 9 circular needles

- Size H crochet hook

- Red Rubber Markers (see "Resources," page 128)

- 4 buttons, 2" diameter

Gauge

Basic Diamond at Widest Point

Small: 25 sts and 24 rows = 5¼"

Medium: 29 sts and 28 rows = 5¾"

Large: 31 sts and 30 rows = 6¼"

X-Large: 35 sts and 34 rows = 6¾"

Body

The following bullet points outline the knitting sequence. For more information, refer to the module instructions.

- Knit BD 1–8 as separate units to form bottom row of coat. For all rem diamonds, PU sts from previously knitted diamonds. See "Joining Modules as You Go" (page 21).

- **LHD 9:** Starting at bottom right of BD 1, PU 13 (15, 16, 18) sts. Finish mod beg at row 2 of LHD.

- **LHD 26, 43, 58:** Work as for LHD 9.

- **BD 10:** PU 13 (15, 16, 18) sts from upper left of BD 1, PU 12 (14, 15, 17) sts from upper right of BD 2. Finish mod beg at row 2 of BD.

- **BD 11–16, 18–25, 27–33, 35–42, 44–49, 51–53, 55–57, 59–62, 65–76:** Work as for BD 10.

- **RHD 17:** Starting at top left of BD 8, PU 13 (15, 16, 18) sts. Finish mod beg at row 2 of RHD.

- **RHD 34, 50, 63:** Work as for RHD 17.

Sleeves

The following bullet points outline the knitting sequence. For more information, refer to the module instructions.

- Knit BD 85 and 86 as separate units.

- **BD 87, 90, 92, 93, 96, 97:** Work as for BD 10 for Body.

- **BD 88, 91, 94, 100:** PU half of sts from BD below, turn work, CO rem sts. Finish mod beg at row 2 of BD.

- **BD 89, 95, 99:** CO half of sts, PU rem half of sts from BD below.

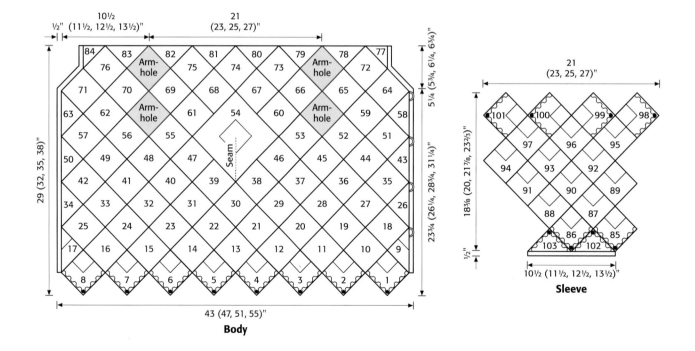

Body

Sleeve

- **BD 98, 101:** Knit as separate units. Sew to other modules, following sleeve schematic.
- **CT 102:** Turn sleeve upside down, PU 25 (29, 31, 35) sts between BD 86 and 85. Finish mod beg at row 2 of CT.
- **CT 103:** CO 13 (15, 16, 18) sts, PU rem sts from side of BD 86. Finish mod beg at row 2 of CT.

Special Abbreviations after Completing Row 2

Knit rows: sK2po = sl 1, SM, K2tog, pass slipped st over

Purl rows: sP2po = sl 1, SM, P2tog, pass slipped st over

Note: Work 1 st fewer on either side of sK2po or sP2po on every WS row.

Basic Diamond (BD)

Change colors on rows 5 and 15. Purl rows 8, 10, 12, and 14. Work 1 st fewer on either side of sK2po or sP2po on every WS row.

Row 1: CO or PU 25 (29, 31, 35) sts.

Row 2 (WS): K1tbl, K10 (12, 13, 15), PM, sK2po, K10 (12, 13, 15), sl 1F.

Row 3 and every RS row: K1tbl, knit across, sl 1F.

Row 4: K1tbl, K9 (11, 12, 14), sK2po, K9 (11, 12, 14), sl 1F.

Rep rows 3 and 4 through rows 23 (27, 29, 33) with 3 sts rem.

Next row: sK2po. Fasten off.

Right Half Diamond (RHD)

Change colors on rows 5 and 15. Purl rows 8, 10, 12, and 14. Work 1 st fewer after K2tog on WS rows.

Row 1: PU 13 (15, 16, 18) sts.

Row 2 (WS): K1tbl, K2tog, K9 (11, 12, 14), sl 1F.

Row 3 and every RS row: K1tbl, knit across, sl 1F.

Row 4: K1tbl, K2tog, K8 (10, 11, 13), sl 1F.

Rep rows 3 and 4 through rows 21 (25, 27, 31) with 3 sts rem.

Next row: K1tbl, P2tog.

Last row: K2tog. Fasten off.

Left Half Diamond (LHD)

Change colors on rows 5 and 15. Purl rows 8, 10, 12, and 14. Work 1 st fewer before K2tog on WS rows.

Row 1: PU 13 (15, 16, 18) sts.

Row 2 (WS): K1tbl, K9 (11, 12, 14), K2tog, sl 1F.

Row 3 and every RS row: K1tbl, knit across, sl 1F.

Row 4: K1tbl, K8 (10, 11, 13), K2tog, sl 1F.

Rep rows 3 and 4 through rows 21 (25, 27, 31) with 3 sts rem.

Next row: K1tbl, P2tog.

Last row: K2tog. Fasten off.

Neck Quarter Diamond (NQD) 77, 84

Change colors on row 5. Work 2 fewer sts between decs on every WS row.

Row 1: NQD 77: PU 13 (15, 16, 18) sts from upper right of BD 72. **NQD 84:** PU 13 (15, 16, 18) sts from upper left of BD 76.

Row 2 (WS): K1tbl, K2tog, K7 (9, 10, 12), K2tog, sl 1F.

Row 3 row and every RS row: K1tbl, knit across, sl 1F.

Row 4: K1tbl, K2tog, K5 (7, 8, 10), K2tog, sl 1F.

Rep rows 3 and 4 through rows 9 (11, 13, 15) with 5 sts rem.

Next row: K1tbl, K2tog, P2tog.

Last row: sK2po. Fasten off.

Shoulder Triangle (ST), 78-83, or Cuff Triangle (CT), 102, 103

Change colors on row 5. Work 2 fewer sts on either side of dec on every WS row.

ST 78: PU 12 (14, 15, 17) sts from upper left of 72, turn work, CO 13 (15, 16, 18) sts.

ST 79: CO 13 (15, 16, 18) sts, PU 12 (14, 15, 17) sts from upper right of 73.

ST 80: PU 12 (14, 15, 17) sts from upper left of 73, PU 13 (15, 16, 18) sts from upper right of 74.

ST 81: PU 12 (14, 15, 17) sts from upper left of 74, PU 13 (15, 16, 18) sts from upper right of 75.

ST 82: PU 12 (14, 15, 17) sts from upper left of 75, turn work, CO 13 (15, 16, 18) sts.

ST 83: CO 13 (15, 16, 18) sts, PU 12 (14, 15, 17) sts from upper right of 76.

CT 102: PU 12 (14, 15, 17) sts from 86, PU 13 (15, 16, 18) sts from 85.

CT 103: CO 13 (15, 16, 18) sts, PU 12 (14, 15, 17) sts from 86.

Row 1: PU or CO 25 (29, 31, 35) sts as indicated above.

Row 2 (WS): K1tbl, K10 (12, 13, 15), PM, sK2po, K10 (12, 13, 15), sl 1F.

Row 3 and every RS row: K2tog tbl, knit across, P2tog.

Row 4: K1tbl, K8 (10, 11, 13), sK2po, K8 (10, 11, 13), sl 1F.

Rep rows 3 and 4 through rows 12 (14, 15, 17) with 3 sts rem.

Next row: sK2po. Fasten off.

Large Diamond (LD) 54

Use circular needles. Change colors on rows 7, 17, and 23. Purl rows 12 and 14.

NOTE: The large center back diamond is worked in a combination of picking up from existing diamonds and casting on. It is not knit in the round. At end of each row, turn work and knit or purl back according to directions. This technique allows colors and pattern stitches to remain symmetrical. When completed, it will have a diagonal opening. Using the same color yarns as they appear in the diamond, sew up seam. If you prefer not to have this large center diamond, you can continue in established fashion and knit four basic diamonds in this same space.

Row 1: Starting at upper-right half of BD 39 and continuing across upper-right half of BD 47, PU 24 (28, 30, 34) sts, turn work, CO 48 (56, 60, 68) sts, PU 24 (28, 30, 34) sts from upper-left halves of BD 46 and BD 38—96 (112, 120, 136) total sts.

Row 2: K1tbl, K22 (26, 28, 32), PM, K2tog, K22 (26, 28, 32), PM, K2tog, K22 (26, 28, 32), PM, K2tog, K22 (26, 28, 32), sl 1F.

Row 3 and every RS row: K1tbl, knit across, sl 1F.

Row 4: K2tog tbl, K20 (24, 26, 30), sK2po, K20 (24, 26, 30), sK2po, K20 (24, 26, 30), sK2po, K20 (24, 26, 30), P2tog.

Rep rows 3 and 4 through rows 25 (29, 31, 35) with 5 sts rem.

Next row: K2tog tbl, sK2po, po. Fasten off.

Finishing

- At shoulder, sew 77 to right half of 80, sew 78 to 79. Sew 84 to left half of 81, sew 83 to 82.

- **Sleeves:** Matching BD placements with schematic, sew sleeves into body. Fold each sleeve in half lengthwise and sew up seams.

- Finish cuffs with 2 rows of hdc followed by 1 row of sc.

- **Front edge:** Refer to "Quick Crocheted Edges" (page 22). Place buttonholes at tops of LHD 58, 43, 26, and 9.

- Sew on 4 wonderful buttons.

Shoulders and Shoulder Pads

- Stabilize shoulder seams inside coat with ch st from neck edge across shoulder for 7" to 9".

- **With leftover yarns, knit 2 shoulder pads:** CO 20 sts, work in garter st for 38 rows, BO. Make two 5½" squares. Fold over each on diagonal to form a half diamond. Whipstitch seams. Tack 3 corners into shoulders of coat. Long expanse is at shoulder and single point is at neck edge.

Dream Coat

Dream Coat represents a real dream come true. In July 2000, I was among ten people in America honored to study under the "Master of Miters," Herr Horst Schulz, in his opulent Berlin flat. Before attending his eight-day workshop, each student was to design and knit an original modular garment. Of course, it had to be a masterpiece in order to pass the judgment of Herr Schulz. After much struggle, indecision, designing, and redesigning, I finally created Dream Coat as my entry piece to the workshop.

This coat was designed on the needles and since I never planned to reproduce it, I didn't take notes on how I did it! Because this has been the most requested piece I have ever knit, I was finally persuaded to write the following pattern. I hope you gain as much pleasure from knitting it and wearing it as I have.

Sizes: Small/Medium (Large/X-Large)

Finished Chest: 41¾ (57¾)"

Finished Hip: 44 (61)"

Finished Length: 26"

NOTE: Using different-sized needles to knit the coat results in subtle shaping, a gentle flare, and extra width at the hip.

Materials

Use worsted-weight yarns as listed below or a variety of yarns to meet gauge.

- 8 to 10 total skeins Great Adirondack Chamois (80% rayon, 20% cotton; 100 yds [91 m] per skein) and/or Noro Silk Garden (45% silk, 45% kid mohair, 10% lamb's wool; 109 yds [100 m] per skein) in 3 to 4 different colorways

- 4 to 6 total skeins Noro Cash Iroha (40% silk, 30% lamb's wool, 20% cashmere, 10% nylon; 99 yds [91 m] per skein) and/or Muench Horstia Maulbeerseide-Schurwolle (50% silk, 50% wool; 108 yds [100 m] per skein) in 4 to 6 different colorways

- Two size 6 double-pointed needles for half diamonds and cuff diamonds

- Two size 6 circular needles for chevrons and cuff bands

- Two size 7 double-pointed needles for first 3 rows of diamonds at hem of coat (or size required to obtain gauge)

- Size 7 circular needles for button band

- Red Rubber Markers (see "Resources," page 128)

- 3 buttons, 1" diameter

Gauge

Basic Diamond: 29 sts and 28 rows = 4½" at widest point on 7 needles

Body Chevron: 4" wide x 17¼" long on size 6 needles

Dazzling Idea!

The body chevrons in this coat are approx 4" wide. Blocking and buttonhole trim net a 42" to 44" finished chest. If you like, you can add two more body chevron panels to the back and one to each front side to increase the finished width to approximately 56" to 60". See diagrams on page 55.

Body

The following bullet points outline the knitting sequence. For more information, refer to the module instructions.

- Knit BD 1–8 as separate units. For all rem BDs, PU sts from previously knit BD. See "Joining Modules As You Go" (page 21).

- **BD 9, 18:** CO 14 sts, PU 15 sts from upper right of BD 1 or 9. Finish mod beg at row 2 of BD.

- **BD 10:** PU 14 sts from upper left of BD 1, PU 15 sts from upper right of BD 2. Finish mod beg at row 2 of BD.

- **BD 11–16 and 19–26:** Work as for BD 10.

- **BD 17, 27:** PU 15 sts from upper left of BD 8 or 17, turn work, CO 14 sts. Finish mod beg at row 2 of BD.

- **LHC 28:** Work as for LHC.

- **BC 29:** Starting at left top of LHC 28, PU 66 sts, PM, PU 14 sts from upper left of BD 18, PU 15 sts from upper right of BD 19, PM, turn work, CO 66 sts. Total: 161 sts. Finish mod beg at row 2 of BC.

- **BC 30, 32–35, 37:** Work as for BC 29.

- **BC 31, 36:** See schematic for armhole opening. CO 33 sts, then 33 sts down from top of BC 30 or 35, PU 33 sts from left side of BC 30 or 35, PM, PU 14 sts from upper left of BD 20 or 25, PU 15 sts from upper right of BD 21 or 26, PM, turn work, CO 66 sts. Total: 161 sts. Finish mod beg at row 2 of BC.

- **RHC 38:** Work as for RHC.

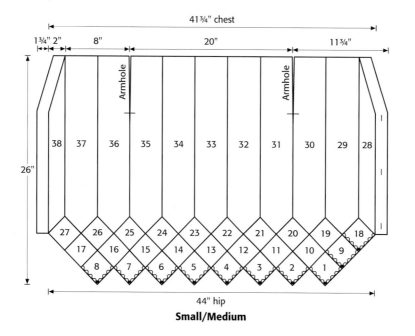

41¾" chest

1¾" 2"   8"   20"   11¾"

Armhole   Armhole

| 38 | 37 | 36 | 35 | 34 | 33 | 32 | 31 | 30 | 29 | 28 |

26"

27 26 25 24 23 22 21 20 19 18
17 16 15 14 13 12 11 10 9
8 7 6 5 4 3 2 1

44" hip

Small/Medium

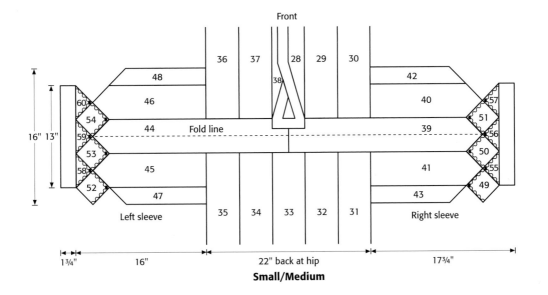

Small/Medium

Front

36 37 28 29 30

48 42

60 57

54 51

59 44   Fold line   39 56

53 50

58 55

52 45   41 49

47 43

Left sleeve   35 34 33 32 31   Right sleeve

16" 13"

1¾" 16" 22" back at hip 17¾"

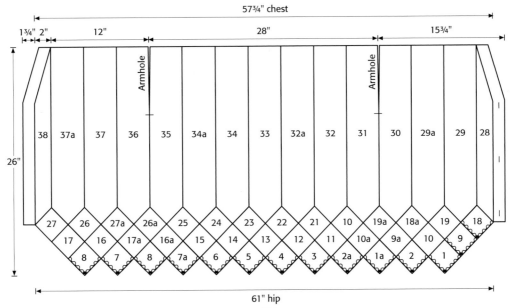

Large/X-Large

57¾" chest

1¾" 2" 12" 28" 15¾"

Armhole   Armhole

38 37a 37 36 35 34a 34 33 32a 32 31 30 29a 29 28

26"

27 26 27a 26a 25 24 23 22 21 10 19a 18a 19 18

17 16 17a 16a 15 14 13 12 11 10a 9a 10 9

8 7 8 7a 6 5 4 3 2a 1a 2 1

61" hip

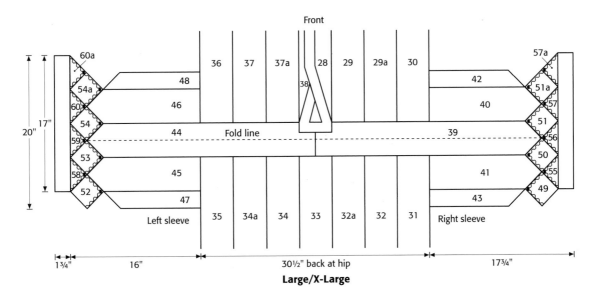

Large/X-Large

Front

60a 57a

60 57 37 37a 28 29 29a 30   42

54a 51a

48 46 38 40 57

60 51

54 56

59 44   Fold line   39 50

53 45 41 55

58 49

52 47 43

Left sleeve   35 34a 34 33 32a 32 31   Right sleeve

20" 17"

1¾" 16" 30½" back at hip 17¾"

Sleeves and Shoulders

The following bullet points outline the knitting sequence. For more information, refer to the module instructions.

- **SC 40, 45:** CO 52 sts, PM, CO 29 sts, PM, PU 52 sts along RSC 39 or LSC 44—133 sts. Finish mod beg at row 2 of SC.

- **SC 41, 46:** PU 52 sts from RSC 39 or LSC 44, PM, turn work, CO 29 sts, PM, CO 52 sts—133 sts. Finish mod beg at row 2 of SC.

- **SHC 42, 47:** PU 52 sts from SC 40 or SC 45. Finish mod beg at row 2 of SHC 42, 47.

- **SHC 43, 48:** PU 52 sts from SC 41 or SC 46. Finish mod beg at row 2 of SHC 43, 48.

- **RSC 39 and LSC 44:** Follow directions for mod.

- **BD 49:** Using size 6 dpn, CO 14 sts, PU 15 sts from SC 41. Finish mod beg at row 2 of BD.

- **BD 50, 51, 53, 54:** Using size 6 dpn, PU 14 sts from one side of a SC, PU 15 sts from another SC or a shoulder chevron. Finish mod beg at row 2 of BD.

- **BD 52:** PU 15 sts from side of SC 45, turn work, CO 14 sts. Finish mod beg at row 2 of BD.

- **CHD 55, 56, 58, 59:** PU 15 sts from upper left of one BD, PU 14 sts from upper right of another BD. Finish mod beg at row 2 of CHD.

- **CHD 57:** PU 15 sts from upper left of BD 51, turn work, CO 14 sts. Finish mod beg at row 2 of CHD.

- **CHD 60:** CO 14 sts, PU 15 sts from upper right of BD 54. Finish mod beg at row 2 of CHD.

Special Abbreviations after Completing Row 2

Knit rows: sK2po = sl 1wyib, SM, K2tog, pass slipped st over

Purl rows: sP2po = sl 1wyib, SM, P2tog, pass slipped st over

Work 1 st fewer either side of sK2po or sP2po on WS rows.

Basic Diamond (BD) 1–27 and 49–54

Use size 7 dpn for BD 1–27. Use size 6 dpn for BD 49–54. Change colors on rows 5 and 15. Purl rows 8, 10, 12, and 14.

Row 1: CO or PU 29 sts.

Row 2 (WS): K1tbl, K12, PM, sK2po, K12, sl 1F—27 sts.

Row 3 and every RS row: K1tbl, knit across, sl 1F.

Row 4: K1tbl, K11, sK2po, K11, sl 1F—25 sts.

Rows 5–27: Rep rows 3 and 4 through row 27 with 3 sts rem.

Row 28: sK2po. Finish off.

Body Chevron (BC) 29–37

Use size 6 circular needles. Change colors on rows 5, 7, 13, and 15. Purl rows 8, 10, and 12.

Row 1: CO or PU 161 sts as follows: 66 sts, PM, 29 sts, PM, 66 sts.

Row 2 (WS): K1tbl, K63, K2tog, SM, K13, PM, sK2po, K13, SM, K2tog, K63, sl 1F—157 sts.

Row 3 and every RS row: K1tbl, knit across, sl 1F.

Row 4: K1tbl, K62, K2tog, SM, K12, sK2po, K12, SM, K2tog, K62, sl 1F—153 sts.

Rows 5–15: Rep rows 3 and 4 through RS row 15 with 133 sts rem. Place 66 sts on size 6 circular needles, place rem 67 sts on other size 6 circular needles. With RS of work facing each other and with size 6 dpn, work a relaxed 3-needle BO on WS of work.

Left Half Chevron (LHC) 28

Use size 6 circular needles. Change colors on rows 5, 7, and 13. Purl rows 8, 10, and 12. Work 1 st fewer after marker on WS rows.

Row 1: PU 15 sts from upper-right half of BD 18, PM, turn work, CO 66 sts—81 sts.

Row 2 (WS): BO 3 sts, K60, K2tog, SM, K13, P2tog—76 sts.

Row 3 and every RS row: K1tbl, knit across, sl 1F.

Row 4: BO 3 sts, K56, K2tog, SM, K12, P2tog—71 sts.

Rows 5–14: Rep rows 3 and 4 through WS row 14. BO rem 46 sts.

Right Half Chevron (RHC) 38

Use size 6 circular needles. Change colors on rows 5, 7, and 13. Purl rows 8, 10, and 12, beg with K2tog tbl. Work 1 st fewer before marker on WS rows.

Row 1: PU 66 sts from left side of BC 37, PM, PU 15 sts from upper-left half of BD 27—81 sts.

Row 2 (WS): K2tog tbl, K13, SM, K2tog, K63, sl 1F—79 sts.

Row 3: BO 6 sts, K71, sl 1F—73 sts.

Row 4: K2tog tbl, K12, SM, K2tog, K56, sl 1F—71 sts.

Row 5: BO 3 sts, K66, sl 1F—68 sts.

Row 6: K2tog tbl, K11, SM, K2tog, K52, sl 1F—66 sts.

Rows 7–14: Rep rows 5 and 6, purling rows 8, 10, and 12, through WS row 14. BO rem 46 sts.

Right Shoulder Chevron (RSC) 39

Use size 6 circular needles. Change colors on rows 5, 7, 13, and 15. Purl rows 8, 10, and 12.

Row 1: PU 36 sts from tops of BC 29 and 30, turn work, CO 52 sts, PM, CO 29 sts, PM, CO 52 sts, PU 36 sts from tops of BC 31 and 32, PU 9 sts from top right half of BC 33—214 sts.

Row 2 (WS): K1tbl, K94, K2tog, SM, K13, PM, sK2po, K13, SM, K2tog, K85, sl 1F—210 sts.

Row 3 and every RS row: K1tbl, knit across, sl 1F.

Row 4: K1tbl, K93, K2tog, SM, K12, sK2po, K12, SM, K2tog, K84, sl 1F—206 sts.

Rows 5–13: Rep rows 3 and 4 through RS row 13 with 190 sts rem. On WS rows, K2tog/P2tog before first marker, K2tog/P2tog after last marker, and knit 1 st fewer on either side of sK2po/sP2po.

Row 14: BO 9 sts, K79, K2tog, SM, K7, sK2po, K7, SM, K2tog, K79, sl 1F—177 sts.

Row 16: Place 89 sts on size 6 circular needles, place rem 88 sts on other size 6 circular needles. With RS facing and size 6 dpn, work relaxed 3-needle BO on WS of work.

Left Shoulder Chevron (LSC) 44

Use size 6 circular needles. Change colors on rows 5, 7, 13, and 15. Purl rows 8, 10, and 12.

Row 1: PU 9 sts from top-left half of BC 33, PU 36 sts from tops of BC 34 and 35, turn work, CO 52 sts, PM, CO 29 sts, PM, CO 52 sts, PU 36 sts from tops of BC 36 and 37—214 sts.

Row 2 (WS): K1tbl, K85, K2tog, SM, K13, PM, sK2po, K13, SM, K2tog, K94, sl 1F—210 sts.

Row 3 and every RS row: K1tbl, knit across, sl 1F.

Row 4: K1tbl, K84, K2tog, SM, K12, sK2po, K12, SM, K2tog, K93, sl 1F—206 sts.

Rows 5–13: Rep rows 3 and 4 through RS row 13 with 190 sts rem. On WS rows, K2tog/P2tog before first marker, K2tog/P2tog after last marker and knit 1 st fewer on either side of sK2po/sP2po.

Row 14: K1tbl, K79, K2tog, SM, K7, sK2po, K7, SM, K2tog, K79, BO 9 sts—176 sts. Fasten off last st and cut yarn.

Row 15: Reattach yarn and K1tbl, knit across, sl 1F.

Row 16: Place 88 sts on size 6 circular needles. Place rem 88 sts on other size 6 circular needles. With RS facing and size 6 dpn, work relaxed 3-needle BO on WS of work.

Sleeve Chevron (SC) 40, 41, 45, 46

Use size 6 circular needles. Change colors on rows 5, 7, 13, and 15. Purl rows 8, 10, and 12.

Row 1: CO or PU 52 sts, PM, CO 29 sts, PM, CO or PU 52 sts—133 sts.

Row 2 (WS): K1tbl, K49, K2tog, SM, K13, PM, sK2po, K13, SM, K2tog, K49, sl 1F—129 sts.

Row 3 and every RS row: K1tbl, knit across, sl 1F.

Row 4: K1tbl, K48, K2tog, SM, K12, sK2po, K12, SM, K2tog, K48, sl 1F—125 sts.

Rows 5–15: Rep rows 3 and 4 through RS row 15 with 105 sts rem.

Place 53 sts on size 6 circular needles. Place rem 52 sts on other size 6 circular needles. With RS facing and size 6 dpn, work relaxed 3-needle BO on WS of work.

Sleeve Half Chevron (SHC) 42, 47

Use size 6 circular needles. Change colors on rows 5, 7, 13, 15, and 17. Purl rows 8, 10, 12, and 16.

Row 1: PU 52 sts from SC 40 or 45.

Row 2 (WS): K1tbl, knit across, P2tog—51 sts.

Row 3 and every RS row: K2tog tbl, knit across, sl 1F.

Row 4: K1tbl, knit or purl across, P2tog.

Rows 5–18: Rep rows 3 and 4 through WS row 18 with 35 sts rem.

Place 35 sts on holder. When completed, place 35 sts of SHC 42 and 43 on 2 sets of size 6 needles. With RS facing and size 6 dpn, work relaxed 3-needle BO on WS of work. Rep for SHC 47 and 48.

Sleeve Half Chevron (SHC) 43 and 48

Use size 6 circular needles. Change colors on rows 5, 7, 13, 15, and 17. Purl rows 8, 10, 12, and 16.

Row 1: PU 52 sts from SC 41 or 46.

Row 2 (WS): K2tog tbl, knit across, sl 1F—51 sts.

Row 3 and every RS row: K1tbl, knit across, P2tog.

Row 4 and every WS row: K2tog tbl, knit or purl across, sl 1F.

Rows 5–18: Rep rows 3 and 4 through WS row 18 with 35 sts rem.

Place 35 sts on holder. When completed, place 35 sts of SHC 42 and 43 on 2 sets of size 6 needles. With RS facing and size 6 dpn, work relaxed 3-needle BO on WS of work. Rep for SHC 47 and 48.

Cuff Half Diamond (CHD) 55–60

Use size 6 dpn. Change colors on rows 5 and 11. Work 2 fewer sts on either side of dec on every WS row.

Row 1: PU or CO 29 sts.

Row 2 (WS): K1tbl, K12, PM, sK2po, K12, sl 1F—27 sts.

Row 3 and every RS row: K2tog tbl, knit across, P2tog.

Row 4: K1tbl, K10, sK2po, K10, sl 1F.

Rows 5–14: Rep rows 3 and 4 through WS row 14.

Row 15: sK2po. Finish off.

Button Band (BB)

Use size 7 circular needles. Cut thirteen 39" lengths of at least 5 different colors of textural yarn for col 3.

Do not use first and last stitch technique for button band.

Sl sts wyib on all RS rows and sl sts wyif on all WS rows.

Row 1: Col 1: PU 202 sts as follows: Starting at lower-right edge of LHC 28, PU 58 sts, PU 34 sts along right front neck edge (beg at slope of LHC 28 and halfway across top of RSC 39), PU 18 sts across back neck, PU 34 sts along left front neck edge (beg halfway across top of LSC 44 and across slope of RHC 38), PU 58 sts across remainder of RHC 38.

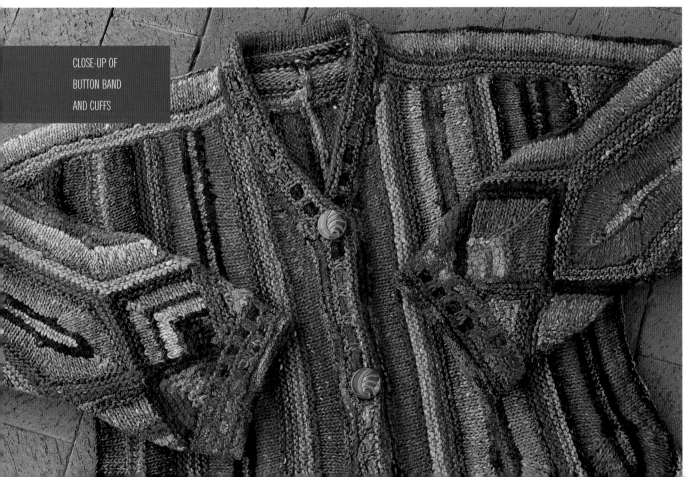

CLOSE-UP OF
BUTTON BAND
AND CUFFS

Row 2 (WS): Knit. Cut col 1.

Row 3 (RS): Col 2: Knit.

Row 4 (WS): Knit.

Row 5 (RS): Knit. Cut col 2.

Row 6 (RS): Col 3: Slide sts to other end of needle. With RS facing and first 39" length of yarn, (K2, sl 2) 4 times. Rep this sequence 11 more times, using 11 different lengths of col. These 12 sequences are knit over 192 sts. Knit 13th col over rem 10 sts, (K2, sl 2) 2 times, K2.

Row 7 (WS): In established col sequence, (K2, sl 2) 50 times, knitting the purls and slipping previously slipped sts wyif, ending with K2. Twist yarns at col changes.

Row 8 (RS): Buttonhole row: P2, sl 2, P2, sl 1, BO 2 sts, sl 2, (P2, sl 2) 4 times, P2, sl 1, BO 2 sts, sl 2, (P2, sl 2) 4 times, P2, sl 1, BO 2 sts, sl 2. Cont (P2, sl 2) across, ending with P2.

Row 9 (WS): *K2, sl 2* in established sequence. At each BO, turn work, CO 2 sts.

Row 10 (RS): Col 2: Knit row, simultaneously knitting in col 3 yarn tails.

Row 11 (WS): Knit.

Row 12 (RS): Col 1: Knit.

Row 13 (WS): Fold-line row: Knit. Cut col 1.

Row 14 (RS): Col 2: Knit.

Row 15 (WS): Purl.

Row 16 (RS): Buttonhole row: K7, BO 2 sts, K21, BO 2 sts, K21, BO 2 sts, knit rem sts.

Row 17 (WS): Purl row: At each BO, turn work, CO 2 sts.

Row 18 (RS): Knit.

Row 19 (WS): Purl.

Row 20: BO 202 sts.

Cuff Bands (CB)

Use size 6 circular needles. Cut eight 39" lengths of 4 different colors of textural yarn for col 2. Cuff bands are knit straight and sewn to CHD.

Do not use first and last st technique for cuff bands. Sl sts wyib on all RS rows and sl sts wyif on all WS rows.

Row 1: Col 1: CO 60 sts.

Row 2 (WS): Knit.

Row 3 (RS): Knit. Cut col 1.

Row 4 (RS): Col 2: Slide sts to other end of needle. With RS work facing and first 39" length of yarn, (K2, sl 2) 4 times. Rep sequence 2 more times, using different colors. These 3 sequences are knit over 48 sts. Knit 4th col over rem 12 sts, (K2, sl 2) 3 times.

Row 5 (WS): In established col sequence, (sl 2, K2) 15 times, knitting the purls and slipping previously slipped sts wyif. Twist yarns at col changes.

Row 6 (RS): (P2, sl 2) 15 times.

Row 7 (WS): (Sl 2, K2) 15 times.

Row 8 (RS): Col 1: Knit row, simultaneously knitting in col 2 yarns.

Row 9 (WS): Knit.

Row 10 (RS): Knit. Cut col 1.

Row 11 (RS): Col 2: Slide sts to other end of needle. This is similar to row 4 except pattern is offset as follows: With RS facing and a length of col, (sl 2, K2) 4 times. Rep sequence 2 more times, using 2 different colors. Knit 4th col over rem 12 sts, (sl 2, K2) 3 times.

Row 12 (WS): (K2, sl 2) 15 times, knitting the purls and slipping previously slipped sts wyif. Twist yarns at col changes.

Row 13 (RS): (Sl 2, P2) 15 times.

Row 14 (WS): (K2, sl 2) 15 times.

Row 15 (RS): Col 1: Knit row, simultaneously knitting in col 2 yarn tails.

Row 16 (WS): Knit.

Row 17 (RS): Knit. Cut col 1.

Row 18 (RS): Col 3: Slide sts to other end of needle. With RS facing, knit.

Row 19 (WS): Knit.

Row 20 (RS): BO 60 sts.

Make 2 cuff bands.

Finishing

- Sew sleeves into coat body.

- Sew open sections of SHC 42 and 43 tog and SHC 47 and 48 tog.

- Sew RSC 39 to LSC 44 at back neck.

- Sew cuff bands to CHDs. Sew button-band facing to inside of coat.

- Sew on 3 traffic-stopping buttons.

DREAM COAT IN RED AND GREEN COLORWAYS USING GREAT ADIRONDACK CHAMOIS, NORO SILK GARDEN, AND MUENCH HORSTIA MAULBEERSEIDE-SCHURWOLLE SILK

Triangles: The Basics

Fun, simple, and fast! What more could a knitter ask? How about the perfect fit! The following two designs offer all these things and many other bonuses for the knitter seeking instant gratification.

Since the pyramid modules in these projects are made with equilateral triangles, each one can be turned any direction you desire to add to the fun. Each pyramid is a simple combination of two alternating rows of color 1 in garter stitch and color 2 in stockinette stitch. Another bonus is that each pyramid takes only a fast 15 to 20 minutes to finish, due to the rapid decreases in the pattern. Use the technique "Double Cast On" (page 20) throughout these two designs.

Thanks to their unique side panels, these projects can be knit in essentially any size desired. Everyone knits the same front and back and then selects the side panel most compatible to a "perfect fit."

It is very important to note on the schematic that sizes Large and XX-Large each have unique side panels in which the pyramid modules continue uninterrupted across the garment. Modules with an asterisk (3, 4, 9, 10, 15, 16, 21, 22, 27, 28, 33, 34, 39, 40, 45, 46) are for sizes Large and XX-Large only. All other sizes omit these 16 basic pyramid (BP) modules and follow directions for "Chevron Side Panels."

When completed, your pyramid module will have two finished edges and one unfinished edge. To pick up the needed stitches along the unfinished edge, it is especially important to start at the extreme right side and end at the extreme left side of this edge. It is also necessary to pick up the sometimes hidden stitches on either side of the finishing-off knot as well as a stitch in the knot itself. Remember that you need to have picked up approximately one-fourth (9 or 11) of the 37 or 43 needed stitches by the time you reach the knot on this edge.

To tumble your pyramids in different directions, cast on half of your stitches and then pick up the remaining stitches. On others, pick up half the stitches, turn your work, and cast on the remaining half.

If you look closely, you will notice that your pyramids form a series of interlocking hexagons. When you have connected four pyramids, it is quite easy to think you need only one more pyramid to close up the opening. Not so! Always be sure you have six, not five, pyramids linking together; otherwise your work will warp and buckle.

THE PROJECTS

Page 65   Page 71

Pyramid Vest

Learn the true secrets to the construction of the pyramids by knitting these very simple equilateral triangles. This lovely vest is the epitome of instant gratification and is one of the easiest patterns in this book. Prepare to stop even the Sphinx in her tracks!

Sizes: X-Small, Small, Medium, Large, (X-Large, XX-Large)

Finished Chest: 35, 37½, 40, 43 (47, 49)"

Finished Length: 18½, 18½, 18½, 18½, (23, 23)"

Materials

Use worsted-weight yarns as listed below or a variety of yarns to achieve gauge.

- **Col 1:** Approx 350, 360, 370, 400 (550, 575) total yds Gedifra Dandy (60% merino, 20% poly-acrylic, 20% polyamide; 71 yds [65 m] per skein), colors 1412, 1420, 1468

- **Col 2:** Approx 280, 290, 300, 310 (375, 390) total yds Noro Cash Iroha (40% silk, 30% lamb's wool, 20% cashmere, 10% nylon; 99 yds [91 m] per skein) and/or Muench Horstia Maulbeerseide-Schurwolle (50% silk, 50% wool; 108 yds [100 m] per skein) in a variety of solid colors

- Two size 6 double-pointed needles (or size required to obtain gauge)

- Size 6 circular needles for larger sizes

- Size G crochet hook

- Tape measure

- 3 buttons, 1" diameter

Dazzling Idea!

Try using a heavier weight or more textured yarn for color 1 and a slightly lighter weight yarn for color 2 to increase the surface dimensionality of your vest.

Gauge for Basic Pyramid

X-Small, Small, Medium, Large: 37 sts and 15 rows = 4" per side

X-Large, XX-Large: 43 sts and 17 rows = 5" per side

Body

The following bullet points outline the knitting sequence. For more information, refer to the module instructions.

Important Note: In the first schematic below, for sizes X-Small, Small, Medium and X-Large, notice that the chevron side panels are worked at the sides below the armholes instead of the modules. In the second schematic below, for sizes Large and XX-Large, notice that the modules are worked at the sides instead of the side panels. Work BP 3, 4, 9, 10, 15, 16, 21, 22, 27, 28, 33, 34, 39, 40, 45, and 46 (which are followed by an * in the schematics) only for sizes Large and XX-Large.

Remember: The pyramid modules are worked in two sizes, 4" per side on the X-Small, Small, Medium, and Large; and 5" per side on the X-Large and XX-Large. Throughout the directions, you will often see 2 sets of stitch numbers. The first set refers to sizes X-Small, Small, Medium, and Large. The stitch numbers in parentheses refer to sizes X-Large and XX-Large.

- Knit BP 1, 5, 7, 11 (1, 3*, 5, 7, 9*, 11) as separate units for bottom row of vest.

- **BP 2, 6, 8, 12 (2, 4*, 6, 8, 10*, 12):** PU sts from knitted BP to form new BP. PU 19 (22) sts from a pyramid, turn work, CO 18 (21) sts. Finish mod beg at row 2 of BP. See "Joining Modules As You Go" (page 21).

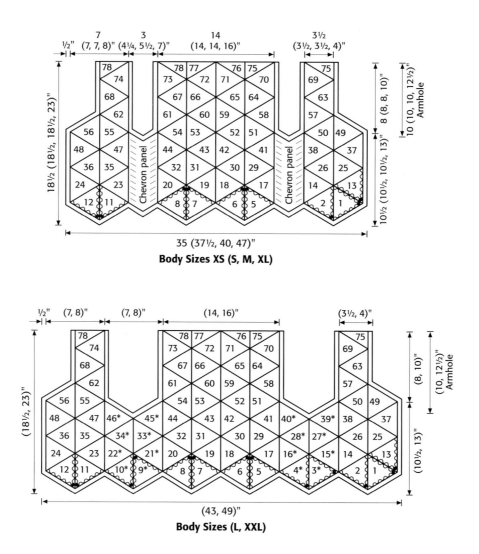

Body Sizes XS (S, M, XL)

Body Sizes (L, XXL)

- **BP 13:** CO 18 (21) sts, PU 19 (22) sts from upper-right side of BP 1. Finish mod beg at row 2 of BP.

- **BP 14, 16*, 18, 20, 22*, 24, 25, 27*, 29, 31, 33*, 35, 37, 38, 40*, 42, 44, 46*, 48, 49, 51, 53, 55, 57–59, 61–64, 66, 68–71, 73, 74:** Work as for BP 13. You can PU, then CO rem sts or you can CO, then PU to provide variety.

- **BP 15*, 17, 19, 21*, 23, 26, 28*, 30, 32, 34*, 36, 39*, 41, 43, 45*, 47, 50, 52, 54, 56, 60, 65, 67, 72:** PU from 2 previously formed pyramids. PU 19 (22) sts from a side of an existing pyramid; then PU 18 (21) sts from another existing pyramid. Finish mod beg at row 2 of BP.

- **BP 75, 78:** In the schematic, it appears these modules are knit in two separate halves. Actually, each is knit as a single, complete BP unit. To knit BP 75, PU 19 (22) sts from upper-right portion of 69, PU 18 (21) sts from upper-left section of 70. Finish mod beg at row 2 of BP. This joins right front of vest to back of vest. Knit BP 78 in same fashion by picking up from BP 73 and 74, joining left front to left back of vest.

Basic Pyramid (BP)

X-Small, Small, Medium, Large (X-Large, XX-Large). All sizes share first 12 rows. Proceed to desired size to finish module.

Row 1: Col 1: CO or PU 37 (43) sts.

Row 2 (WS): K1tbl, K16 (19), sK2po, K16 (19), sl 1F—35 (41) sts.

Row 3: Col 2: K2tog tbl, K14 (17), sK2po, K15 (18), sl 1F—32 (38) sts.

Row 4: K2tog tbl, P13 (16), sP2po, P13 (16), sl 1F—29 (35) sts.

Row 5: Col 1: K2tog tbl, knit across, sl 1F—28 (34) sts.

Row 6: K2tog tbl, K11 (14), sK2po, K11 (14), sl 1F—25 (31) sts.

Row 7: Col 2: K2tog tbl, K9 (12), sK2po, K10 (13), sl 1F—22 (28) sts.

Row 8: K2tog tbl, P8 (11), sP2po, P8 (11), sl 1F—19 (25) sts.

Row 9: Col 1: K2tog tbl, knit across, sl 1F—18 (24) sts.

Row 10: K2tog tbl, K6 (9), sK2po, K6 (9), sl 1F—15 (21) sts. Cut col 1 for smaller sizes.

Row 11: Col 2: K2tog tbl, K4 (7), sK2po, K5 (8), sl 1F—12 (18) sts.

Row 12: K2tog tbl, P3 (6), sP2po, P3 (6), sl 1F—9 (15) sts.

BP: X-Small, Small, Medium, Large

Row 13: Col 2: K2tog tbl, K1, sK2po, K2, sl 1F—6 sts.

Row 14: K2tog tbl, sP2po, sl 1F—3 sts.

Row 15: K1tbl, K2tog, po. Fasten off.

BP: X-Large, XX-Large

Row 13: Col 1: K2tog tbl, K4, sK2po, K5, sl 1F—12 sts.

Row 14: K2tog tbl, K3, sK2po, K3, sl 1F—9 sts. Cut col 1 yarn.

Row 15: Col 2: K2tog tbl, K1, sK2po, K2, sl 1F—6 sts.

Row 16: K2tog tbl, sP2po, sl 1F—3 sts.

Row 17: K1tbl, K2tog, po. Fasten off.

Neck Half Pyramids (NHP) 76, 77

X-Small, Small, Medium, Large (X-Large, XX-Large). All sizes share first 12 rows. Proceed to desired size to finish module.

Row 1: Col 1: PU 19 (22) sts from BP 71 or BP 72. PU NHP 76 from upper right of BP 71. PU NHP 77 from upper left of BP 72.

Rows 2, 6, 10 (WS): Col 1: K2tog tbl, knit across, sl 1F—18, 13, 8 (21, 16, 11) sts. Cut col 1 after row 10 for smaller sizes.

Rows 3, 7, 11: Col 2: K2tog tbl, knit across, P2tog—16, 11, 6 (19, 14, 9) sts.

Rows 4, 8, 12: Col 2: K2tog tbl, purl across, sl 1F—15, 10, 5 (18, 13, 8) sts.

Rows 5, 9: Col 1: K2tog tbl, knit across, sl 1F—14, 9 (17, 12) sts.

NHP: X-Small, Small, Medium, Large

Row 13: Col 2: K2tog tbl, K1, P2tog—3 sts.

Row 14: K1tbl, P2tog, po. Fasten off.

NHP: X-Large, XX-Large

Row 13: Col 1: K2tog tbl, K5, sl 1F—7 sts.

Row 14: K2tog tbl, K4, sl 1F—6 sts. Cut col 1.

Row 15: Col 2: K2tog tbl, K2, P2tog—4 sts.

Row 16: K2tog tbl, P2tog, po. Fasten off.

Chevron Side Panels

For X-Small, Small, Medium, and X-Large Only

When vest fronts and back are completed, measure existing width. Crochet button band will add another ½" to 1" to width of each front. This measurement will determine the additional width needed to complete your vest. Choose side panel that most closely matches final width needed. Knit two panels. Single crochet down each side of finished panel if desired.

NOTE: When knitting chevron side panels, do not use my standard technique for first and last stitches on page 20.

Extra Small: 3" wide

Row 1: Col 1: CO 19 sts for bottom row of chevron point.

Row 2 (WS): K8, sK2po, K8—17 sts.

Row 3: Col 2: K1, M1, K15, M1, K1—19 sts.

Row 4: P8, sP2po, P8—17 sts.

Row 5: Col 1: K1, M1, K15, M1, K1—19 sts.

Row 6: K8, sK2po, K8—17 sts.

Rep rows 3–6 approx 11 more times or until desired length, ending with completed row 6. BO rem sts.

Small: 4¼" wide

Row 1: Col 1: CO 27 sts for bottom row of chevron point.

Row 2 (WS): K12, sK2po, K12—25 sts.

Row 3: Col 2: K1, M1, K23, M1, K1—27 sts.

Row 4: P12, sP2po, P12—25 sts.

Row 5: Col 1: K1, M1, K23, M1, K1—27 sts.

Row 6: K12, sK2po, K12—25 sts.

Rep rows 3–6 approx 11 more times or until desired length, ending with completed row 6. BO rem sts.

Medium: 5½" wide

Row 1: Col 1: CO 35 sts for bottom row of chevron point.

Row 2 (WS): K16, sK2po, K16—33 sts.

Row 3: Col 2: K1, M1, K31, M1, K1—35 sts.

Row 4: P16, sP2po, P16—33 sts.

Row 5: Col 1: K1, M1, K31, M1, K1—35 sts.

Row 6: K16, sK2po, K16—33 sts.

Rep rows 3–6 approx 11 more times or until desired length, ending with completed row 6. BO rem sts.

X-Large: 7" wide

Row 1: Col 1: CO 43 sts for bottom row of chevron point.

Row 2 (WS): K20, sK2po, K20—41 sts.

Row 3: Col 2: K1, M1, K39, M1, K1—43 sts.

Row 4: P20, sP2po, P20—41 sts.

Row 5: Col 1: K1, M1, K39, M1, K1—43 sts.

Row 6: K20, sK2po, K20—41 sts.

Rep rows 3–6 until panel is desired length, ending with completed row 6. BO rem sts.

Dazzling Idea!

Use the chevron side panels to alter the size or appearance of any design presented in this book. I make each side panel in a different colorway. Yes!

Finishing

- Sew NHP 77 to half of 78. Sew NHP 76 to half of 75.

- For sizes X-Small, Small, Medium, and X-Large, sew chevron side panels to front and back of vest.

- Work front and bottom edge, referring to "Quick Crocheted Edges" (page 22). Start at center back neck between NHP 76 and 77, work 2 continuous rows hdc, followed by 1 row sc around entire garment. Place buttonholes at bottom of BP 13, 37, and point of 49.

- **Armhole trim:** Work 1 row hdc, followed by 1 row sc around each armhole.

- Sew on 3 extraordinary buttons.

PYRAMID VEST IN
BLUE COLORWAY

Pyramid Jacket

Using the modular concept, it is so simple to allow your Pyramid Vest to grow sleeves! In fact, I wore the jacket shown in the photo as a vest for many months. One day, I just decided to add sleeves by picking up and knitting additional modules to the vest. As with any garment shown in this book, you can add length, width, sleeves, collars, and trim to your wearable art pieces. The possibilities never cease!

The sleeves can be knit flat as displayed on the schematic or they can be connected in the round as you knit. For a distinctive fashion statement, I also added the collar from "Maya's Creative Crocheted Collar" (page 40) and the cuff bands from Dream Coat (page 60).

Sizes: X-Small, Small, Medium, Large (X-Large, XX-Large)
Finished Chest: 35, 37½, 40, 43 (47, 49)"
Finished Length: 18½, 18½, 18½, 18½ (23, 23)"

Materials

Use worsted-weight yarns as listed below or a variety of yarns to achieve gauge.

- **Col 1:** Approx 680, 690, 700, 750 (1050, 1075) total yds Stacy Charles Baci (62% wool, 20% acrylic, 18% rayon; 71 yds [65 m] per skein), color 5

- **Col 2:** Approx 520, 530, 550, 570 (700, 710) total yds Noro Cash Iroha (40% silk, 30% lamb's wool, 20% cashmere, 10% nylon; 99 yds [91 m] per skein) and/or Muench Horstia Maulbeerseide-Schurwolle (50% silk, 50% wool; 108 yds [100 m] per skein) in a variety of colors

- Two size 6 double-pointed needles (or size required to obtain gauge)

- Size 6 circular needles for larger sizes

- Size G crochet hook

- 3 buttons, ¾" to 1" diameter

Gauge for Basic Pyramid

X-Small, Small, Medium, Large: 37 sts and 15 rows = 4" per side
X-Large and XX-Large: 43 sts and 17 rows = 5" per side

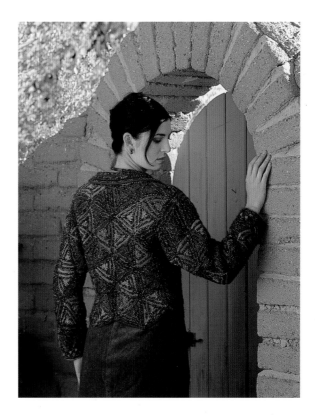

Jacket

The following bullet points outline the knitting sequence. For more information, refer to the module instructions.

- Knit Pyramid Vest on pages 65–69.

- Knit UP 79, 87, 116, and 124 according to module directions.

- Knit rem sleeve pyramids as for vest BP (page 67).

Underarm Pyramid (UP) 79, 124

For X-Small (Small, Medium, X-Large), combine with 3" (4½", 5½", 7") chevron panels.

Row 1: Col 1: CO or PU 18 (18, 18, 20) sts, PU 9 (13, 17, 21) sts from upper right or left half of chevron panel—27 (31, 35, 41) sts.

Row 2 (WS): K1tbl, K6 (10, 14, 18), sK2po, K16 (16, 16, 18), sl 1F—25 (29, 33, 39) sts.

Row 3: Col 2: K2tog tbl, K14 (14, 14, 16), sK2po, K5 (9, 13, 17), sl 1F—22 (26, 30, 36) sts.

Row 4: K1tbl, P4 (8, 12, 16), sP2po, P13 (13, 13, 15), sl 1F—20 (24, 28, 34) sts.

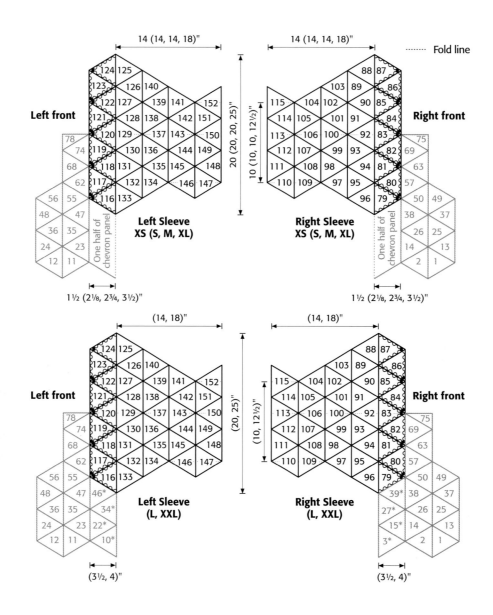

Rows 5, 9: Col 1: K2tog tbl, knit across, sl 1F—19, 11 (23, 15; 27, 19; 33, 25) sts.

Row 6: K1tbl, K3 (7, 11, 15), sK2po, K11 (11, 11, 13), sl 1F—17 (21, 25, 31) sts.

Row 7: Col 2: K2tog tbl, K9 (9, 9, 11), sK2po, K2 (6, 10, 14), sl 1F—14 (18, 22, 28) sts.

Row 8: K1tbl, P1 (5, 9, 13), sP2po, P8 (8, 8, 10), sl 1F—12 (16, 20, 26) sts.

Row 10: Col 1: K1tbl, K0 (4, 8, 12), sK2po, K6 (6, 6, 8), sl 1F—9 (13, 17, 23) sts.

3" Chevron Panel (cont 79, 124)

Row 11: Col 2: K2tog tbl, K4, sK2po—6 sts.

Row 12: K1tbl, P2, sP2po—4 sts.

Row 13: K2tog tbl, P2tog—2 sts.

Row 14: K2tog tbl. Fasten off.

(4½", 5½", 7") Chevron Panels (cont 79, 124)

Row 11: Col 2: K2tog tbl, K (4, 4, 6), sK2po, K (3, 7, 11), sl 1F—(10, 14, 20) sts.

Row 12: K1tbl, P (2, 6, 10) sP2po, P (3, 3, 5), sl 1F—(8, 12, 18) sts.

Row 13: K2tog tbl, K (1, 1, 3), sK2po, K (1, 5, 9), sl 1F—(5, 9, 15) sts.

Row 14: K1tbl, P (0, 4, 8), sP2po, P (0, 0, 2), sl 1F—(3, 7, 13) sts.

Row 15: BO rem sts.

Underarm Pyramid (UP) 87, 116

For X-Small (Small, Medium, X-Large), combine with 3", 4½", 5½", 7" chevron panels.

Row 1: Col 1: PU 9 (13, 17, 21) sts from upper right or left half of chevron panel, turn work, CO or PU 18 (18, 18, 20) sts—27 (31, 35, 41) sts.

Row 2 (WS): K1tbl, K16 (16, 16, 18), sK2po, K6 (10, 14, 18), sl 1F—25 (29, 33, 39) sts.

Row 3: Col 2: K1tbl, K5 (9, 13, 17), sK2po, K14 (14, 14, 16), P2tog—22 (26, 30, 36) sts.

Row 4: K1tbl, P13 (13, 13, 15), sP2po, P4 (8, 12, 16), sl 1F—20 (24, 28, 34) sts.

Rows 5, 9: Col 1: K1tbl, knit across, P2tog—19, 11 (23, 15; 27, 19; 33, 25) sts.

Row 6: K1tbl, K11 (11, 11, 13), sK2po, K3 (7, 11, 15), sl 1F—17 (21, 25, 31) sts.

Row 7: Col 2: K1tbl, K2 (6, 10, 14), sK2po, K9 (9, 9, 11), P2tog—14 (18, 22, 28) sts.

Row 8: K1tbl, P8 (8, 8, 10), sP2po, P1 (5, 9, 13), sl 1F—12 (16, 20, 26) sts.

Row 10: Col 1: K1tbl, K6 (6, 6, 8), sK2po, K0 (4, 8, 12), sl 1F—9 (13, 17, 23) sts.

3" Chevron Panel (cont 87, 116)

Row 11: Col 2: sK2po, K4, P2tog—6 sts.

Row 12: sP2po, P2, sl 1F—4 sts.

Row 13: K2tog tbl, P2tog—2 sts.

Row 14: K2tog tbl. Fasten off.

(4½", 5½", 7") Chevron Panels (cont 87, 116)

Row 11: Col 2: K1tbl, K (3, 7, 11), sK2po, K (4, 4, 6), P2tog—(10, 14, 20) sts.

Row 12: K1tbl, P (3, 3, 5), sP2po, P (2, 6, 10), sl 1F—(8, 12, 18) sts.

Row 13: K1tbl, K (1, 5, 9), sK2po, K (1, 1, 3), P2tog—(5, 9, 15) sts.

Row 14: K1tbl, P (0, 0, 2), sP2po, P (0, 4, 8), sl 1F—(3, 7, 13) sts.

Row 15: BO rem sts.

Finishing

- Sew sleeve seams tog if not knit tog.
- Work front edge trim as for Pyramid Vest (page 69).
- **Work cuffs as follows:** With crochet hook, hdc 2 or more rows in the round. For a more decorative finish as shown in photo, adapt cuff from Dream Coat (page 60).
- Add collar from "Maya's Creative Crocheted Collar" (page 40) if desired.
- Sew on 3 glorious buttons.

Shells: The Basics

These lovely shells may appear complex, but they are surprisingly simple to knit. After casting on the foundation row, each shell is shaped by decreases on wrong-side rows. If you desire a size in between those offered, go up or down a needle size. This will net a finished garment size approximately 2" larger or smaller, depending upon needle size, than the size given in the pattern. Multiply the width of one shell by the number of shells around the garment and add 1" to 2" for crochet finishing to determine the final garment width.

The lacy appearance of the shells in the first three projects is accomplished with slipped stitches. Since it can be easy to get off track with slip stitches, remember you are knitting stitches with the color of yarn in your hand and slipping stitches of the opposite color. The slipped stitches are always color A and the background stitches are always color B. Using a lighter weight yarn for color A, as in "Fan" Dango Vest, gives the illusion of an even lacier fabric.

While some of these patterns suggest alternating with only two different colors, don't feel constrained by this. Change colors as often as you like, preferably only on right-side rows. The seed-stitch section of these shells can be knit in yet a totally different color. If you use only two different colors within each shell, carry the yarn up the side of your work. Use the technique "Double Cast On" (page 20) for the three shell patterns and the "Knitted Cast On" (page 20) for the two Mola designs.

Your first row of shells may look angular rather than curvy. Don't despair; the sensuous shaping occurs as other shells are joined to them.

THE PROJECTS

Concha Vest

This lovely vest of concha shells is as unlimited in its potential colorways as there are delicately tinted shells on the beach. Many admirers of this vest insist that it is crocheted, but you will know the treasures that lie hidden just beneath the surface of the shimmering waters of your charming creation. You will change colors every two rows on right-side rows only. Vary the yarn colors as you knit your shells, so that—as in nature—each is unique.

Sizes: Small (Medium, Large)

Finished Chest: 29½ (39, 48½)"

Finished Length: 16½ (16½, 18)"

Materials

Use worsted-weight yarns as listed below or a variety of yarns to achieve gauge.

- **Col A:** 3 (4, 4) skeins Noro Silk Garden (45% silk, 45% kid mohair, 10% lamb's wool; 109 yds [100 m] per skein), color 50

- **Col B:** 3 (3, 4) skeins Noro Silk Garden in several different colorways

- Two size 8 double-pointed needles (or size required to obtain gauge)

- Size G crochet hook

- 3 buttons, ¾" to 1" diameter

Gauge

Basic Shell (BSh): 25 sts and 24 rows = 4¾" wide x 3" high

Body

The following bullet points outline the knitting sequence. For more information, refer to the module instructions.

- Knit 6 (8, 10) BSh as separate units for bottom row of vest. For all rem shells, PU from previously knit shells. See "Joining Modules As You Go" (page 21).

- **BSh 8 (10, 12):** PU 13 sts from left side of BSh 1, PU 12 sts from right side of BSh 2. Finish mod beg at row 2 of BSh.

- **Small: BSh 9–12, 14–19, 21–25, 27–32, 34–38, 40–43, 46, 50, 51, 55:** Work as for BSh 8.

- **Medium: BSh 11–16, 18–25, 27–33, 35–42, 44–48, 50, 53, 54, 57–62, 66, 67, 71–75:** Work as for BSh 10.

- **Large: BSh 13–20, 22–31, 33–41, 43–52, 54–62, 64–72, 75–77, 80–86, 90–92, 96–101:** Work as for BSh 12.

- **LHS 7 (9, 11):** Working from bottom to top, PU 13 sts from right side of BSh 1. Finish mod beg at row 2 of LHS.

- **Small: LHS 20, 33, 45, 48, 49, 54, 57:** Work as for LHS 7.

- **Medium: LHS 26, 43, 52, 56, 63, 65, 69:** Work as for LHS 9.
- **Large: LHS 32, 53, 74, 79, 87, 89, 94:** Work as for LHS 11.
- **RHS 13 (17, 21):** Working from top to bottom, PU 13 sts from left side of BSh 6 (8, 10). Finish mod beg at row 2 of RHS.
- **Small: RHS 26, 39, 44, 47, 52, 53, 56:** Work as for RHS 13.
- **Medium: RHS 34, 49, 51, 55, 64, 68, 70:** Work as for RHS 17.
- **Large: RHS 42, 63, 73, 78, 88, 93, 95:** Work as for RHS 21.
- **Small: QS 58; Medium: QS 76, 78, 82; Large: QS 102, 104, 109:** Working from bottom to top, PU 13 sts from right side of RHS or BSh below. Finish mod beg at row 2 of QS.
- **Small: QS 61; Medium: QS 77, 81, 83; Large: QS 103, 108, 110:** Working from top to bottom, PU 13 sts from left side of LHS or BSh below. Finish mod beg at row 2 of QS.
- **Small: BHSh 59 and 60; Medium: BHSh 79 and 80; Large: BHSh 105–107:** PU as for BSh 8 (10, 12). Finish mod beg at row 2 of BHSh.

Dazzling Idea!

Can't decide which two colors to use in each concha? Take two different contrasting colorways of Noro Silk Garden. Label one color A and the other color B. Every time the pattern calls for color A, use whatever color pops up next from that skein. Do the same with the yarn designated as color B. This will take the indecision out of your knitting and you can happily glide ahead.

Basic Shell (BSh)

Rows 3, 4, 7, 8, and 12 end with 2 slipped sts.

Row 1: Col A: CO or PU 25 sts from 2 shells in row below.

Row 2 (WS): K1tbl, knit across, sl 1F.

Rows 3, 7: Col B: K1tbl, sl 1 wyib, (K1, sl 1 wyib) 11 times, sl 1F.

Rows 4, 8: Col B: K1tbl, sl 1 wyif, (K1 wyib, sl 1 wyif) 11 times, sl 1F.

Rows 5, 6, 9, 13: Col A: K1tbl, knit across, sl 1F.

Row 10: Col A: K2tog tbl, (K1, K2tog) 7 times, P2tog—16 sts.

Row 11: Col B: K1tbl, (sl 1 wyib, K1) 7 times, sl 1F.

Row 12: Col B: K1tbl, (K1 wyib, sl 1 wyif) 7 times, sl 1F.

Row 14: Col A: K2tog tbl, (K1, K2tog) 4 times, P2tog—10 sts. Cut col A.

Row 15: Col B: K1tbl, knit across, sl 1F.

Rows 16, 18, 20: K2tog tbl, seed st across, P2tog—8, 6, 4 sts.

Rows 17, 19, 21, 23: K1tbl, seed st across, sl 1F—8, 6, 4, 3 sts.

Row 22: K1tbl, P2tog, sl 1F—3 sts.

Row 24: sK2po. Fasten off.

Left Half Shell (LHS)

Row 1: Col A: PU 13 sts from right side of shell below.

Row 2 (WS): K1tbl, knit across, P2tog—12 sts.

Row 3: Col B: K1tbl, (sl 1 wyib, K1) 5 times, sl 1F.

Row 4: K1tbl, K1, (sl 1 wyif, K1 wyib) 4 times, P2tog—11 sts.

Rows 5, 9, 13: Col A: K1tbl, knit across, sl 1F.

Rows 6, 10, 14: Col A: K1tbl, knit across, P2tog—10, 8, 6 sts. Cut col A after row 14.

Row 7: Col B: K1tbl, (sl 1 wyib, K1) 4 times, sl 1F.

Row 8: K1tbl, K1, (sl 1 wyif, K1 wyib) 3 times, P2tog—9 sts.

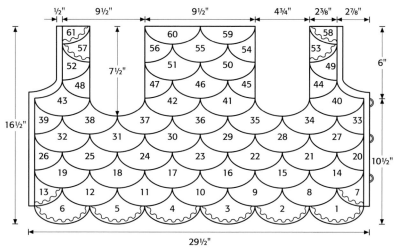

Small

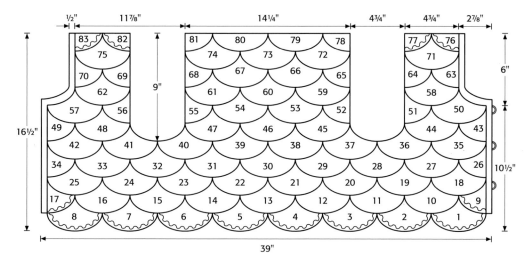

Medium

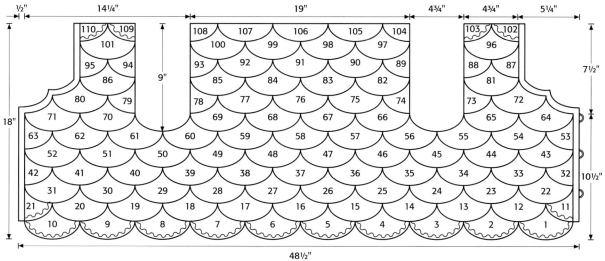

Large

Row 11: Col B: K1tbl, (sl 1 wyib, K1) 3 times, sl 1F.

Row 12: K1tbl, K1, (sl 1 wyif, K1 wyib) 2 times, P2tog—7 sts.

Row 15: Col B: K1tbl, knit across, sl 1F.

Rows 16, 18, 20: K1tbl, seed st across, P2tog—5, 4, 3 sts.

Rows 17, 19, 21: K1tbl, seed st across, sl 1F.

Row 22: sK2po. Finish off.

Right Half Shell (RHS)

Rows 4, 8, and 12 end with 2 slipped sts.

Row 1: Col A: PU 13 sts from left side of shell below.

Row 2 (WS): K2tog tbl, knit across, sl 1F—12 sts.

Row 3: Col B: K1tbl, (sl 1 wyib, K1) 5 times, sl 1F.

Row 4: K2tog tbl, (sl 1 wyif, K1 wyib) 4 times, sl 1 wyif, sl 1F—11 sts.

Rows 5, 9, 13: Col A: K1tbl, knit across, sl 1F.

Rows 6, 10, 14: Col A: K2tog tbl, knit across, sl 1F—10, 8, 6 sts. Cut col A after row 14.

Row 7: Col B: K1tbl, (sl 1 wyib, K1) 4 times, sl 1F.

Row 8: K2tog tbl, (sl 1 wyif, K1 wyib) 3 times, sl 1 wyif, sl 1F—9 sts.

Row 11: Col B: K1tbl, (sl 1 wyib, K1) 3 times, sl 1F.

Row 12: K2tog tbl, (sl 1 wyif, K1 wyib) 2 times, sl wyif, sl 1F—7 sts.

Row 15: Col B: K1tbl, knit across, sl 1F.

Rows 16, 18, 20: K2tog tbl, seed st across, sl 1F—5, 4, 3 sts.

Rows 17, 19, 21: K1tbl, seed st across, sl 1F.

Row 22: sK2po. Fasten off.

Quarter Shell (QS)

Rows 3, 4, 7, and 8 end with 2 slipped sts.

Row 1: Col A: PU 13 sts from right or left side of shell below.

Row 2 (WS): K2tog tbl, knit across, sl 1F—12 sts.

Row 3: Col B: K2tog tbl, sl 1, (K1, sl 1 wyib) 4 times, sl 1F—11 sts.

Row 4: K2tog tbl, (K1 wyib, sl 1 wyif) 4 times, sl 1F—10 sts.

Rows 5, 9, 11: Col A: K2tog tbl, knit across, sl 1F—9, 5, 3 sts.

Rows 6, 10: Col A: K2tog tbl, knit across, sl 1F—8, 4 sts.

Row 7: Col B: K2tog tbl, sl 1, (K1, sl 1 wyib) 2 times, sl 1F—7 sts.

Row 8: K2tog tbl, (K1 wyib, sl 1 wyif) 2 times, sl 1F—6 sts. Cut col B.

Row 12: Col A: sK2po. Fasten off.

Bottom Half Shell (BHSh)

Row 1: Col A: PU 25 sts from 2 shells in row below.

Row 2 (WS): K2tog tbl, knit across, P2tog—23 sts.

Row 3: Col B: K2tog tbl, sl 1, (K1, sl 1 wyib) 9 times, P2tog—21 sts.

Row 4: K2tog tbl, K1, (sl 1 wyif, K1 wyib) 8 times, P2tog—19 sts.

Rows 5, 9: Col A: K2tog tbl, knit across, P2tog—17, 9 sts.

Rows 6, 10: Col A: K2tog tbl, knit across, P2tog—15, 7 sts.

Row 7: Col B: K2tog tbl, sl 1, (K1, sl 1 wyib) 5 times, P2tog—13 sts.

Row 8: K2tog tbl, K1, (sl 1 wyif, K1 wyib) 4 times, P2tog—11 sts. Cut col B.

Row 11: Col A: K1tbl, K2tog twice, P2tog—4 sts.

Row 12: K2tog tbl, P2tog, po. Fasten off.

Finishing

- Sew shoulder seams tog.
- Work front edge and armhole trim, referring to "Quick Crocheted Edges" (page 22). Place buttonhole loops at top of LHS 33 (43, 53); 20 (26, 32); and 7 (9, 11).
- Sew on 3 lovely buttons.

USING IDEAS FROM "ACHIEVING A FLAWLESS FIT," DESIGNER AND ARTIST SHERIE SPITZ ADDED SLEEVES TO HER BLUE CONCHA VEST.

Concha Short-Sleeve Top

So you might experience the versatility of yarn types and colorways that can make essentially the same garment look totally different, I knit the Concha Vest as a short-sleeve top. It is a combination of many different weights of cottons, silks, linens, and rayons, which all happily join in a lively symphony of festive colors.

Sizes: Small (Medium, Large)

Finished Chest: 29½ (39, 48½)"

Finished Length: 16½ (16½, 18)"

Materials

- Approx 1000 (1200, 1400) total yds of a variety of cottons, silks, rayons, and linens, in varying weights
- Two size 8 double-pointed needles (or size required to obtain gauge)
- Size G crochet hook
- 3 buttons, ¾" to 1" diameter

Gauge

Basic Shell (BSh): 25 sts and 24 rows = 4¾" wide x 3" high

Body

Knit the Concha Vest as directed on pages 77–80.

Sleeves

The following bullet points outline the knitting sequence. For more information, refer to the module instructions.

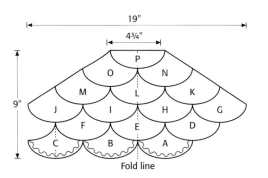

- Knit the same sleeves for each size using BSh directions on page 78 and BHSh directions on page 80, eliminating mod P for size Small.

- Fold mod C in half at underarm. Sew left side of mod C to right underside of mod D.

- **Left sleeve (Small, Medium, Large):** Sew left side of J to right side of mod 38 (41, 61). Sew left side of M to right side of 48 (56, 79). Sew left side of O to right side of 57 (69, 94). Top of mod P spans (81–82, 109–108). Sew right side of N to left side of 56 (68, 93). Sew right side of K to left side of 47 (55, 78). Sew right side of G to left side of 37 (40, 60).

- **Right sleeve:** Work as for left sleeve.

Finishing

- Finish as for Concha Vest (page 80).

- Sew sleeves into body.

- **Small:** Sew right side of mod O to left side of mod N.

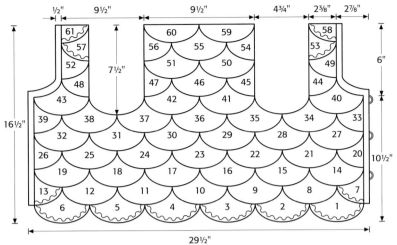

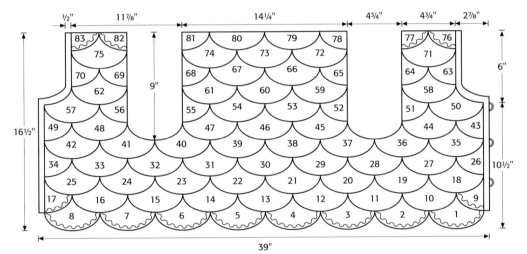

Small

Medium

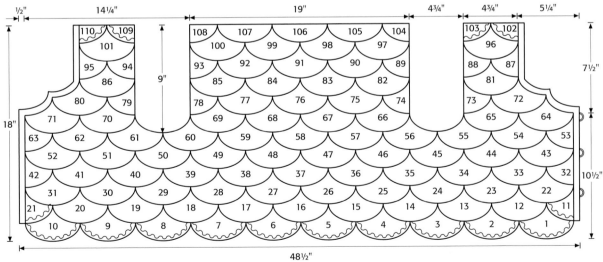

Large

"Fan" Dango Vest

This very lacy, feminine vest is nothing more than the Concha Vest turned on its head. Rather than working from the bottom to the top, you will start at the shoulders and work your way down to the beautiful scalloped edging that finishes the vest.

Since you will be knitting this vest from top to bottom, you will need to turn your knitted work upside down as shown in the schematic.

Sizes: Small (Medium, Large)

Finished Chest: 29½ (39, 48½)"

Finished Length: 17½ (17½, 19)"

Materials

- Approx 800 (900, 1000) total yds of a wide variety of cottons, silks, rayons, and linens in any weight yarn
- Two size 8 double-pointed needles (or size required to obtain gauge)
- Size G crochet hook
- 3 buttons, ¾" to 1" diameter

Gauge

Basic Shell: 25 sts and 24 rows = 4¾" wide x 3" high

Dazzling Idea!

To create a more distinct concha, I worked rows 1 and 2 of every module twice in this vest. First CO or PU 25 sts and work rows 1 and 2 in color B; then work BSh directions as written, starting with row 1 in color A.

Body

The following bullet points outline the knitting sequence. For more information, refer to the module instructions.

Follow directions for BSh, LHS, RHS, BHSh, and QS on pages 78–80.

- Knit 2 (5, 6) BSh as separate units for shoulders and top back of vest. For all rem BSh, PU from previously knit shells. See "Joining Modules As You Go" (page 21). **Small:** Knit RHS 1 and LHS 4, following RHS and LHS directions.

- **BSh 7 (9, 10):** PU 13 sts from left side of BSh 3, PU 12 sts from right side of BSh 2. Finish mod beg at row 2 of BSh. All rem BSh are worked in this same fashion.

- **LHS 5 (7, 8):** Starting at bottom right of BSh/RHS 1, PU 13 sts. Finish mod beg at row 2 of LHS.

- **Small: LHS 8, 13, 14, 17, 29, 42, 55:** Work as for LHS 5.

- **Medium: LHS 11, 13, 20, 24, 26, 48, 65:** Work as for LHS 7.

- **Large: LHS 13, 15, 23, 28, 49, 70, 91:** Work as for LHS 8.

- **RHS 9 (12, 14):** Working from top to bottom, PU 13 sts from left side of LHS 4 (BSh 5, BSh 6). Finish mod beg at row 2 of RHS.

- **Small: RHS 6, 10, 15, 18, 23, 36, 49:** Work as for RHS 9.

- **Medium: RHS 6, 8, 19, 21, 25, 40, 57:** Work as for RHS 12.

- **Large: RHS 7, 9, 24, 29, 39, 60, 81:** Work as for RHS 14.

- **Medium and Large only: QS (82, 112):** Working from bottom to top, PU 13 sts from right side of BSh (73, 101). Finish mod beg at row 2 of QS.

- **Medium and Large only: QS (74, 102):** Working from top to bottom, PU 13 sts from left side of BSh (66, 92). Finish mod beg at row 2 of QS.

- **BHSh 61 (81, 111):** PU 13 sts from left side of LHS 55 (BSh 73, BSh 101), PU 12 sts from right side of BSh 54 (72, 100). Finish mod beg at row 2 of BHSh.

- **BHSh 56–60 (75–80, 103–110):** Work as for BHSh 61 (81, 111).

- **QS 62 (83, 113):** Turn work and schematic RS up to work QS modules. Working from bottom to top, PU 13 sts from right side of BSh 2. Finish mod beg at row 2 of QS.

- **QS 63 (84, 114):** Working from top to bottom, PU 13 sts from left side of BSh 3 (2, 2). Finish mod beg at row 2 of QS.

- **Medium and Large only: QS (85, 115):** Work as for QS (83, 113).

- **Medium and Large only: QS (86, 116):** Work as for QS (84, 114).

Finishing

- Finish as for Concha Vest (page 80).

- Finish bottom with scalloped crochet edge as follows:

> **Row 1: Col 1:** With RS facing, beg at lower-left front edge of vest, *work 3 hdc, skip 1 st*, rep from * to * across entire bottom edge of vest.
>
> **Row 2: Col 2:** With RS facing, beg at lower-left front edge. Work hdc in established sts across bottom edge.
>
> **Row 3: Col 3: Scallop row:** With RS facing, beg at lower-left front edge, *work 5 dc into same st, skip 1 st, sc, skip 1 st*, rep from * to * across entire width of vest bottom.

- Voilà! An ultra feminine touch to a very flirty, girly-girl vest!

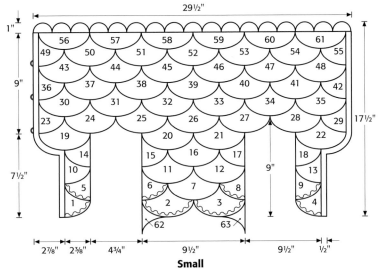

Small

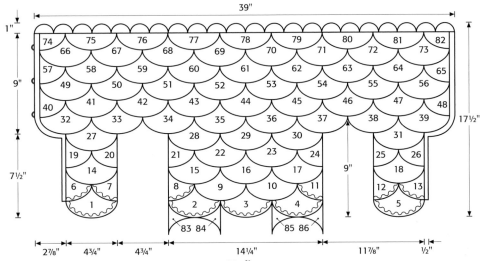

Medium

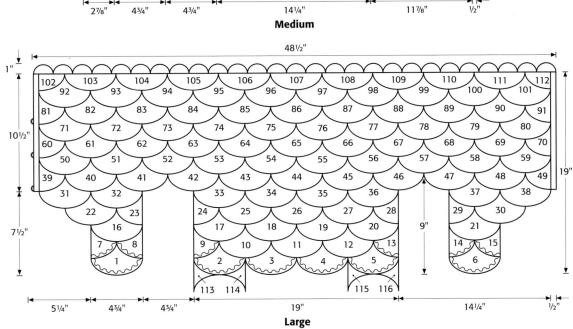

Large

Mola Jacket

This whimsical design fulfilled my longing to reproduce in knitting the amazing images created by the San Blas Island Indians in their reverse appliqué work. These imaginative people craft their vision of the universe, their spirituality, and their daily encounters with life onto the canvas of their colorful Molas.

I own a large collection of Molas and delight every day seeing what representations have been depicted in this tedious process. To create this marvelous effect, the Indians stack multiple layers of colorful fabric on top of one another and then meticulously cut away through varying tiers of fabric. Each layer is folded back and stitched to reveal colors and fanciful imagery.

Sizes: Small (Medium, Large)

Finished Chest: 37 (43, 48)"

Finished Length: 18 (21, 23½)"

Materials

Use DK-weight yarns as listed below or a variety of yarns to achieve gauge.

- Dale of Norway Heilo (100% wool; 109 yds [100 m] per skein) in the following amounts and colors:
- **BG Col:** 5 (6, 7) skeins (will be darkest color)
- **Col 1:** 5 (6, 7) skeins of assorted medium colors for *horizontal* motifs
- **Col 1:** 5 (5, 6) skeins Stahl Wolle Limbo (100% wool; 135 yds per skein), color 2539, for *vertical* motifs
- **Col 2:** 5 or more skeins of assorted dark colors
- **Col 3:** 5 or more skeins of assorted bright colors for center squares
- Three size 6 double-pointed needles (or size required to obtain gauge)
- Size F or G crochet hook
- Tapestry needle
- 3 buttons, 1½" to 2" diameter

Gauge for Basic Mola

Small: 32 sts and 64 rows = 5" x 8", including 1" center square

Medium: 36 sts and 70 rows = 6" x 9", including 1½" center square

Large: 40 sts and 78 rows = 7" x 10", including 1¾" center square

Special Notes

- Each full Basic Mola (BM) is knit in two separate parts and joined by 3-needle bind off.
- Use the technique "Knitted Cast On" (page 20) for all Mola motifs.
- Unlike many of my other designs, this pattern is not constructed from bottom to top. While most Molas can be picked up from other Molas, it is almost impossible to eliminate the need to sew some together after they are knit. Of the 88 modules, some 20 will need to be sewn together. To create a coherent piece of work, sew these modules together immediately by keeping a tapestry needle threaded with background color.

- In the jacket shown on pages 90 and 93, note that I have used a variegated yarn (color 1) on *vertical* motifs. Color 1 in these motifs is consistently alternated with the purple background color. *Horizontal* motifs are knit with medium value solid colors (also color 1) alternated with a darker value (color 2). All Mola motifs consistently begin and end with a purple background color. This is just one way of approaching the design. As always, I strongly encourage you to create your own color scheme and combinations.

Body

The following bullet points outline the knitting sequence. For more information, refer to the module instructions.

- Knit BM 1 and 2, joining centers with 3-needle BO to create first full Mola. All rem Molas are joined to one another by 3-needle BO, sewing, or picking up sts from previously knitted Molas. See "Joining Modules As You Go" (page 21).

- **BM 3, 4:** With RS facing and working from right to left across BM 1, then BM 2, PU 32 (36, 40) sts. Finish mod beg at row 2 of BM. Knit BM 4 by casting on 32 (36, 40) sts, taking care not to rep the seed-st section that creates the center square. Join BM 3 and 4 with 3-needle BO.

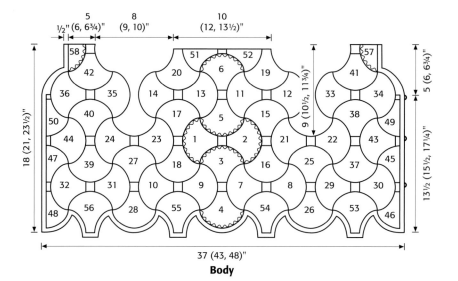

Body

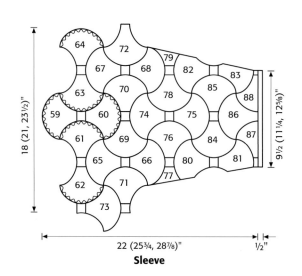

Sleeve

- **BM 5–42:** Work as for BM 3, 4.
- BM 19 joins shoulder to BM 41 same as BM 3, 4.
- BM 20 joins shoulder to BM 42 same as BM 3, 4.
- **BM 41 and 42:** Join to BM 19 and 20 using 3-needle BO to join shoulders.
- **BM 43, 44:** BO after rows 32 (35, 39).
- **BM 53–56:** BO after rows 26 (28, 32).
- **HM 45:** Using HM instructions, work HM 45: PU 15 (18, 20) sts from BM 43. Finish mod beg at row 2 of HM.
- **HM 46–52:** Work as for HM 45: CO or PU 15 (18, 20) sts. Finish mod beg at row 2 of HM.

Sleeves

Join sleeves to body by sewing and picking up from other Molas as follows:

- **BM 59, 60:** Using BM instructions, PU 32 (36, 40) sts between BM 19 and 41 for right sleeve and BM 20 and 42 for left sleeve. Finish mod beg at row 2 of BM.
- **BM 61–72, 74–76, 78, 84–85:** Work as for BM 59 and 60.
- **BM 86:** Eliminate seed-st section.
- **HM 87, 88:** Using HM instructions, PU 15 (18, 20) sts from BM 86. Finish mod beg at row 2 of HM.
- **SLM 73, 77, 79–83:** Refer to specific pattern directions for details.

Basic Mola (BM)

Small (Medium, Large)

First 10 rows are shared by all sizes. Proceed to desired size to finish module.

Row 1: BG col: CO or PU 32 (36, 40) sts.

Row 2 (WS): K1tbl, purl across, sl 1F. Cut BG col.

Row 3: Col 1: K2tog tbl, knit across, sl 1F—31 (35, 39) sts.

Row 4: K2tog tbl, knit across, sl 1F—30 (34, 38) sts.

Rows 5–8: K1tbl, knit across, sl 1F.

Row 9: Col 2: K1tbl, knit across, sl 1F.

Row 10: K1tbl, P1, (P2, P2tog) 7 (8, 9) times—23 (26, 29) sts.

BM: Small

Rows 11–14: Col 1: K1tbl, knit across, sl 1F—23 sts for all rows.

Row 15: Col 2: K1tbl, knit across, sl 1F.

Row 16: K1tbl, (P2tog, P1) 7 times, sl 1F—16 sts.

Rows 17–20: Col 1: K1tbl, knit across, sl 1F.

Row 21: Col 2: K1tbl, knit across, sl 1F.

Row 22: K2tog tbl, (P2tog) 7 times—8 sts. Cut col 2.

Rows 23–26: Col 1: K1tbl, knit across, sl 1F. Cut col 1.

Row 27: BG col: K1tbl, knit across, sl 1F.

Row 28: K2tog tbl, purl across, sl 1F—7 sts. Cut BG col.

Row 29: Col 3: K1tbl, knit across, sl 1F.

Rows 30–36: K1tbl, seed st across, sl 1F. Cut col 3. Leave 7 sts on needle.

The first half of BM is complete. For other half, rep rows 1–28 only. Leave 7 sts on needle. With RS facing, hold 2 modules on needles tog and work 3-needle BO on WS.

BM: Medium

Rows 11–16: Col 1: K1tbl, knit across, sl 1F—26 sts for all rows.

Row 17: Col 2: K1tbl, knit across, sl 1F.

Row 18: K1tbl, (P1, P2tog) 8 times, sl 1F—18 sts.

Rows 19–22: Col 1: K1tbl, knit across, sl 1F.

Row 23: Col 2: K1tbl, knit across, sl 1F.

Row 24: K2tog tbl, (P2tog) 8 times—9 sts. Cut col 2.

Rows 25–28: Col 1: K1tbl, knit across, sl 1F. Cut col 1.

Row 29: BG col: K1tbl, knit across, sl 1F.

Row 30: K2tog tbl, purl across, sl 1F—8 sts. Cut BG col.

Row 31: Col 3: K1tbl, knit across, sl 1F.

Rows 32–40: K1tbl, seed st across, sl 1F. Cut col 3. Leave 8 sts on needle.

The first half of BM is complete. For other half, rep rows 1–30 only. Leave 8 sts on needle. With RS facing, hold 2 modules on needles tog and work 3-needle BO on WS.

BM: Large

Rows 11–16: Col 1: K1tbl, knit across, sl 1F—29 sts for all rows.

Row 17: Col 2: K1tbl, knit across, sl 1F.

Row 18: K1tbl, (P1, P2tog) 9 times, sl 1F—20 sts.

Rows 19–24: Col 1: K1tbl, knit across, sl 1F.

Row 25: Col 2: K1tbl, knit across, sl 1F.

Row 26: K2tog, (P2tog) 9 times—10 sts. Cut col 2.

Rows 27–32: Col 1: K1tbl, knit across, sl 1F. Cut col 1.

Row 33: BG col: K1tbl, knit across, sl 1F.

Row 34: K2tog tbl, purl across, sl 1F—9 sts. Cut BG col.

Row 35: Col 3: K1tbl, knit across, sl 1F.

Rows 36–44: K1tbl, seed st, sl 1F. Cut col 3. Leave 9 sts on needle.

The first half of BM is complete. For other half, rep rows 1–34 only. Leave 9 sts on needle. With RS facing, hold 2 modules on needles tog and work 3-needle BO on WS.

Half Mola (HM) 45–52, 87, 88

First 9 rows are shared by all sizes. Proceed to desired size to finish module.

Row 1: BG col: CO or PU 15 (18, 20) sts.

Row 2 (WS): K1tbl, purl across, sl 1F. Cut BG col.

Rows 3–8: Col 1: K1tbl, knit across, sl 1F.

Row 9: Col 2: K1tbl, knit across, sl 1F.

HM: Small

Row 10: Col 2: K1tbl, P1 (P2, P2tog) 3 times, sl 1F—12 sts.

Rows 11–14: Col 1: K1tbl, knit across, sl 1F.

Row 15: Col 2: K1tbl, knit across, sl 1F.

Row 16: K1tbl, (P2tog, P1) 3 times, P2tog—8 sts.

Rows 17–20: Col 1: K1tbl, knit across, sl 1F.

Row 21: Col 2: K1tbl, knit across, sl 1F.

Row 22: K2tog tbl, (P2tog) 3 times—4 sts. Cut col 2.

Rows 23–26: Col 1: K1tbl, knit across, sl 1F. Cut col 1 after row 26.

Row 27: BG col: K1tbl, knit across, sl 1F.

Row 28: K1tbl, purl across, sl 1F. Cut BG col.

Row 29: Col 3: K1tbl, knit across, sl 1F.

Rows 30–36: K1tbl, seed st across, sl 1F. Leave 4 sts on needle.

The first half of HM is complete. For other half, rep rows 1–28 only. Leave 4 sts on needle. With RS facing, hold 2 modules on needles tog and work 3-needle BO on WS.

HM: Medium

Row 10: Col 2: K1tbl, P1, (P2, P2tog) 4 times—14 sts.

Rows 11–16: Col 1: K1tbl, knit across, sl 1F.

Row 17: Col 2: K1tbl, knit across, sl 1F.

Row 18: K1tbl, (P2tog, P1) 4 times, sl 1F—10 sts.

Rows 19–22: Col 1: K1tbl, knit across, sl 1F.

Row 23: Col 2: K1tbl, knit across, sl 1F.

Row 24: K2tog tbl, (P2tog) 4 times—5 sts. Cut col 2.

Rows 25–28: Col 1: K1tbl, knit across, sl 1F. Cut col 1 after row 28.

Row 29: BG col: K1tbl, knit across, sl 1F.

Row 30: K2tog, purl across, sl 1F—4 sts. Cut BG col.

Row 31: Col 3: K1tbl, knit across, sl 1F.

Rows 32–40: K1tbl, seed st across, sl 1F. Leave 4 sts on needle.

The first half of HM is complete. For other half, rep rows 1–30 only. Leave 4 sts on needle. With RS facing, hold 2 modules on needles tog and work 3-needle BO on WS.

HM: Large

Row 10: Col 2: K2tog tbl, (P2, P2tog) 4 times, P1, sl 1F—15 sts.

Rows 11–16: Col 1: K1tbl, knit across, sl 1F.

Row 17: Col 2: K1tbl, knit across, sl 1F.

Row 18: K2tog tbl, (P1, P2tog) 4 times, sl 1F—10 sts.

Rows 19–24: Col 1: K1tbl, knit across, sl 1F.

Row 25: Col 2: K1tbl, knit across, sl 1F.

Row 26: K2tog tbl, (P2tog) 4 times—5 sts. Cut col 2.

Rows 27–32: Col 1: K1tbl, knit across, sl 1F. Cut col 1 after row 32.

Row 33: BG col: K1tbl, knit across, sl 1F.

Row 34: K2tog tbl, purl across, sl 1F—4 sts. Cut BG col.

Row 35: Col 3: K1tbl, knit across, sl 1F.

Rows 36–44: K1tbl, seed st across, sl 1F. Leave 4 sts on needle.

The first half of HM is complete. For other half, rep rows 1–34 only. Leave 4 sts on needle. With RS facing, hold 2 modules on needles tog and work 3-needle BO on WS.

Quarter Neckline Mola (QNM) 57

First 14 rows are shared by all sizes. Proceed to desired size to finish module.

When completed, sew QNM 57 to right half of HM 52.

Row 1: BG col: Starting at bottom right of BM 41, PU 18 (20, 22) sts.

Row 2 (WS): K2tog tbl, purl across, sl 1F—17 (19, 21) sts. Cut BG col.

Rows 3, 4, 5, 7, 11, 13: Col 1: K2tog tbl, knit across, sl 1F—16, 15, 14, 13, 11, 10 (18, 17, 16, 15, 13, 12; 20, 19, 18, 17, 15, 14) sts.

Rows 6, 8, 12, 14: Col 1: K1tbl, knit across, sl 1F. **Small:** Cut col 1 after row 14.

Row 9: Col 2: K2tog tbl, knit across, sl 1F—12 (14, 16) sts.

Row 10: Col 2: K1tbl, purl across, sl 1F.

QNM 57: Small

Row 15: Col 2: K2tog tbl, knit across, sl 1F—9 sts.

Row 16: K1tbl, purl across, sl 1F.

Row 17: BO rem 9 sts.

QNM 57: Medium

Row 15: Col 1: K2tog tbl, knit across, sl 1F—11 sts.

Row 16: K1tbl, knit across, sl 1F. Cut col 1.

Row 17: Col 2: K2tog tbl, knit across, sl 1F—10 sts.

Row 18: K1tbl, purl across, sl 1F.

Row 19: BO rem 10 sts.

QNM 57: Large

Rows 15, 19, 21: Col 1: K2tog tbl, knit across, sl 1F—13, 11, 10 sts.

Rows 16, 20, 22: Col 1: K1tbl, knit across, sl 1F.

Row 17: Col 2: K2tog tbl, knit across, sl 1F—12 sts.

Row 18: Col 2: K1tbl, purl across, sl 1F. Cut col 2.

Row 23: BO rem 12 sts.

Quarter Neckline Mola (QNM) 58

First 14 rows are shared by all sizes. Proceed to desired size to finish module.

When completed, sew QNM 58 to left half of HM 51.

Row 1: BG Col: Starting at top left of BM 42, PU 18 (20, 22) sts.

Row 2 (WS): K2tog tbl, purl across row, sl 1F—17 (19, 21) sts. Cut BG col.

Row 3: Col 1: K2tog tbl, knit across, sl 1F—16 (18, 20) sts.

Rows 5, 7, 11, 13: Col 1: K1tbl, K across row, sl 1F.

Rows 4, 6, 8, 12, 14: Col 1: K2tog tbl, K across row, sl 1F—15, 14, 13, 11, 10 (17, 16, 15, 13, 12; 19, 18, 17, 15, 14) sts. **Small:** Cut col 1 after row 14.

Row 9: Col 2: K1tbl, knit across row, sl 1F—13 (15, 17) sts.

Row 10: K2tog tbl, purl across row, sl 1F—12 (14, 16) sts.

QNM 58: Small

Row 15: Col 2: K1tbl, knit across row, sl 1F—10 sts.

Row 16: K2tog tbl, purl across row, sl 1F—9 sts.

Row 17: BO rem 9 sts.

QNM 58: Medium

Row 15: Col 1: K1tbl, knit across row, sl 1F—12 sts.

Row 16: Col 1: K2tog tbl, knit across row, sl 1F—11 sts. Cut col 1.

Row 17: Col 2: K1tbl, knit across row, sl 1F.

Row 18: K2tog tbl, purl across row, sl 1F—10 sts

Row 19: BO rem 10 sts.

QNM 58: Large

Rows 15, 19, 21: Col 1: K1tbl, knit across row, sl 1F—14, 12, 11 sts.

Rows 16, 20, 22: Col 1: K2tog tbl, knit across row, sl 1F—13, 11, 10 sts. Cut col 1 after row 22.

Row 17: Col 2: K1tbl, knit across row, sl 1F—13 sts.

Row 18: Col 2: K2tog tbl, purl across row, sl 1F—12 sts.

Row 23: BO rem 12 sts.

Sleeve Module (SLM) 73

First 14 rows are shared by all sizes. Proceed to desired size to finish module.

When body and sleeves are completed, sew bound-off edge of SLM 73 seed-st section to the side of the seed-st section between BM 21 and 22 at right armhole and between BM 23 and 24 at left armhole.

Row 1: BG col: PU 12 (13, 15) sts from BM 71, turn work, CO 11 (13, 14) sts.

Row 2 (WS): K1tbl, purl across, sl 1F. Cut BG col.

Rows 3–8: Col 1: K1tbl, knit across, sl 1F.

Row 9: Col 2: K1tbl, knit across, sl 1F.

Row 10: K1tbl, purl across, sl 1F.

Rows 11–14: Col 1: K1tbl, knit across, sl 1F.

SLM 73: Small

Rows 15, 21: Col 2: K1tbl, knit across, sl 1F. Cut col 2 after row 21.

Row 16: Col 2: K1tbl, (P2tog, P1) 7 times, sl 1F—16 sts.

Rows 17–20, 23–26: Col 1: K1tbl, knit across, sl 1F. Cut col 1 after row 26.

Row 22: Col 2: K2tog tbl, (P2tog) 7 times—8 sts. Cut col 2.

Row 27: BG col: K1tbl, knit across, sl 1F.

Row 28: K2tog tbl, purl across, sl 1F—7 sts. Cut BG col.

Row 29: Col 3: K1tbl, knit across, sl 1F.

Rows 30–36: K1tbl, seed st across, sl 1F.

BO rem 7 sts.

SLM 73: Medium

Rows 15, 16, 19–22, 25–28: Col 1: K1tbl, knit across, sl 1F. Cut col 1 after row 28.

Rows 17, 23: Col 2: K1tbl, knit across, sl 1F.

Row 18: Col 2: K1tbl, (P2tog, P1) 8 times, sl 1F—18 sts.

Row 24: Col 2: K2tog tbl, (P2tog) 8 times—9 sts. Cut col 2.

Row 29: BG col: K1tbl, knit across, sl 1F.

Row 30: K2tog tbl, purl across, sl 1F—8 sts. Cut BG col.

Row 31: Col 3: K1tbl, knit across, sl 1F.

Rows 32–40: K1tbl, seed st across, sl 1F.

BO rem 8 sts.

SLM 73: Large

Rows 15, 16, 19–24, 27–32: Col 1: K1tbl, knit across, sl 1F. Cut col 1 after row 32.

Rows 17, 25: Col 2: K1tbl, knit across, sl 1F.

Row 18: Col 2: K1tbl, (P2tog, P1) 9 times, sl 1F—20 sts.

Row 26: Col 2: K2tog tbl, (P2 tog) 9 times—10 sts. Cut col 2.

Row 33: BG col: K1tbl, knit across, sl 1F.

Row 34: K2tog tbl, purl across, sl 1F—9 sts. Cut BG col.

Row 35: Col 3: K1tbl, knit across, sl 1F.

Rows 36–44: K1tbl, seed st across, sl 1F.

BO rem 9 sts.

Sleeve Modules: (SLM) 77, 79

First 6 rows are shared by all sizes. Proceed to desired size to finish module.

When SLM 77 and 79 are completed, leave rem 7 (8, 9) sts on needle. Use 3-needle BO to connect SLM 77 to sleeve BM 76 and SLM 79 to sleeve BM 78.

Row 1: BG col: CO 18 (20, 22) sts.

Row 2 (WS): K1tbl, purl across, sl 1F. Cut BG col.

Rows 3, 4: Col 1: K2tog tbl, knit across, sl 1F—17, 16 (19, 18; 21, 20) sts.

Rows 5, 6: K1tbl, knit across, sl 1F.

SLM 77, 79: Small

Rows 7, 13: Col 2: K1tbl, knit across, sl 1F.

Row 8: K1tbl, purl across, sl 1F.

Rows 9–12, 15–18: Col 1: K1tbl, knit across, sl 1F. Cut col 1 after row 18.

Row 14: Col 2: K2tog tbl, (P2tog) 7 times—8 sts. Cut col 2.

Row 19: BG col: K1tbl, knit across, sl 1F.

Row 20: K2tog tbl, purl across, sl 1F—7 sts.

SLM 77, 79: Medium

Rows 7, 8, 11–16, 19–22: Col 1: K1tbl, knit across, sl 1F. Cut col 1 after row 22.

Rows 9, 17: Col 2: K1tbl, knit across, sl 1F.

Row 10: K1tbl, purl across, sl 1F.

Row 18: K2tog tbl, (P2tog) 8 times—9 sts. Cut col 2.

Row 23: BG col: K1tbl, knit across, sl 1F.

Row 24: K2tog tbl, purl across, sl 1F—8 sts.

SLM 77, 79: Large

Rows 7, 8, 11–16, 19–24: Col 1: K1tbl, knit across, sl 1F. Cut col 1 after row 24.

Rows 9, 17: Col 2: K1tbl, knit across, sl 1F.

Row 10: Col 2: K1tbl, purl across, sl 1F.

Row 18: Col 2: K2tog tbl, (P2tog) 9 times—10 sts. Cut col 2.

Row 25: BG col: K1tbl, knit across, sl 1F.

Row 26: K2tog tbl, purl across, sl 1F—9 sts.

Sleeve Modules (SLM) 80, 82

First 14 rows are shared by all sizes. Proceed to desired size to finish module.

When SLM 80 and 82 are completed, leave rem 7 (8, 9) sts on needle. Use 3-needle BO to join SLM 80 to SLM 81 and SLM 82 to SLM 83.

Row 1: BG col: PU 27 (30, 33) sts from SLM 77 and BM 76 or BM 78 and SLM 79.

Row 2 (WS): K1tbl, purl across, sl 1F. Cut BG col.

Rows 3–6: Col 1: K2tog tbl, knit across, sl 1F—26, 25, 24, 23 (29, 28, 27, 26; 32, 31, 30, 29) sts.

Rows 7, 8: K1tbl, knit across, sl 1F.

Row 9: Col 2: K1tbl, knit across, sl 1F.

Row 10: K1tbl, purl across, sl 1F.

Rows 11–14: Col 1: K1tbl, knit across, sl 1F.

SLM 80, 82: Small

Rows 15, 21: Col 2: K1tbl, knit across, sl 1F.

Row 16: K1tbl, (P2tog, P1) 7 times, sl 1F—16 sts.

Rows 17–20, 23–26: Col 1: K1tbl, knit across, sl 1F. Cut col 1 after row 26.

Row 22: Col 2: K2tog tbl, (P2tog) 7 times—8 sts. Cut col 2.

Row 27: BG col: K1tbl, knit across, sl 1F.

Row 28: K2tog tbl, purl across, sl 1F—7 sts. Cut BG col.

Row 29: Col 3: K1tbl, knit across, sl 1F.

Rows 30–36: K1tbl, seed st across, sl 1F.

SLM 80, 82: Medium

Rows 15, 16, 19–22, 25–28: Col 1: K1tbl, knit across, sl 1F. Cut col 1 after row 28.

Rows 17, 23: Col 2: K1tbl, knit across, sl 1F.

Row 18: K1tbl, (P2tog, P1) 8 times, sl 1F—18 sts.

Row 24: Col 2: K2tog tbl, (P2tog) 8 times—9 sts. Cut col 2.

Row 29: BG col: K1tbl, knit across, sl 1F.

Row 30: K2tog tbl, purl across, sl 1F—8 sts. Cut BG col.

Row 31: Col 3: K1tbl, knit across, sl 1F.

Rows 32–40: K1tbl, seed st across, sl 1F.

SLM 80, 82: Large

Rows 15, 16, 19–24, 27–32: Col 1: K1tbl, knit across, sl 1F. Cut col 1 after row 32.

Rows 17, 25: Col 2: K1tbl, knit across, sl 1F.

Row 18: Col 2: K1tbl, (P1, P2tog) 9 times, sl 1F—20 sts.

Row 26: Col 2: K2tog tbl, (P2tog) 9 times—10 sts. Cut col 2.

Row 33: BG col: K1tbl, knit across, sl 1F.

Row 34: K2tog tbl, purl across, sl 1F—9 sts. Cut BG col.

Row 35: Col 3: K1tbl, knit across, sl 1F.

Rows 36–44: K1tbl, seed st across, sl 1F.

Sleeve Modules (SLM) 81, 83

First 9 rows are shared by all sizes. Proceed to desired size to finish module.

When SLM 81 and 83 are completed, leave rem 7 (8, 9) sts on needle. Use 3-needle BO to join SLM 81 to SLM 80 and SLM 83 to SLM 82.

Row 1: BG col: CO 16 (18, 20) sts.

Row 2 (WS): K2tog tbl, purl across, sl 1F—15 (17, 19) sts. Cut BG col.

Rows 3–8: Col 1: K1tbl, knit across, sl 1F.

Row 9: Col 2: K1tbl, knit across, sl 1F.

SLM 81, 83: Small

Row 10: Col 2: K1tbl, (P2, P2tog) 3 times, P1, sl 1F—12 sts.

Rows 11–14, 17–20, 23–26: Col 1: K1tbl, knit across, sl 1F. Cut col 1 after row 26.

Rows 15, 21: Col 2: K1tbl, knit across, sl 1F.

Row 16: Col 2: K2tog tbl, (P1, P2tog) 3 times, sl 1F—8 sts.

Row 22: Col 2: K1tbl, purl across, sl 1F. Cut col 2.

Row 27: BG col: K1tbl, knit across, sl 1F.

Row 28: K2tog tbl, purl across, sl 1F—7 sts.

SLM 81, 83: Medium

Row 10: Col 2: K1tbl, (P2, P2tog) 4 times—13 sts.

Rows 11–16, 19–22, 25–28: Col 1: K1tbl, knit across, sl 1F. Cut col 1 after row 28.

Rows 17, 23: Col 2: K1tbl, knit across, sl 1F.

Row 18: Col 2: K1tbl, (P1, P2tog) 4 times—9 sts.

Row 24: Col 2: K1tbl, purl across, sl 1F. Cut col 2.

Row 29: BG col: K1tbl, knit across, sl 1F.

Row 30: K2tog tbl, purl across, sl 1F—8 sts.

SLM 81, 83: Large

Row 10: Col 2: K1tbl, P1, (P2tog, P2) 4 times, sl 1F—15 sts.

Rows 11–16, 19–24, 27–32: Col 1: K1tbl, knit across, sl 1F. Cut col 2 after row 32.

Rows 17, 25: Col 2: K1tbl, knit across, sl 1F.

Row 18: Col 2: K2tog tbl, (P1, P2tog) 4 times, sl 1F—10 sts.

Row 26: Col 2: K1tbl, purl across, sl 1F. Cut col 2.

Row 33: BG col: K1tbl, knit across, sl 1F.

Row 34: K2tog tbl, purl across, sl 1F—9 sts.

Maya's Shortened-Sleeve Module 86 (Small Only)

NOTE: Use the following instructions only if you are knitting size Small sleeves and you wish to shorten the sleeve length from the original 22½" to 19". I also deleted SLM 81, HM 87, and HM 88 to shorten the length and achieve appropriate tapering of the sleeve.

Row 1: BG col: PU 32 sts from BM 84 and 85.

Row 2 (WS): K2tog tbl, purl across, P2tog—30 sts. Cut BG col.

Rows 3–8: Col 1: K2tog tbl, knit across, P2tog—28, 26, 24, 22, 20, 18 sts.

Row 9: Col 2: K2tog tbl, knit across, P2tog—16 sts.

Row 10: K2tog tbl, purl across, P2tog—14 sts. Cut col 2.

Rows 11–14: Col 1: K2tog tbl, knit across, P2tog—12, 10, 8, 6 sts.

Row 15: BO rem 6 sts.

Finishing

- When sleeves are completed, fold lengthwise and sew SLM 77 to SLM 79, SLM 80 to SLM 82, SLM 81 to SLM 83, and HM 87 to HM 88.

- At underarm, sew bound-off edge of SLM 73 seed-st section to the side of the seed-st section between BM 21 and BM 22 at right armhole and between BM 23 and BM 24 at left armhole.

- For front edge trim and buttonholes, refer to "Quick Crocheted Edges" (page 22). Start at center back neck, work 2 continuous rows of hdc, followed by 1 row of sc around neck edges, fronts of jacket, and bottom scallops. On row 2 of hdc, work 3 buttonholes at top of HM 49, seed-st section of BM 43, and seed-st section between HM 45 and 46.

- Sew on 3 dazzling buttons.

SOME OF MY
MOLA COLLECTION

Mola Vest

As a variation to Mola Jacket, I knit this vest in cottons. Review the schematic on page 104 and follow module instructions for Mola Jacket on pages 92-96.

Sizes: Small (Medium, Large)

Finished Chest: 37 (43, 48)"

Finished Length: 18 (21, 23½)"

Materials

Use DK-weight yarns or a variety of yarns to achieve gauge.

- **BG Col:** Approx 400 (500, 625) total yds of darkest color

- **Col 1:** Approx 400 (500, 625) total yds of variegated yarn for *vertical* motifs

- **Col 1:** Approx 400 (500, 625) total yds of 4 or more assorted medium colors for *horizontal* motifs

- **Col 2:** Approx 400 (500, 625) total yds of 4 or more assorted dark colors

- **Col 3:** Approx 120 total yds of 4 or more assorted bright colors for center squares

- Three size 6 double-pointed needles (or size required to obtain gauge)

- Size F or G crochet hook

- Tapestry needle

- 3 buttons, 1½" to 2" diameter

Gauge for Basic Mola

Small: 32 sts and 64 rows = 5" x 8", including 1" center square

Medium: 36 sts and 70 rows = 6" x 9", including 1½" center square

Large: 40 sts and 78 rows = 7" x 10", including 1¾" center square

Body

The following bullet points outline the knitting sequence. For more information, refer to the module instructions.

- Work all modules as for Mola Jacket body (pages 92–96).

- For modules 12, 14, 33, and 35, knit as for SLM 77, 79 (pages 97–98). BO rem 7 (8, 9) sts.

- For shoulder modules A and B, knit BM rows 1–16 (1–18; 1–18) and BO. **Mod A:** Beg at bottom of mod 42 and cont across mod 20, PU 32 (36, 40) sts. **Mod B:** Beg at top of mod 41 and cont across mod 19, PU 32 (36, 40) sts.

- Finish body as for Mola Jacket. Finish armholes with 1 row hdc, followed by 1 row sc.

- Sew on 3 festive buttons.

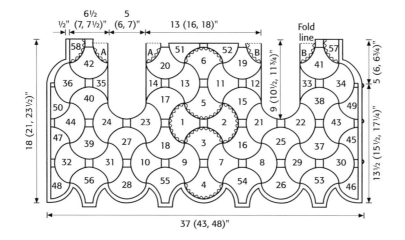

Cubes: The Basics

The assembly techniques employed in the following two projects are unique. These modules are knit by stacking one on top of the other in diagonal rows that slant from right to left, bottom to top. The first diagonal row begins at the lower-left edge of the garment. Each successive diagonal row begins at the bottom edge of the garment and always to the right of the previous diagonal row of modules.

In these two designs, it is especially important to knit each diagonally slanting row in the proper numerical sequence indicated at the bottom of each schematic. Twist yarns when changing colors so that you leave no hole in your work. Use the technique "Double Cast On" in these two designs (page 20).

Each completed module consists of three shades of one color plus a variegated yarn that flows consistently throughout the work. The main color (MC), a variegated yarn, is the garter row, which is superimposed over each module. The lid or top of each module is knit in the lightest color. The right side of each module is always the darkest color, and the left side is the medium value. Maintaining this color rhythm throughout the design creates the three-dimensional effect.

Color and Design Options

- Use one continuous dark, solid color—such as black, navy, or dark purple—for the main color.

- Repeat the same three shades of one color for every motif in the garment.

- Make one diagonal row of cubes in the same color family—say reds—and the next row yellows, the next greens, and so on.

- Knit each module in stockinette stitch with no alternating main color in the garter rows. If you choose this option, you might wish to outline the modules in the main color by starting each with two garter rows in the main color.

- Knit each module completely in garter stitch.

- Regardless of which option you choose, it is essential to maintain consistent use of three shades of the same color to achieve the three-dimensional effect.

Page 107   Page 113

3-D Cubist Vest

This vest is an original project inspired by elements of an old quilt and a Kaffe Fassett design. However, this modular approach is much easier, faster, and more flexible. This is a chance to use lots of beautiful, lingering yarns to create a striking new masterpiece for your wardrobe.

    Each cube consists of one double row of garter followed by a double row of stockinette. Carefully review the cube basics (page 105) prior to starting this unique design.

Sizes: X-Small (Small, Medium, Large, X-Large)
Finished Chest: 34 (36¾, 39½, 45, 47¾)"
Finished Length: 19 (19, 19, 22⁹⁄₁₆, 22⁹⁄₁₆)"

Materials

Use worsted-weight yarns or a variety of yarns to achieve gauge.

- **MC:** Approx 350 (375, 390, 490, 525) total yds of Noro Silk Garden by Noro (45% silk, 45% kid mohair, 10% lamb's wool; 109 yds [100 m] per skein), color 51 brown variegated

- **Lt:** Approx 115 (120, 130, 180, 190) total yds Noro Cash Iroha (40% silk, 30% lamb's wool, 20% cashmere, 10% nylon; 99 yds [91 m] per skein) and/or Muench Horstia Maulbeerseide-Schurwolle (50% silk, 50% wool; 108 yds [100 m] per skein) in several light shades

- **Md:** Approx 115 (120, 130, 180, 190) total yds Noro Cash Iroha and/or Muench Horstia Maulbeerseide-Schurwolle in several medium shades

- **Dk:** Approx 115 (120, 130, 180, 190) total yds Noro Cash Iroha and/or Muench Horstia Maulbeerseide-Schurwolle in several dark shades

- Two size 6 double-pointed needles (or size required to obtain gauge)

- Size F crochet hook

- 3 buttons, 1" diameter

Gauge

Cube: 19 sts and 37 rows = approx 2¾" wide x 4¾" high

NOTE: To connect many modules, you will be knitting with stitches from the right half of your work. At the end of right-side rows, when designated, you will join the right module to the left module as follows:
Special Abbreviation: ◄= join modules by slipping next st pw wyib, K1 from left needle and pass slipped st over, turn work, beg next row.

Body

While in some sizes you will start your first cube using the instructions for mod A, a majority of remaining cubes will be knit following directions for mod C. See schematic to determine which module to knit. If there is no designation within a cube shape, follow directions for mod C.

Module A: Cube

Row 1: MC: CO or PU 19 sts.

Row 2 (WS): MC: K1tbl, K7, sK2po, K7, sl 1F—17 sts.

Rows 3, 7, 11, 15: Dk: K1tbl, M1, K8; **Md:** K7, M1, sl 1F—19 sts for all rows.

Rows 4, 8, 12, 16: Md: K1tbl, P7, sP2po; **Dk:** P7, sl 1F—17 sts for all rows. Cut Md/Dk after row 16.

X-Small and Small

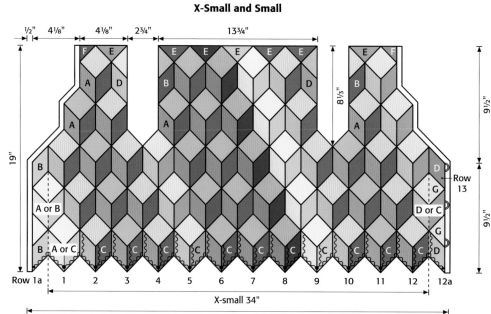

Medium

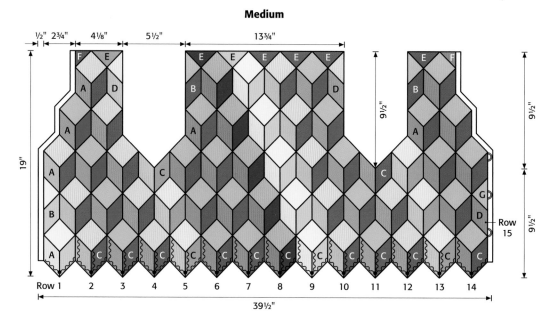

Note: Begin each diagonal row of modules at bottom edge of garment. Work each consecutive shape on top of previous module below, forming rows that slant from right to left.

Rows 5, 9, 13, 17: MC: K1tbl, M1, K15, M1, sl 1F—19 sts for all rows.

Rows 6, 10, 14, 18: MC: K1tbl, K7, sK2po, K7, sl 1F—17 sts for all rows.

Row 19: Lt: K1tbl, M1, K6, ◀.

Row 20: K1tbl, P7, sl 1F.

Rows 21, 25, 29, 33: MC: K1tbl, K7, ◀.

Rows 22, 26, 30, 34: K1tbl, K7, sl 1F.

Rows 23, 27, 31, 35: Lt: K1tbl, K7, ◀.

Rows 24, 28, 32, 36: K1tbl, P7, sl 1F. Cut Lt after row 36.

Row 37: MC: K1tbl, K7, sl 1F.

Row 38: K1tbl, K7, sl 1F.

Do not cut MC yarn. With 9 sts on needle, beg mod B if indicated on schematic. If this is last mod in row, BO rem 9 sts.

Large

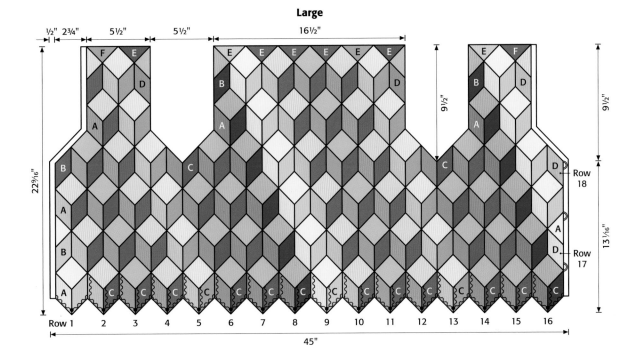

X-Large

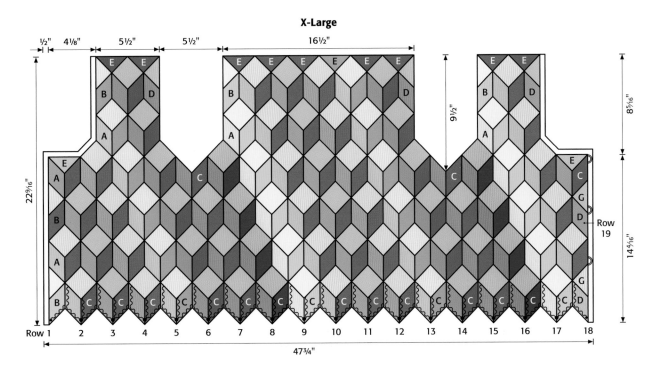

Module B: Right Half Cube

Rows 1, 5, 9, 13: From 9 sts on needle, Dk: K1tbl, M1, K7 sts, sl 1F—10 sts for all rows.

Rows 2, 6, 10, 14 (WS): Dk: K2tog tbl, P7, sl 1F—9 sts for all rows. Cut Dk after row 14.

Rows 3, 7, 11, 15: MC: K1tbl, M1, K7, sl 1F—10 sts for all rows.

Rows 4, 8, 12, 16: MC: K2tog tbl, K7, sl 1F—9 sts for all rows.

Row 17: Lt: K1tbl, M1, K7, sl 1F—10 sts.

Row 18: K1tbl, P8, sl 1F.

Rows 19, 23, 27, 31, 35: MC: K1tbl, knit across, sl 1F.

Rows 20, 24, 28, 32: K2tog tbl, knit across, sl 1F—9, 7, 5, 3 sts.

Rows 21, 25, 29, 33: Lt: K1tbl, knit across, sl 1F.

Rows 22, 26, 30, 34: Lt: K2tog tbl, purl across, sl 1F—8, 6, 4, 2 sts. Cut Lt after row 34.

Row 36: MC: K2tog. Fasten off.

Module C: Cube

Mod C begins a new diagonal row of cubes in which you PU from the right side of cubes to the left of your work. Follow this pattern for cubes with "C" or with no alphabetical designation.

Row 1: MC: CO or PU 19 sts; then PU 9 sts along right side of cube to left—28 sts.

Row 2 (WS): MC: K1tbl, K16, sK2po, K7, sl 1F.

Rows 3, 7, 11, 15: Dk: K1tbl, M1, K8; **Md:** K7, M1, ◀—19 sts for all rows.

Rows 4, 8, 12, 16: Md: K1tbl, P7, sP2po; **Dk:** P7, sl 1F—17 sts for all rows. Cut Md/Dk after row 16.

Rows 5, 9, 13: MC: K1tbl, M1, K15, M1, ◀—19 sts for all rows.

Rows 6, 10, 14: MC: K1tbl, K7, sK2po, K7, sl 1F—17 sts for all rows.

Row 17: MC: K1tbl, M1, K15, M1, ◀, K1, turn work—20 sts.

Row 18: MC: K1tbl, K8, sK2po, K7, sl 1F—18 sts.

Row 19: Lt: K1tbl, M1, K6, ◀.

Row 20: Lt: K1tbl, P7, sl 1F.

Rows 21, 25, 29, 33: MC: K1tbl, K7, ◀.

Rows 22, 26, 30, 34: MC: K1tbl, K7, sl 1F.

Rows 23, 27, 31, 35: Lt: K1tbl, K7, ◀.

Rows 24, 28, 32, 36: Lt: K1tbl, P7, sl 1F. Cut Lt after row 36.

Row 37: MC: K1tbl, K7, ◀, do not turn work.

Do not cut MC yarn. Leave 9 sts on needle. To continue making cubes, PU 10 sts from right side of cube lid (CL) to left, PU 9 sts along right side of cube base (CB) to left or CO 9 sts if no cube exists. With 28 sts on needle, beg row 2 of mod C. If this finished cube is the last mod in row, disregard PU directions above, BO rem 9 sts.

Module D: Left Half Cube

Row 1: MC: PU 10 sts from right side of CL to left, PU 9 sts from right side of CB to left.

Row 2 (WS): MC: K1tbl, K17, sl 1F.

Rows 3, 7, 11, 15: Md: K2tog tbl, K8, M1, ◀.

Rows 4, 8, 12, 16: Md: K1tbl, P9, sl 1F. Cut Md after row 16.

Rows 5, 9, 13, 17: MC: K2tog tbl, K8, M1, ◀.

Rows 6, 10, 14, 18: MC: K1tbl, K9, sl 1F.

If this is for right front edge of vest, cut MC and beg mod G; otherwise cont to row 19.

Row 19: Lt: K2tog tbl, K8, sl 1F—10 sts.

Row 20: Lt: K1tbl, P8, sl 1F.

Rows 21, 25, 29, 33: MC: K2tog tbl, knit across, sl 1F—9, 7, 5, 3 sts.

Rows 22, 26, 30, 34: MC: K1tbl, knit across, sl 1F.

Rows 23, 27, 31, 35: Lt: K2tog tbl, knit across, sl 1F—8, 6, 4, 2 sts.

Rows 24, 28, 32, 36: Lt: K1tbl, purl across, sl 1F.

Row 37: MC: K2tog tbl. Cut both yarns. Fasten off.

Module E: One-Quarter Cube or Triangle

Mod E finishes shoulders and back neckline. It can also fill in bottom of vest for an even hemline.

Row 1: MC: PU 9 sts from left side of CL below, PU 10 sts from right side of CL below—19 sts.

Row 2 (WS): MC: K1tbl, K7, sK2po, K7, sl 1F—17 sts.

Row 3: Dk: K2tog tbl, K7; **Md:** K7, sl 1F—16 sts.

Row 4: Md: K2tog tbl, P5, sP2po; **Dk:** P5, sl 1F—13 sts.

Rows 5, 9: MC: K2tog tbl, knit across, sl 1F—12, 4 sts.

Row 6: MC: K2tog tbl, K3, sK2po, K3, sl 1F—9 sts.

Row 7: Dk: K2tog tbl, K3; **Md:** K3, sl 1F—8 sts.

Row 8: Md: K2tog tbl, P1, sP2po; **Dk:** P1, sl 1F—5 sts.

Row 10: MC: K2tog tbl, P2tog, po. Fasten off.

Module F: Half Triangle for X-Small, Small, and Medium

Mod F finishes front necklines. Use Md color for right side of vest and Dk color for left side of vest.

Row 1: MC: PU 10 sts from right or left side of CL below—10 sts.

Row 2 (WS): MC: K1tbl, K8, sl 1F—10 sts.

Rows 3, 7: Md or Dk: K2tog tbl, knit across, sl 1F—9, 5 sts.

Rows 4, 8: Md or Dk: K2tog tbl, purl across, sl 1F—8, 4 sts.

Rows 5, 6, 9: MC: K2tog tbl, knit across, sl 1F—7, 6, 3 sts.

Row 10: MC: sK2po. Fasten off.

Module G: Alternate Left Half Cube Lid

Mod G occurs only on right front side of vest as an alternate lid for mod D. It is knit differently than other modules to mirror the corresponding lid on left side of the vest. You will connect G and D at the end of every WS row.

Row 1: With 11 sts on needle from mod D, turn work to WS, join MC yarn, and CO 8 sts—19 sts.

Row 2 (WS): MC: K1tbl, K7, ◄.

Rows 3, 7, 11, 15: Lt: K1tbl, knit across, sl 1F—9, 7, 5, 3 sts.

Rows 4, 8, 12, 16: Lt: K2tog tbl, purl 6, 4, 2, 0 ◄—8, 6, 4, 2 sts.

Rows 5, 9, 13, 17: MC: K1tbl, knit across, sl 1F—8, 6, 4, 2 sts.

Rows 6, 10, 14, 18: MC: K2tog tbl, knit 5, 3, 1, 0 ◄—7, 5, 3, 2 sts.

Row 19: MC: K2tog tbl. Fasten off.

Finishing

- Sew shoulder seams tog.

- Front edge and armhole trims: Refer to "Quick Crocheted Edges" (page 22). Place buttonholes as indicated on schematic.

- Sew on 3 spectacular buttons.

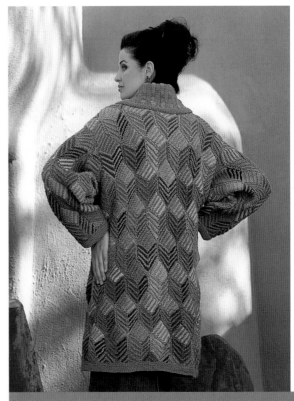

EVER THE INNOVATOR, NANCY NICKERSON HAS EXPANDED THE 3-D CUBIST VEST TO A LONG-SLEEVED COAT WITH COLLAR BY EMPLOYING TECHNIQUES SUGGESTED IN THE SECTION "PAPER DOLL CUTOUT" (PAGE 27).

Metropolis Coat

The design for this coat took root in my imagination while I was in the city of Berlin. This ancient city, with its centuries-old cathedral spires juxtaposed with futuristic skyscrapers, spoke volumes to my architectural background. This coat consists of two different modules, one representing the primeval structures and the other the contemporary edifices, which live side by side in sharp contrast in many a metropolis.

The modules incorporated in this dazzling coat link beautifully together in a symphony of color. The pattern for each module in this coat is almost consistently one double row of garter followed by two double rows of stockinette. The cube lids are all garter.

Sizes: Small/Medium (Large, X-Large)
Finished Chest: 45½ (51, 56½)"
Finished Length: 26 (26, 32)"

Materials

Use worsted-weight yarns as listed below or a variety of yarns to achieve gauge.

- **MC:** Approx 680 (820, 1050) total yds of Noro Silk Garden (45% silk, 45% kid mohair, 10% lamb's wool; 109 yds [100 m] per skein), color 65

- **Lt:** Approx 650 (750, 1000) total yds Noro Cash Iroha (40% silk, 30% lamb's wool, 20% cashmere, 10% nylon; 99 yds [100 m] per skein) OR Muench Horstia Maulbeerseide-Schurwolle (50% silk, 50% wool; 108 yds [100 m] per skein) in several light shades

- **Md:** Approx 600 (675, 860) total yds Noro Cash Iroha AND/OR Muench Horstia Maulbeerseide-Schurwolle in several medium shades

- **Dk:** Approx 600 (675, 860) total yds Noro Cash Iroha AND/OR Muench Horstia Maulbeerseide-Schurwolle in several dark shades

- Two size 5 double-pointed needles for modules (or size required to obtain gauge)

- Size 5 circular needles for modules and collar

- Two size 6 double-pointed needles for I-Cord and frog closures

- Red Rubber Markers (see "Resources," page 128)

- 10 stitch holders or large safety pins

Gauge

Y: 17 sts and 32 rows = 5½" wide x 6" high on size 5 needles

V: 33 sts and 16 rows = 5½" wide x 3½" high on size 5 needles

Cube: 17 sts and 30 rows = 2¾" wide x 4½" high on size 5 needles

NOTE: To connect many of the modules, you will be knitting with stitches from the right half of your work. At the end of right-side rows, when designated, you will join the right module to the left module as follows:

Special Abbreviation: ◀ = join modules by slipping next st pw wyib, K1 from left needle and pass slipped st over, turn work, beg next row.

Body

While each size garment may start with a different module shape, a majority of shapes will be knit following instructions for modules Y, V, or C designated on the schematic. If there is no indication within a module, follow instructions for module Y for the Y shapes, V for the V shapes, and C for the cube shapes. Do not cut the main-color yarn unless so directed. Once you are in the flow of knitting the diagonal rows, you will notice you are knitting a recurring sequence of a diagonal row of cubes followed by a diagonal row of Ys and Vs. This rhythm prevails throughout the design.

Generally speaking, half of the 17 stitches of the first row of a cube are picked up from the right side of the indent of the V below. The remaining stitches are picked up from the left side of the indent of the same V below. Half of the 17 stitches of the first row of a Y shape are picked up from the left top of the V below. The remaining stitches are picked up from the right top of the other V immediately below.

Use size 5 double-pointed or circular needles for all modules.

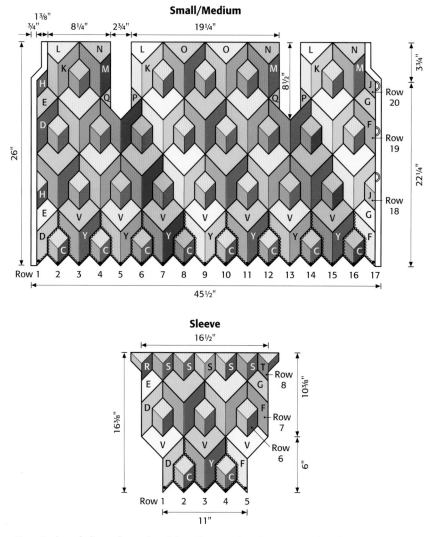

Note: Begin each diagonal row of modules at bottom edge of garment. Work each consecutive shape on top of previous module below, forming rows that slant from right to left.

Module Y

While working module Y, you will also pick up off other modules to the left.

This module begins a new diagonal row in which you PU from the right side of the module to the left of your work. Knit every Y-shaped module on schematic (except the first Y at the cuff of size Large sleeve) with or without an alphabetical designation as follows:

Row 1: MC: CO or PU 17, PU 7 sts from right side of cube base (CB) to left, PU 8 sts from right side of cube lid (CL), PU 8 sts from right side of Y or CO 8 if no Y exists—40 sts.

Row 2 (WS): K1tbl, K6, K2tog, K21, sK2po, K6, sl 1F—37 sts.

Rows 3, 5, 9, 11, 15: Dk: K1bf, K6; **Md:** K7, M1, ◄—17 sts for all rows.

Rows 4, 6, 10, 12, 16: Md: K1tbl, P6, sP2po; **Dk:** P6, sl 1F—15 sts for all rows.

Rows 7, 13: MC: K1bf, K13, M1, ◄—17 sts for both rows.

Rows 8, 14: MC: K1tbl, K6, sK2po, K6, sl 1F—15 sts for both rows.

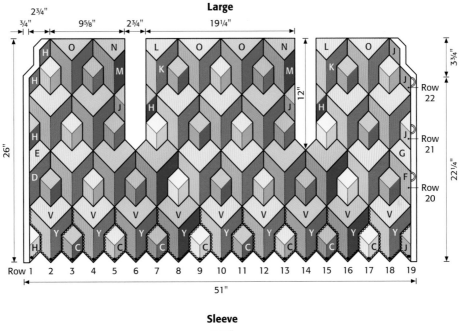

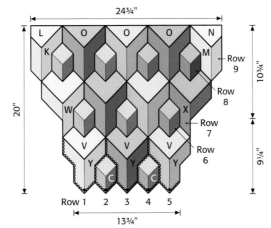

Note: Begin each diagonal row of modules at bottom edge of garment. Work each consecutive shape on top of previous module below, forming rows that slant from right to left.

Row 17: Dk: First CO 9 sts; then K1tbl, K15; **Md:** K7, M1, K1, K8 sts from left needle, turn work—33 sts.

Row 18: Md: K1tbl, P14, sP2po; **Dk:** P14, sl 1F—31 sts. AT SAME TIME, work MC back to edge.

Rows 19, 25, 31: MC: K1bf, K29, M1, ◀—33 sts for all rows.

Rows 20, 26, 32: MC: K1tbl, K14, sK2po, K14, sl 1F—31 sts for all rows.

Rows 21, 23, 27, 29: Dk: K1bf, K14; **Md:** K15, M1, ◀—33 sts for all rows.

Rows 22, 24 28, 30: Md: K1tbl, P14, sP2po;

Dk: P14, sl 1F—31 sts for all rows. Cut Md/Dk after row 30. With 31 sts on needle, beg mod V.

Module Y for Large Sleeve Only

First Y at sleeve cuff.

Row 1: MC: CO 17 sts.

Row 2 (WS): K1tbl, K6, sK2po, K6, sl 1F—15 sts.

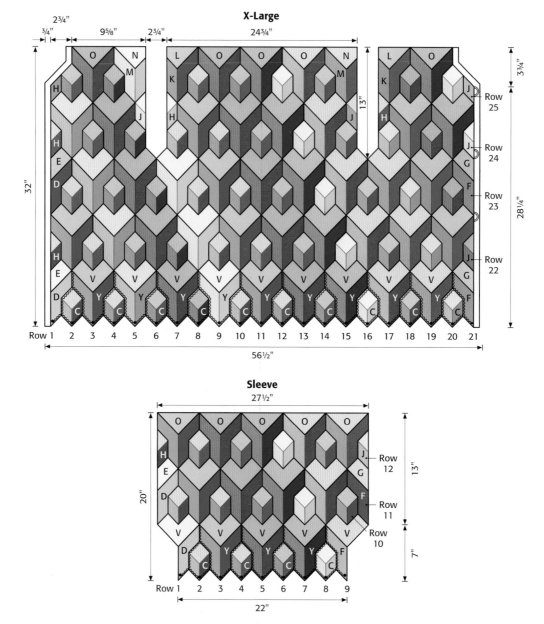

Note: Begin each diagonal row of modules at bottom edge of garment. Work each consecutive shape on top of previous module below, forming rows that slant from right to left.

Rows 3, 5, 9, 11, 15: Dk: K1bf, K6; **Md:** K7, M1, sl 1F—17 sts for all rows.

Rows 4, 6, 10, 12, 16: Md: K1tbl, P6, sP2po; **Dk:** P6, sl 1F—15 sts for all rows.

Rows 7, 13: MC: K1bf, K13, M1, sl 1F—17 sts for both rows.

Rows 8, 14: MC: K1tbl, K6, sK2po, K6, sl 1F—15 sts for both rows.

Row 17: Dk: First CO 9 sts; then over those 24 sts K1tbl, K15; **Md:** K7, M1, sl 1F—25 sts.

Row 18: Md: First CO 8 sts; then over those 33 sts K1tbl, P14, sP2po; **Dk:** P14, sl 1F—31 sts. AT SAME TIME, work MC back to edge.

Rows 19, 25, 31: MC: K1bf, K29, M1, sl 1F—33 sts for all rows.

Rows 20, 26, 32: MC: K1tbl, K14, sK2po, K14, sl 1F—31 sts for all rows.

Rows 21, 23, 27, 29: Dk: K1bf, K14; **Md:** K15, M1, sl 1F—33 sts for all rows.

Rows 22, 24, 28, 30: Md: K1tbl, P14, sP2po; **Dk:** P14, sl 1F—31 sts for all rows. Cut Md/Dk after row 30.

With 31 sts on needle, beg mod V.

Module V

Knit every V-shaped module on schematic with or without alphabetical designation as follows:

Row 1: Lt: K1bf, K29, M1, sl 1F—33 sts.

Row 2 (WS): Lt: K1tbl, P14, sP2po, P14, sl 1F—31 sts.

Rows 3, 7, 9 13, 15: Lt: K1tbl, knit across, sl 1F—31, 27, 25, 21, 19 sts.

Row 4: Lt: K1tbl, P13, sP2po, P13, sl 1F—29 sts.

Rows 5, 11: MC: K1tbl, knit across, sl 1F—29, 23 sts.

Row 6: MC: K1tbl, K12, sK2po, K12, sl 1F—27 sts.

Row 8: Lt: K1tbl, P11, sP2po, P11, sl 1F—25 sts.

Row 10: Lt: K1tbl, P10, sP2po, P10, sl 1F—23 sts.

Row 12: MC: K1tbl, K9, sK2po, K9, sl 1F—21 sts. Cut MC.

Row 14: Lt: K1tbl, P8, sP2po, P8, sl 1F—19 sts.

Row 16: Lt: K1tbl, P7, sP2po, P7, sl 1F—17 sts. Cut Lt.

Place 17 sts on holder until time to knit cube module on next diagonal row.

Module C: Cube

Special Abbreviation starting with row 18:
sK2po = sl 1wyib, SM, K2tog, pass slipped st over

Knit every cube shape on schematic with or without alphabetical designation as follows:

Row 1: MC: CO or PU 17; or from 17 sts on holder, K1tbl, K16. Then PU 7 sts from right side of base of Y to the left, PU 8 sts from underside of Y to left—32 sts.

Row 2 (WS): K1tbl, K12, K2tog, K7, sK2po, K6, sl 1F—29 sts.

Rows 3, 5, 9, 11: Dk: K1bf, K6; **Md:** K7, M1, ◄—17 sts for all rows.

Rows 4, 6, 10, 12: Md: K1tbl, P6, sP2po; **Dk:** P6, sl 1F—15 sts for all rows. Cut Md/Dk after row 12.

Rows 7, 13: MC: K1bf, K13, M1, ◄—17 sts for both rows.

Rows 8, 14: MC: K1tbl, K6, sK2po, K6, sl 1F—15 sts for both rows. Cut MC after row 14.

Row 15: Lt: K1bf, K13, M1, ◄—17 sts.

Row 16: K1tbl, K6, PM, sK2po, K6, sl 1F—15 sts.

Row 17: K1tbl, knit across, with 1 st in Lt rem on needle, ◄.

Row 18: K1tbl, K5, sK2po, K5, sl 1F—13 sts.

Rows 19–29: Rep rows 17 and 18 through row 29 when 3 sts rem. On every WS row, knit 1 less st on either side of sK2po.

Row 30: sK2po. Cut Lt yarn. Fasten off.

Module D: Right Half of Module Y

Row 1: MC: CO or PU 9 sts.

Row 2 (WS): K2tog tbl, K6, sl 1F—8 sts.

Rows 3, 5, 9, 11, 15: Dk: K1bf, K6, sl 1F—9 sts for all rows.

Rows 4, 6, 10, 12, 16: Dk: K2tog tbl, P6, sl 1F—8 sts for all rows.

Rows 7, 13: MC: K1bf, K6, sl 1F—9 sts for both rows.

Rows 8, 14: MC: K2tog tbl, K6, sl 1F—8 sts for both rows.

Row 17: Dk: First CO 9 sts. Then K1tbl, K15, sl 1F—17 sts.

Row 18: Dk: K2tog tbl, P14, sl 1F—16 sts. AT SAME TIME, work MC back to edge.

Rows 19, 25, 31: MC: K1bf, K14, sl 1F—17 sts for all rows.

Rows 20, 26, 32: MC: K2tog tbl, K14, sl 1F—16 sts for all rows.

Rows 21, 23, 27, 29: Dk: K1bf, K14, sl 1F—17 sts for all rows.

Rows 22, 24, 28, 30: Dk: K2tog tbl, P14, sl 1F—16 sts for all rows. Cut Dk after row 30.

Finish row 32. With 16 sts on needle, beg mod V or mod E as diagram designates.

Module E: Right Half of Module V

Row 1: Lt: From 16 sts on needle, K1bf, K14, sl 1F—17 sts.

Row 2 (WS): Lt: K2tog tbl, P14, sl 1F—16 sts.

Rows 3, 7, 9, 13, 15: Lt: K1tbl, knit across, sl 1F—16, 14, 13, 11, 10 sts.

Rows 4, 8, 10, 14, 16: Lt: K2tog tbl, purl across, sl 1F—15, 13, 12, 10, 9 sts. Cut Lt after row 16.

Rows 5, 11: MC: K1tbl, knit across, sl 1F—15, 12 sts.

Rows 6, 12: MC: K2tog tbl, knit across, sl 1F—14, 11 sts. Cut MC after row 12.

Finish row 16. Place 9 sts on holder until time to knit mod C on next diagonal row, or immediately beg mod H or R if diagram designates.

Module F: Left Half of Module Y

Row 1: MC: CO or PU 9 sts; then PU 7 sts from right side of CB to left, PU 8 sts from right side of CL, PU 8 sts from right side of Y to left—32 sts.

Row 2 (WS): MC: K1tbl, K6, K2tog, K21, P2tog—30 sts.

Rows 3, 5, 9, 11, 15: Md: K1tbl, K6, M1, ◄—9 sts for all rows.

Rows 4, 6, 10, 12, 16: Md: K1tbl, P6, P2tog—8 sts for all rows.

Rows 7, 13: MC: K1tbl, K6, M1, ◄—9 sts for both rows.

Rows 8, 14: MC: K1tbl, K6, P2tog—8 sts for both rows.

Row 17: Md: K1tbl, K6, M1, K1, K8 sts off left needle—17 sts.

Rows 18, 22, 24, 28, 30: Md: K1tbl, P14, P2tog—16 sts for all rows. Cut Md after row 30.

Rows 19, 25, 31: MC: K1tbl, K14, M1, ◄—17 sts for all rows.

Rows 20, 26: MC: K1tbl, K14, P2tog—16 sts for both rows.

Rows 21, 23, 27, 29: Md: K1tbl, K14, M1, ◄—17 sts for all rows.

Row 32: MC: K1tbl, K15, sl 1F—17 sts.

With 17 sts on needle, beg mod V or mod G as diagram designates.

Module G: Left Half of Module V

Row 1: Lt: From 17 sts on needle, K1tbl, K15, sl 1F—17 sts.

Row 2 (WS): Lt: K1tbl, P14, P2tog—16 sts.

Rows 3, 7, 9, 13, 15: Lt: K1tbl, knit across, sl 1F—16, 14, 13, 11, 10 sts.

Rows 4, 8, 10, 14, 16: Lt: K1tbl, purl across, P2tog—15, 13, 12, 10, 9 sts. Cut Lt after row 16.

Rows 5, 11: MC: K1tbl, knit across, sl 1F—15, 12 sts.

Rows 6, 12: MC: K1tbl, knit across, P2tog—14, 11 sts.

Finish row 16. Place 9 sts on holder until time to knit mod J or mod T on next diagonal row.

Module H: Right Half of Module C

Row 1: MC: From 9 sts on needle or holder, K1tbl, K7, sl 1F—9 sts.

Rows 2, 8, 14 (WS): MC: K2tog tbl, K6, sl 1F—8 sts for all rows. Cut MC after row 14.

Rows 3, 5, 9, 11: Dk: K1bf, K6, sl 1F—9 sts for all rows.

Rows 4, 6, 10, 12: K2tog tbl, P6, sl 1F—8 sts for all rows. Cut Dk after row 12.

Rows 7, 13: MC: K1bf, K6, sl 1F—9 sts for both rows.

Do NOT knit beyond row 14 for mod H at neckline. Instead, BO rem 8 sts.

Row 15: Lt: K1bf, K6, sl 1F—9 sts.

Row 16: K2tog tbl, K6, sl 1F—8 sts.

Rows 17, 19, 21, 23, 25, 27, 29: K1tbl, knit across, sl 1F—8, 7, 6, 5, 4, 3, 2 sts.

Rows 18, 20, 22, 24, 26, 28: K2tog tbl, knit across, sl 1F—7, 6, 5, 4, 3, 2 sts.

Row 30: K2tog tbl. Fasten off.

Module J: Left Half of Module C

For mod J at neckline only:

Row 1: MC: From 9 sts on needle or holder, K1tbl, K8, PU 7 sts from RS of mod to the left—16 sts.

Row 2 (WS): K1tbl, K5, K2tog, K6, K2tog—14 sts.

Proceed to row 3 pattern directions on page 120.

All other mod J:

Row 1: MC: From 9 sts on needle or holder, K1tbl, K8; then PU 7 sts from RS of Y base, PU 8 sts from right underside of Y—24 sts.

Row 2 (WS): MC: K1tbl, K12, K2tog, K7, P2tog—22 sts.

Rows 3, 5, 9, 11: Md: K1tbl, K6, M1, ◄—9 sts for all rows.

Rows 4, 6, 10, 12: Md: K1tbl, P6, P2tog—8 sts for all rows. Cut Md after row 12.

Rows 7, 13: MC: K1tbl, K6, M1, ◄—9 sts for both rows.

Rows 8, 14: MC: K1tbl, K6, P2tog—8 sts for both rows. Cut MC after row 14.

Do NOT knit beyond row 14 for mod J at neckline. Instead, BO 8 sts.

Row 15: Lt: K1tbl, knit across, M1, ◄—9 sts.

Rows 16, 18, 20, 22, 24, 26, 28: K1tbl, knit across, P2tog—8, 7, 6, 5, 4, 3, 2 sts.

Rows 17, 19, 21, 23, 25, 27, 29: K1tbl, knit across, ◄.

Row 30: K2tog tbl. Fasten off.

Module K: Partial Y Module

Small/Medium: left front neck only

Row 1: MC: PU 17 sts; then PU 7 sts from cube base to left—24 sts.

Row 2: (WS): K1tbl, K5, K2tog, K6, sK2po, K6, sl 1F—21 sts.

Rows 3, 5, 9, 11: Dk: K1bf, K6; **Md:** K7, M1, ◄—17 sts.

Rows 4, 6, 10, 12: Md: K1tbl, P6, sP2po; **Dk:** P6, sl 1F—15 sts.

Rows 7, 13: MC: K1bf, K13, M1, ◄—17 sts.

Rows 8, 14: MC: K1tbl, K6, sK2po, K6, sl 1F—15 sts.

Proceed to row 15 of mod K above right to finish:

All Sizes: right front armhole, left back armhole; **Large:** upper left sleeve

Row 1: MC: PU 17 sts

Rows 2, 8, 14: (WS): K1tbl, K6, sK2po, K6, sl 1F—15 sts for all rows.

Rows 3, 5, 9, 11, 15: Dk: K1bf, K6, **Md:** K7, M1, sl 1F—17 sts for all rows.

Rows 4, 6, 10, 12, 16: Md: K1tbl, P6, sP2po, **Dk:** P6, sl 1F—15 sts for all rows.

Rows 7, 13: MC: K1bf, K13, M1, sl 1F—17 sts for both rows.

Row 17: Dk: CO 9 sts. K16; **Md:** K7, M1, sl 1F—25 sts.

Row 18: Md: K1tbl, P6, sP2po; **Dk:** P14, sl 1F—23 sts. AT SAME TIME, knit MC back to edge.

Rows 19, 25, 31: MC: K1bf, K21, M1, sl 1F—25 sts for all rows.

Rows 20, 26, 32: MC: K1tbl, K6, sK2po, K14, sl 1F—23 sts for all rows.

Rows 21, 23, 27, 29: Dk: K1bf, K14; **Md:** K7, M1, sl 1F—25 sts for all rows.

Rows 22, 24, 28, 30: Md: K1tbl, P6, sP2po; **Dk:** P14, sl 1F—23 sts for all rows. Cut Dk/Md after row 30.

Finish row 32. With 23 sts on needle, beg mod L.

Module L: Partial V Module

All Sizes: right front armhole, left back armhole; **Small/Medium:** left front neck; **Large:** upper left sleeve

Rows 1, 3: From 23 sts on needle, Lt: K2tog tbl, knit to last st, M1, sl 1F—23, 21 sts.

Row 2 (WS): Lt: K1tbl, P6, sP2po, P12, sl 1F—21 sts.

Row 4: Lt: K1tbl, P6, sP2po, P10, sl 1F—19 sts.

Row 5: MC: K2tog tbl, K16, M1, sl 1F—19 sts.

Row 6: MC: K1tbl, K6, sK2po, K8, sl 1F—17 sts.

Rows 7, 9, 13: Lt: K2tog tbl, knit across, sl 1F—16, 13, 7 sts.

Row 8: Lt: K1tbl, P6, sP2po, P5, sl 1F—14 sts.

Row 10: Lt: K1tbl, P6, sP2po, P2, sl 1F—11 sts.

Row 11: MC: K2tog tbl, K8, sl 1F—10 sts.

Row 12: MC: K1tbl, K6, sK2po—8 sts. Cut MC.

Row 14: Lt: BO 7 sts.

Module M: Partial Y Module

All Sizes: left front armhole, right back armhole;
Small/Medium: right front neck; **Large:** upper right
sleeve

Row 1: MC: PU 17 sts, PU 7 sts from right side of
cube base to left, PU 8 sts from cube lid, PU 8 sts
from right side of Y—40 sts.

Row 2 (WS): K1tbl, K6, K2tog, K21, sK2po, K6,
sl 1F—37 sts.

Rows 3, 5, 7, 9, 11, 15: Dk: K1bf, K6; **Md:** K7,
M1, ◄—17 sts for all rows.

Rows 4, 6, 10, 12, 16: Md: K1tbl, P6, sP2po;
Dk: P6, sl 1F—15 sts for all rows.

Rows 7, 13: MC: K1bf, K13, M1, ◄—17 sts for
both rows.

Rows 8, 14: MC: K1tbl, K6, sK2po, K6, sl 1F—
15 sts for both rows.

Row 17: Dk: K1bf, K6; **Md:** K7, M1, K1; K8 sts from
left needle, turn work—25 sts.

Row 18: Md: K1tbl, P14, sP2po; **Dk:** P6, sl 1F—
23 sts.

Rows 19, 25, 31: MC: K1bf, K21, M1, ◄—25 sts
for all rows.

Rows 20, 26, 32: MC: K1tbl, K14, sK2po, K6,
sl 1F—23 sts for all rows.

Rows 21, 23, 27, 29: Dk: K1bf, K6; **Md:** K15, M1,
◄—25 sts for all rows.

Rows 22, 24, 28, 30: Md: K1tbl, P14, sP2po;
Dk: P6, sl 1F—23 sts for all rows. Cut Md/Dk after
row 30.

Finish row 32. With 23 sts on needle, beg mod N.

Module N: Partial V Module

All Sizes: left front armhole, right back armhole;
Small/Medium: right front neck; **Large:** upper right
sleeve

Row 1: With 23 sts on needle, **Lt:** K1bf, K20, P2tog—
23 sts.

Row 2 (WS): K1tbl, P12, sP2po, P6, sl 1F—21 sts.

Row 3: K1bf, K18, P2tog—21 sts.

Row 4: K1tbl, P10, sP2po, P6, sl 1F—19 sts.

Row 5: MC: K1bf, K16, P2tog—19 sts.

Row 6: K1tbl, K8, sK2po, K6, sl 1F—17 sts.

Rows 7, 9, 13: Lt: K1tbl, knit across, P2tog—16,
13, 7 sts.

Row 8: Lt: K1tbl, P5, sP2po, P6, sl 1F—14 sts.

Row 10: Lt: K1tbl, P2, sP2po, P6, sl 1F—11 sts.

Row 11: MC: K1tbl, K8, P2tog—10 sts.

Row 12: MC: sK2po, K6, sl 1F—8 sts. Cut MC.

Row 14: Lt: BO 7 sts.

Module O: Decapitated V

All Sizes: top of coat; **Large, X-Large:** top of sleeves

Row 1: From 31 sts on needle, Lt: K2tog tbl, knit
across, P2tog—29 sts.

Row 2 (WS): K1tbl, P12, sP2po, P12, sl 1F—27 sts.

Rows 3, 7, 9, 13: Lt: K2tog tbl, knit across, P2tog—
25, 17, 13, 5 sts.

Row 4: Lt: K1tbl, P10, sP2po, P10, sl 1F—23 sts.

Rows 5, 11: MC: K2tog tbl, knit across, P2tog—21,
9 sts.

Row 6: MC: K1tbl, K8, sK2po, K8, sl 1F—19 sts.

Row 8: Lt: K1tbl, P6, sP2po, P6, sl 1F—15 sts.

Row 10: Lt: K1tbl, P4, sP2po, P4, sl 1F—11 sts.

Row 12: MC: K1tbl, K2, sK2po, K2, sl 1F—7 sts. Cut MC.

Row 14: Lt: K1tbl, sP2po, sl 1F—3 sts.

Row 15: sK2po. Fasten off.

Module P: Underarm Fill-In (¼ V)

Small/Medium: right front armhole and left back armhole

Row 1: Lt: PU 9 sts.

Row 2 (WS): Lt: K2tog tbl, P6, M1, sl 1F—9 sts.

Rows 3, 7, 9, 13, 15: Lt: K1tbl, knit across, sl 1F—9, 7, 6, 4, 3 sts.

Rows 4, 8, 10, 14: Lt: K2tog tbl, purl across, sl 1F—8, 6, 5, 3 sts.

Rows 5, 11: MC: K1tbl, knit across, sl 1F—8, 5 sts.

Rows 6, 12: MC: K2tog tbl, knit across, sl 1F—7, 4 sts. Cut MC after row 12.

Row 16: Lt: sP2po. Fasten off.

Module Q: Underarm Fill-In (¼ V)

Small/Medium: left front armhole and right back armhole

Row 1: Lt: PU 9 sts.

Row 2 (WS): Lt: K1bf, P6, P2tog—9 sts.

Rows 3, 7, 9, 13, 15: Lt: K1tbl, knit across, sl 1F—9, 7, 6, 4, 3 sts.

Rows 4, 8, 10, 14: Lt: K1tbl, purl across, P2tog—8, 6, 5, 3 sts.

Rows 5, 11: MC: K1tbl, knit across, sl 1F—8, 5 sts.

Rows 6, 12: MC: K1tbl, knit across, P2tog—7, 4 sts. Cut MC after row 12.

Row 16: Lt: sP2po. Fasten off.

Module R: Partial Cube

Small/Medium: left top of sleeves

Row 1: MC: From 9 sts on holder, K1tbl, K7, sl 1F.

Row 2 (WS): K2tog tbl, K6, M1, sl 1F—9 sts.

Rows 3, 5: Dk: K1tbl, K7, sl 1F.

Rows 4, 6: Dk: K2tog tbl, P6, M1, sl 1F—9 sts for both rows.

Row 7: MC: K1tbl, K8, turn work, CO 8 sts—17 sts.

Row 8: MC: K1tbl, K6, sK2po, K6, sl 1F—15 sts.

Rows 9, 11: Dk: K1bf, K6; **Md:** K7, M1, sl 1F—17 sts for both rows.

Rows 10, 12: Md: K1tbl, P6, sP2po; **Dk:** P6, sl 1F—15 sts for both rows. Cut Md/Dk after row 12.

Row 13: MC: K1bf, K12, P2tog—15 sts.

Row 14: MC: K1tbl, K5, sK2po, K5, sl 1F—13 sts. Cut MC.

Rows 15, 17, 19: Lt: K2tog tbl, knit across, P2tog—11, 7, 3 sts.

Row 16: Lt: K1tbl, P3, sP2po, P3, sl 1F—9 sts.

Row 18: Lt: K1tbl, P1, sP2po, P1, sl 1F—5 sts.

Row 20: sP2po. Fasten off.

Module S: Decapitated Cube

Small/Medium: top of sleeves

Row 1: MC: PU 17 sts; or from sts on holder, K1tbl, K16; then PU 7 sts from cube base to left—24 sts.

Row 2 (WS): K1tbl, K4, K2tog, K7, sK2po, K6, sl 1F—21 sts.

Rows 3, 5, 9, 11: Dk: K1bf, K6; **Md:** K7, M1, ◄—17 sts for all rows.

Rows 4, 6, 10, 12: Md: K1tbl, P6, sP2po; **Dk:** P6, sl 1F—15 sts for all rows. Cut Md/Dk after row 12.

Row 7: MC: K1bf, K13, M1, ◀—17 sts.

Row 8: MC: K1tbl, K6, sK2po, K6, sl 1F—15 sts.

Row 13: MC: K1tbl, K13, ◀—15 sts.

Row 14: MC: K1tbl, K5, sK2po, K5, sl 1F—13 sts. Cut MC.

Rows 15, 17, 19: Lt: K2tog tbl, knit across, P2tog—11, 7, 3 sts.

Row 16: Lt: K1tbl, P3, sP2po, P3, sl 1F—9 sts.

Row 19: Lt: K1tbl, P1, sP2po, P1, sl 1F—5 sts.

Row 20: Lt: sP2po. Fasten off.

Module T: Partial Cube

Small/Medium: right top of sleeves

Row 1: MC: From 9 sts on holder, K1tbl, K8, PU 7 sts from mod S to left—16 sts.

Row 2 (WS): K1tbl, K4, K2tog, K7, P2tog—14 sts.

Rows 3, 5: Md: K1tbl, K6, M1, ◀—9 sts for both rows.

Row 4: Md: K1tbl, P6, P2tog—8 sts.

Row 6: Md: K1tbl, P8, turn work, CO 7 sts in Dk—16 sts.

Row 7: MC: K1tbl, K14, M1, ◀—17 sts.

Row 8: MC: K1tbl, K6, sK2po, K6, sl 1F—15 sts.

Rows 9, 11: Dk: K1bf, K6; **Md:** K7, M1, ◀—17 sts for both rows.

Rows 10, 12: Md: K1tbl, P6, sP2po; **Dk:** P6, sl 1F—15 sts for both rows. Cut Md/Dk after row 12.

Row 13: MC: K1tbl, K13, ◀—15 sts.

Row 14: MC: K1tbl, K5, sK2po, K5, sl 1F—13 sts. Cut MC.

Rows 15, 17, 19: Lt: K2tog tbl, knit across, P2tog—11, 7, 3 sts.

Row 16: K1tbl, P3, sP2po, P3, sl 1F—9 sts.

Row 18: K1tbl, P1, sP2po, P1, sl 1F—5 sts.

Row 20: sP2po. Fasten off.

Module W: ¾ Right Portion of Y

Large: for sleeve

Row 1: MC: PU 9 sts from top left of V below—9 sts.

Row 2 (WS): MC: K2tog tbl, K6, sl 1F—8 sts.

Rows 3, 5, 9, 11, 15: Dk: K1bf, K6, sl 1F—9 sts for all rows.

Rows 4, 6, 10, 12, 16: Dk: K2tog tbl, P6, sl 1F—8 sts for all rows.

Rows 7, 13: MC: K1bf, K6, sl 1F—9 sts for both rows.

Rows 8, 14: MC: K2tog tbl, K6, sl 1F—8 sts for both rows.

Row 17: Dk: CO 8 sts. K1tbl, K15, turn work; **Md:** CO 17 sts—33 sts.

Row 18: Md: K1tbl, P14, sP2po; **Dk:** P14, sl 1F—31 sts. AT SAME TIME, work MC back to edge.

Rows 19, 25, 31: MC: K1bf, K29, M1, sl 1F—33 sts for all rows.

Rows 20, 26, 32: MC: K1tbl, K14, sK2po, K14, sl 1F—31 sts for all rows.

Rows 21, 23, 27, 29: Dk: K1bf, K14; **Md:** K15, M1, sl 1F—33 sts for all rows.

Rows 22, 24, 28, 30: Md: K1tbl, P14, sP2po; **Dk:** P14, sl 1F—31 sts for all rows. Cut Dk after row 30.

Finish row 32. With 31 sts on needle, beg mod V.

Module X: ¾ Left Portion of Y

Large: for sleeve

Row 1: MC: PU 9 sts from top right of V below, PU 7 sts from right side of cube base to left, PU 8 sts from right side of cube lid, PU 8 sts from right side of Y to left—32 sts.

Row 2 (WS): K1tbl, K6, K2tog, K21, P2tog—30 sts.

Rows 3, 5, 9, 11: Md: K1tbl, K6, M1, ◄—9 sts for all rows.

Rows 4, 6, 10, 12, 16: Md: K1tbl, P6, P2tog—8 sts for all rows.

Rows 7, 13: MC: K1tbl, K6, M1, ◄—9 sts for both rows.

Rows 8, 14: MC: K1tbl, K6, P2tog—8 sts for both rows.

Row 15: Md: K1tbl, K6, M1, ◄—9 sts.

Row 17: Dk: CO 16 sts. K1tbl, K15; **Md:** K7, M1, K1; K8 off left needle—33 sts.

Row 18: Md: K1tbl, P14, sP2po; **Dk:** P14, sl 1F—31 sts. AT SAME TIME, knit MC back to edge.

Rows 19, 25, 31: MC: K1bf, K29, M1, ◄—33 sts for all rows.

Rows 20, 26, 32: MC: K1tbl, K14, sK2po, K14, sl 1F—31 sts for all rows.

Rows 21, 23, 27, 29: Dk: K1bf, K14; **Md:** K15, M1, ◄—33 sts for all rows.

Rows 22, 24, 28, 30: Md: K1tbl, P14, sP2po; **Dk:** P14, sl 1F—31 sts for all rows. Cut Md/Dk after row 30.

Finish row 32. With 31 sts on needle, beg mod V.

Finishing

- Sew shoulder seams tog. Sew sleeves into armholes. Sew sleeve seams tog if not knit tog.

- Place I-cord buttons and loops at locations designated on schematic (pages 114–16) and photo (pages 112 and 125).

- **Collar:** With size 5 circular needles, PU approx 8 (16, 16) sts across mod(s) J (and cube lid for X-Large) at front right neck; PU approx 20 sts to shoulder seam; PU approx 20 (20, 30) sts across neck back; another 20 sts from shoulder seam to mod H at left front neck and approx 8 (16, 16) sts across mod(s) H (and cube lid for X-Large). **Approx total:** 76 (92,102) sts. Work K1, P1 ribbing for 2" or height desired for collar.

- **Trim:** Finishing includes 2 rows of 4-st I-cord knitted onto front of coat. Knit and attach I-cord to garment as follows: Beg at lower-right front edge of coat, CO 4 sts using size 6 dpn. *With RS of garment facing you, PU 1 st from garment with left end of dpn that has the 4 sts on it. Without turning work, slide 5 sts to right-hand end of needle and pull yarn around back. Knit 3 sts; then knit last st tog with first st picked up from garment.* With left end of needle holding sts, PU 1 st from garment and rep from * to *, up right side of coat, around necklines, and down left side. BO I-cord at bottom left edge of coat. For second row of attached I-cord, rep above instructions, picking up 5th st from first col row of I-cord.

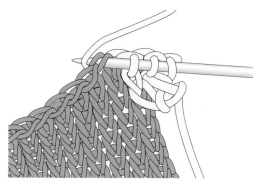

Attached I-Cord

- Frog buttons and buttonhole closures: These fun frogs are unattached I-cord that is knit and then sewn onto the coat.

- With size 6 dpn, CO 3 sts for frogs. *Without turning work, slide sts to other end of needle, pull yarn around back and knit sts.* Rep from * to * until reaching desired length of cord. Knit 3 separate 14" lengths of I-cord and BO. These will form the three 4-petal clover motifs to be sewn to right side of coat.

- Knit 3 separate 10" lengths of unattached I-cord and BO. These will form the three 3-petal clover motifs to be sewn to left side of coat.

- Referring to drawing below, shape clover petals and sew into place.

- CO 4 sts for buttons. Knit 3 separate 4" lengths of unattached I-cord and BO. Tie each of these lengths into a knot to form 3 buttons. Sew knotted buttons onto left side of coat at center of 3-petal clover motifs.

Unattached I-Cord

Four-Petal Clover

Three-Petal Clover
with Knot

Dazzling Design Options

With the No Limits, No Boundaries Knitting concept, the options never end. However, here are a few of my favorites that I suggest you try.

- Choose colors in daylight and place selections in a basket. When knitting under artificial light, without looking, reach into the basket, pick up any ball of yarn and start knitting with it. If the colors are complementary and beautiful in daylight, they will all look wonderful together.

- Knit an extra module or two. Sew it to the inside of the garment as a little secret pocket.

- Mix the stitch patterns and colors used in every module to make each unique.

- Start the first two to four rows of garter stitch with the same color for every module, perhaps black or dark purple. Using black with all remaining rows in bright colors gives the illusion of stained glass.

- Try using only three or four colors repeated in the same sequence and stitch pattern in every module for a more subdued effect. See the Ojo de Dios vests on page 35.

- Create new color combinations by holding two different colors of yarn together for a few rows.

- If you do not like an area of color, embroider over it, sew on beads or small buttons, or mark over the area with a colored permanent marker. Yes! I do it all the time with great results!

- Can't stand one of your modules? Start at the finishing-off row and begin unraveling that module. In doing so, you may encounter live stitches on adjacent modules. Use stitch holders or double-pointed needles to hold stitches until you bind them off. Knit a replacement module and sew it into the existing hole. No one will ever know.

- Shape your masterpiece by using smaller-size modules at the waistline or perhaps larger ones at the hips. It really works!

- If your swatch is larger than the size suggested in the pattern, just knit the next smaller-size garment and/or use smaller needles or finer-gauge yarn. Conversely, if your swatch is smaller, knit the next size larger and/or use larger needles or heavier yarn.

- Add a mitered or crocheted collar. How about some sleeves or external pockets?

- Embellish some modules with amulets, sequins, or charms, sewing them on after the garment has been completed.

- Don't limit yourself to only one style of button. I often use three to five different colors and/or styles of buttons on my garments. I also sew on each button with a different color of yarn or thread. Buttons are your garment's jewelry!

- Before crocheting the last row of your edging, think about what shirt you might be wearing with your garment and choose a contrasting color for the last row so that it stands out rather than blends in.

- When knitting for toddlers, it is quite easy to add length or width to a growing child's garment by simply adding more modules.

Tackling Blocking: Finishing in 15 Minutes

I am first and foremost a knitter. Anything that takes time away from knitting has a very low priority. So, the following are my fast, effective blocking techniques that will have you back knitting in less than 15 minutes.

NOTE: Many people never block their knitted treasures. However, I feel that it is imperative to lightly block mitered designs. Due to the distortion that this style of knitting creates on the surface of your garment, it is essential to allow the fibers to gently relax in their new environment. My methods of blocking maintain the wonderful surface textures while allowing your knitwear to drape naturally over the structure of your body. You will wear your vest or jacket rather than it wearing you!

Method A: Spray Blocking

This versatile technique provides immediate gratification with minimal effort.

Supplies

Finished garment
Tape measure
Pencil and paper
Spray bottle filled with cool water or wet towel
Dry towel

1. Lay finished garment on flat surface and measure width, length, armhole depth, and shoulder width. On paper, sketch a rudimentary outline of garment, including dimensions.

2. Next, lay the garment on a dry towel and spritz lightly with water or dab lightly with a wet towel. Referring to your sketch, stretch, tug, and persuade the garment to the desired measurements.

Method B: Steam Blocking

Thanks to my Rowenta Steam Generator, the following technique is the fastest and my favorite. Quite by accident, I discovered a way to relax the pesky seams of modular sleeves. These sculptural shapes often undulate rather than form straight lines. To circumvent this peculiarity, turn sleeves wrong side out. Lay seam line face up and steam heavily along the seam. Eventually, the rippling seam line will relax.

Supplies

Finished garment
Tape measure
Pencil and paper
Steam iron
Ironing board
Nonrusting straight pins

1. See Method A, step 1.

2. With garment on an ironing board, hold steam iron 2" to 3" above the surface of the garment until it is moist. Never, never, never touch a garment directly with an iron, not even through a towel. This flattens the life out of your dazzling, textural garment forever.

3. Allow the garment to dry on the ironing board. This technique is great for really cranky mitered areas. If a section refuses to behave, I give it a thorough steaming and then insert straight pins around that section to hold it in place until it dries.

Resources

My gratitude to the following companies, many of whom generously shared materials used to create the projects in this book. For a list of shops in your area that carry the yarns, buttons, and other supplies mentioned in the book, contact the following companies.

Common Thread Uncommon Fabrics
120A Bent St.
Taos, NM 87571
505-758-8987
retail buttons, fabrics, and more

Durango Button Company
11384 E. Cimmarron Dr.
Englewood, CO 80111
Orders: 800-834-2001
Fax: 303-779-7994
www.DurangoButton.com
durangobutton@yahoo.com
wholesale only

Fiesta Yarns
5401 San Diego NE
Albuquerque, NM 87113
www.fiestayarns.com
wholesale only

Great Adirondack Yarn
950 County Hwy 126
Amsterdam, NY 12010
518-843-3381
wholesale only

Knitting Fever, Inc.
www.knittingfever.com
wholesale only

MAYA, Patricia Werner
www.dazzlingknits.com
retail kits, workshops, yarn, and beaded necklaces

Muench Yarns, Inc.
285 Bel Marin Keys Blvd., Unit J
Novato, CA 94949
www.muenchyarns.com
wholesale only

Needle's Eye
839 Paseo de Peralta, Ste. O
Santa Fe, NM 87501
800-883-0706
www.needleseyesantafe.com
retail yarns

Patternworks
Route 25, PO Box 1618
Center Harbor, NH 03226-1618
800-438-5464
www.patternworks.com
retail yarns and knitting supplies

Rowenta, Inc.
196 Boston Ave.
Medford, MA 02155
www.rowentausa.com
wholesale only

Weaving Southwest
216-B Paseo del Pueblo Norte
Taos, NM 87571
800-765-1272
www.weavingsouthwest.com
retail yarns

NOTE: I use a large variety of yarns in my garments, Noro's Silk Garden and Cash Iroha, Great Adirondack's Chamois, and Muench's Horstia Mulbeerseide-Schurwolle in particular. You may know, however, how rapidly these and other stunning yarns are replaced or discontinued. Therefore, it is with great hesitancy that I offer you the color numbers used in my designs, since they may soon be discontinued. However, these same companies and many others are constantly offering new and wonderful colorways that can easily be substituted to knit these garments. So please don't be disappointed if the exact yarns are not currently available.

Laboratory Manual
to accompany

Seventh Edition

puntos
de partida

An Invitation to Spanish

María Sabló-Yates
Delta College

McGraw Hill

Boston   Burr Ridge, IL   Dubuque, IA   Madison, WI   New York
San Francisco   St. Louis   Bangkok   Bogotá   Caracas   Kuala Lumpur
Lisbon   London   Madrid   Mexico City   Milan   Montreal   New Delhi
Santiago   Seoul   Singapore   Sydney   Taipei   Toronto

Mc
Graw
Hill

This is an book.

Laboratory Manual to accompany
Puntos de partida: An Invitation to Spanish

Published by McGraw-Hill, an imprint of The McGraw-Hill Companies, Inc., 1221 Avenue of the Americas, New York, NY 10020. Copyright © 2005, 2001, 1997, 1993, 1989, 1985, 1981. The McGraw-Hill Companies, Inc. All rights reserved. No part of this publication may be reproduced or distributed in any form or by any means, or stored in a data base or retrieval system, without the prior written permission of The McGraw-Hill Companies, Inc., including, but not limited to, in any network or other electronic storage or transmission, or broadcast for distance learning.

1 2 3 4 5 6 7 8 9 0 QPD QPD 0 9 8 7 6 5 4

ISBN 0-07-295128-1

Editor-in-chief: *Thalia Dorwick*
Publisher: *William R. Glass*
Sponsoring editor: *Christa Harris*
Director of development: *Scott Tinetti*
Development editor: *Pennie Nichols-Alem*
Executive marketing manager: *Nick Agnew*
Production supervisor: *Randy Hurst*
Project manager: *Mel Valentín*
Editorial assistant: *Daniela Reissmann*
Compositor: *The GTS Companies/York, PA Campus*
Typeface: *Palatino*
Printer: *Quebecor Printing Dubuque, Inc.*
Illustrators: *Wayne Clark, David Bohn, Axelle Fortier, Lori Heckelman, Judith Macdonald, Stephanie O'Shaughnessy, Barbara Reinerison, Katherine Tillotson, Stan Tusan, and Joe Veno.*

http://www.mhhe.com

Contents

To the Student

The purpose of the audio program that accompanies *Puntos de partida* is to give you as much practice as possible in listening to, speaking, reading, and writing, and, above all, understanding the Spanish language in a variety of contexts. This edition of the Laboratory Manual contains a variety of exercises to help you accomplish that goal. To get the most out of the audio program, you should listen to the CDs after your instructor covers the corresponding material in class, and you should listen as often as possible. You will need the Laboratory Manual much of the time when you listen to the CDs, since many of the exercises are based on visuals, realia (real things—such as advertisements, classified ads, and so on—that you would encounter in a Spanish-speaking country), and written cues.

The audio program follows the format of chapters in the main text. Each chapter begins with a section (**Vocabulario: Preparación**) in which you can practice vocabulary in a variety of contexts. This preliminary vocabulary study is followed by pronunciation exercises (**Pronunciación y ortografía**). Each chapter includes exercises to practice the grammatical concepts of the chapters (**Gramática**), and functional dialogue (**Videoteca: Minidramas**). In addition, there is a section that combines grammar points and vocabulary introduced in the chapter (**Un poco de todo: Para entregar**). This section is to be handed in to your instructor for correction; no answers are provided on the CD, or in the answers Appendix at the back of the Manual. In addition, some exercises give you the option of answering in writing. Since writing the answers to these exercises is an option only, you should ask your instructor how she or he would prefer these to be handled. Finally, each chapter concludes with a brief quiz, **Prueba corta.** Each quiz allows you to check your mastery of the vocabulary and grammatical structures learned in that specific chapter.

The exercises in most sections progress from controlled to more open-ended and personalized or interactive, to give you a chance to be more creative in Spanish while practicing the skills you have learned. With the exception of the **Para entregar** portions of the Laboratory Manual, the **Dictados,** and other writing-based exercises, you will hear the answers to most exercises on the CD immediately after the item or at the end of a series of items. You will find the answers to most written exercises (except those called **Para entregar**) in the answers Appendix.

Although the audio program includes some material taken directly from *Puntos de partida,* it also contains many new exercises: surveys (**Encuestas**); dictations; personalized questions and interviews; visually based listening comprehension exercises; cultural listening passages, some based on survey questions answered by native speakers; exercises based on realia; and brief interactive dialogues. Whenever possible, the exercises are presented in a context.

The following types of exercises are a regular feature of the *Puntos de partida* audio program and are found in most chapters.

- **Definiciones, Situaciones,** and **Asociaciones** use a multiple choice or matching format in order to test listening comprehension and vocabulary.
- **Identificaciones** and **Descripción,** as their names imply, will ask you to generate responses based on visuals, with or without written or oral cues. Although these are more controlled in nature, they are contextualized and related to the theme of the current or a previous chapter. You will find these types of exercises throughout the Laboratory Manual.
- **Encuestas** are personalized surveys in which you need only check an answer that is true for you. These surveys are offered for listening comprehension and are related to the theme of the chapter or to specific grammar points. You will find these at the beginning of both the vocabulary and the grammar sections.
- **Los hispanos hablan** is found after **Vocabulario: Preparación,** and presents comments from native speakers on a variety of topics: clothing, pastimes, favorite foods, and so on. Each section of **Los hispanos hablan** is tied to the theme and/or the vocabulary of the chapter in which it is found. The passages offer listening comprehension that is based on cultural information. The follow-up activities include taking notes, evaluating true or false statements, making comparisons, completing charts, and answering questions.

- The **Minidiálogos** offer examples of real-life situations and often convey cultural information. Most of them are the same ones that appear in *Puntos de partida*. The follow-up exercises include cloze dictations, true or false statements, summarizing statements, identifying the person who made a statement, inferring information from the dialogue, and writing information about the dialogue (in **¿Qué recuerdas?**). The minidialogues appear at the beginning of many grammar sections.

- There are two types of question and answer sequences. The first will offer you an oral or written cue, and you will hear the correct answer on the CD after each item. **Entrevista** activities, in contrast, offer no cues or answers. The questions are more open-ended and personalized, and you will be able to stop the CD to write your answers. The **Entrevista** is a regular feature of the **Un poco de todo** section that is for handing in to your instructor.

- The **Videoteca: Minidramas** dialogues are taken from the Video on CD to accompany *Puntos de partida,* which is available to adopters and their students. Like the minidialogues, they offer examples of real-life conversations and situations, as well as some cultural information. After they are read, you will usually have the opportunity to participate in a similar conversation, interactive in nature, in which you use the cues that are provided. In some instances, you may have the option of writing your answers. You will always hear a correct answer on the CD. In earlier chapters, you will have the opportunity to repeat portions of the dialogue.

- Listening passages appear in the **Un poco de todo** section. These passages are cultural in nature and contain information on a variety of topics related to the Hispanic world. Their themes are related to the theme of each chapter. The passages are usually preceded by a section called **Antes de escuchar** in which you will practice listening strategies: guessing content, gisting, making inferences about the passage, and so on. Following each passage is a **Después de escuchar** section that offers a variety of comprehension or follow-up exercises.

- The Laboratory Manual also includes many types of dictations (**Dictados**) and other writing activities. You will be asked to listen for and write down specific information: letters, words, phrases, or entire sentences. In some instances, you will be asked to jot down notes about the content of brief passages. Answers are generally provided in the Appendix.

Sound effects are used throughout the audio program, when appropriate. You will hear a variety of native speakers, so that you can get used to different accents and voice types found in the Spanish-speaking world, but no accent will be so pronounced as to be difficult for you to understand. In approximately the first third of the audio program, the speakers will speak at a slower rate. The rate of speech will increase gradually until it reaches natural or close to natural speed in the final third of the audio program.

Learning another language requires hard work and patience, as well as an open mind. We hope that the variety of exercises and the cultural information in the Laboratory Manual will provide a natural and stimulating context within which you will begin to communicate in Spanish!

We offer our sincere thanks to the following individuals: to Ana María Pérez-Gironés (Wesleyan University), who wrote the listening passages in **Un poco de todo**; to Manuela González-Bueno, who made many helpful suggestions for improving the **Pronunciación y ortografía** sections; to the Hispanic exchange students whose answers were the bases of the passages in the **Los hispanos hablan;** to William R. Glass, who provided welcome suggestions and advice; to Thalia Dorwick, Christa Harris, Scott Tinetti, and Pennie Nichols-Alem, whose comments, suggestions, and superior editing made this Laboratory Manual and audio program possible; and to my family for their support and understanding throughout the writing process.

María Sabló-Yates

PRIMERA PARTE

■■■Saludos y expresiones de cortesía

A. Diálogos

Paso 1. In the following dialogues, you will practice greeting others appropriately in Spanish. The dialogues will be read with pauses for repetition. After each dialogue, you will hear two summarizing statements. Circle the letter of the statement that best describes each dialogue. First, listen.

1. MANOLO: ¡Hola, Maricarmen!
   MARICARMEN: ¿Qué tal, Manolo? ¿Cómo estás?
   MANOLO: Muy bien. ¿Y tú?
   MARICARMEN: Regular. Nos vemos, ¿eh?
   MANOLO: Hasta mañana.

Comprensión: a. b.

2. ELISA VELASCO: Buenas tardes, señor Gómez.
   MARTÍN GÓMEZ: Muy buenas, señora Velasco. ¿Cómo está?
   ELISA VELASCO: Bien, gracias. ¿Y usted?
   MARTÍN GÓMEZ: Muy bien, gracias. Hasta luego.
   ELISA VELASCO: Adiós.

Comprensión: a. b.

3. LUPE: Buenos días, profesor.
   PROFESOR: Buenos días. ¿Cómo te llamas?
   LUPE: Me llamo Lupe Carrasco.
   PROFESOR: Mucho gusto, Lupe.
   LUPE: Igualmente.

Comprensión: a. b.

4. MIGUEL: Hola, me llamo Miguel René. ¿Y tú? ¿Cómo te llamas?
   KARINA: Me llamo Karina. Mucho gusto.
   MIGUEL: Mucho gusto, Karina. Y, ¿de dónde eres?
   KARINA: Yo soy de Venezuela. ¿Y tú?
   MIGUEL: Yo soy de México.

Comprensión: a. b.

Paso 2. Now you will participate in a conversation, partially printed in your Manual, in which you play the role of Karina. Complete the conversation using the written cues. When you hear the corresponding number, say Karina's line. Then you will hear Miguel's response. Continue until you complete the conversation. (If you wish, pause and write the answers.) Here are the cues for your conversation.

buenas tardes   cómo te llamas   de dónde eres

me llamo   mucho gusto   yo soy

Now, begin the conversation.

KARINA: 1. _____.

MIGUEL: Muy buenas.

KARINA: 2. _____ Karina. 3. ¿_____?

MIGUEL: Me llamo Miguel.

KARINA: 4. _____, Miguel. 5. ¿_____?

MIGUEL: Soy de Puerto Rico. ¿Y tú?

KARINA: 6. _____ de Puerto Rico también.

B. ¿Formal o informal? You will hear a series of expressions. Indicate whether each expression would be used in a formal or in an informal situation.

1. a. formal   b. informal
2. a. formal   b. informal
3. a. formal   b. informal
4. a. formal   b. informal
5. a. formal   b. informal

C. Situaciones

Paso 1. You will hear a series of questions or statements. Each will be said twice. Circle the letter of the best response or reaction to each.

1. a. Me llamo Ricardo Barrios.   b. Bien, gracias.
2. a. Encantada, Eduardo.   b. Muchas gracias, Eduardo.
3. a. Regular. ¿Y tú?   b. Mucho gusto, señorita Paz.
4. a. Con permiso, señor.   b. No hay de qué.
5. a. De nada, señora Colón.   b. Buenas noches, señora Colón.
6. a. Soy de Guatemala.   b. ¿Y tú?

Paso 2. Now, listen to the questions and statements again and read the correct answers in the pauses provided. You will hear each item only once. Be sure to repeat the correct answer after you hear it.

1. ... 2. ... 3. ... 4. ... 5. ... 6. ...

D. ¿Qué dicen estas personas? (*What are these people saying?*) Circle the letter of the drawing that is best described by the sentences you hear. Each will be said twice.

1. a.

b.

2. a.

b.

3. a.

b.

4. a.

b.

■■■¿Cómo es usted?

A. Dictado:* ¿Cómo son? (*What are they like?*) You will hear five sentences. Each will be said twice. Listen carefully and write the missing words.

1. El hotel es _____. 4. El museo es muy _____

2. El estudiante es muy _____. 5. Íñigo no es _____

3. El _____ no es difícil (*difficult*).

B. Descripción. In this exercise, you will practice gisting, that is, getting the main idea—an important skill in language learning. Although some of the vocabulary you hear will not be familiar to you, concentrate on the words that you *do* know. After the exercise, pause and choose the statement that best describes the passage.

1. ☐ This person is describing her country and the sports that are played there.
2. ☐ This person is describing herself, her studies, and her outside interests.

Now resume listening.

C. Encuesta (*Survey*). You will hear a series of questions. For each question, check the appropriate answer. No answers will be given. The answers you choose should be correct for you!

1. ☐ Sí, soy independiente. 3. ☐ Sí, soy eficiente.
   ☐ No, no soy independiente.   ☐ No, no soy eficiente.
2. ☐ Sí, soy sentimental. 4. ☐ Sí, soy flexible.
   ☐ No, no soy sentimental.   ☐ No, no soy flexible.

D. Preguntas (*Questions*). Ask the following persons about their personalities, using **¿Eres... ?** or **¿Es usted... ?** as appropriate, and the cues you will hear. Follow the model. (Remember to repeat the correct question. If you prefer, pause and write the questions.) You will hear answers to your questions.

MODELO: (*you see*) Marcos (*you hear*) tímido →
(*you say*) Marcos ¿eres tímido? (*you hear*) Sí, soy tímido.

1. Ramón, ¿ _____?

2. Señora Alba, ¿ _____?

3. Señor Castán, ¿ _____?

4. Anita, ¿ _____?

---

*Answers to all **Dictado** exercises are given in the Appendix.

■■■Pronunciación y ortografía • El alfabeto español

A. El alfabeto español. You will hear the names of the letters of the Spanish alphabet, along with a list of place names. Listen and repeat, imitating the speaker. Notice that most Spanish consonants are pronounced differently than in English. In future chapters, you will have the opportunity to practice the pronunciation of most of these letters individually.

a	a	la Argentina	ñ	eñe	España
b	be	Bolivia	o	o	Oviedo
c	ce	Cáceres	p	pe	Panamá
d	de	Durango	q	cu	Quito
e	e	el Ecuador	r	ere	el Perú
f	efe	Florida	rr	erre	Monterrey
g	ge	Guatemala	s	ese	San Juan
h	hache	Honduras	t	te	Toledo
i	i	Ibiza	u	u	el Uruguay
j	jota	Jalisco	v	ve	Venezuela
k	ca	(*Kansas*)	w	doble ve	(*Washington*)
l	ele	Lima	x	equis	Extremadura
m	eme	México	y	i griega	el Paraguay
n	ene	Nicaragua	z	zeta	Zaragoza

B. Repeticiones. Repeat the following words, phrases, and sentences. Imitate the speaker and pay close attention to the difference in pronunciation between Spanish and English.

1.	c/ch	Colón	Cecilia	Muchas gracias.	Buenas noches.
2.	g/gu	Ortega	gusto	Miguel	guitarra
3.	h	La Habana	Héctor	hotel	historia
4.	j/g	Jamaica	Jiménez	Geraldo	Gilda
5.	l/ll	Lupe	Manolo	Sevilla	me llamo
6.	y	Yolanda	yate	Paraguay	y
7.	r/rr	Mario	arte	Roberto	carro
8.	ñ	Begoña	Toño	señorita	Hasta mañana.

C. Más repeticiones. Repeat the following Spanish syllables, imitating the speaker. Try to pronounce each vowel with a short, tense sound.

1.	ma	fa	la	ta	pa
2.	me	fe	le	te	pe
3.	mi	fi	li	ti	pi
4.	mo	fo	lo	to	po
5.	mu	fu	lu	tu	pu
6.	sa	se	si	so	su

D. Las vocales. Compare the pronunciation of the following words in both English and Spanish. Listen for the schwa, the *uh* sound in English, and notice its absence in Spanish.

English: *banana*   Spanish: **banana**

capital   **capital**

Now, repeat the following words, imitating the speaker. Be careful to avoid the English schwa. Remember to pronounce each vowel with a short and tense sound.

1. hasta	tal	nada	mañana	natural
2. me	qué	Pérez	usted	rebelde
3. sí	señorita	permiso	imposible	tímido
4. yo	con	cómo	noches	profesor
5. tú	uno	mucho	Perú	Lupe

E. ¿Español o inglés? You will hear a series of words. Each will be said twice. Circle the letter of the word you hear, either a Spanish word (**español**) or an English word (**inglés**). Note that Spanish vowels are short and tense; they are never drawn out with a *u* or *i* glide as in English.

ESPAÑOL   INGLÉS

1. a. mi   b. me
2. a. fe   b. Fay
3. a. es   b. ace
4. a. con   b. cone
5. a. ti   b. tea
6. a. lo   b. low

F. Dictado

Paso 1. You will hear a series of words that are probably unfamiliar to you. Each will be said twice. Listen carefully, concentrating on the vowel sounds, and write in the missing vowels.

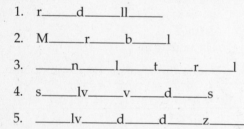

1. r____d____ll____

2. M____r____b____l

3. ____n____l____t____r____l

4. s____lv____v____d____s

5. ____lv____d____d____z____

Paso 2. Imagine that you work as a hotel receptionist in Miami. Listen to how some Hispanic guests spell out their last names for you. Write down the names as you hear them.

1. _____

2. _____

3. _____

4. _____

SEGUNDA PARTE

■■■Los números 0–30; hay

A. ¿Cuánto es? (*How much does it cost?*) You will hear the price of three different brands of items you want to purchase in pesos (the unit of currency in many Hispanic countries). Repeat the price of the *least* expensive brand. In this exercise, you will practice listening for specific information. (Remember to repeat the correct answer.)

1. ...   2. ...   3. ...   4. ...

B. ¿Cuántos hay? (*How many are there?*) Read the following phrases when you hear the corresponding numbers. (Remember to repeat the correct answer.)

1. 21 personas (*f.*)
2. 18 profesores
3. 1 señora (*f.*)
4. 21 días (*m.*)
5. 30 cafés

C. ¿Qué hay en la sala de clase? (*What is there in the classroom?*) You will hear a series of questions. Each will be said twice. Answer based on the following drawing. (Remember to repeat the correct answer.)

1. ...   2. ...   3. ...   4. ...

■■■Gustos y preferencias

A. ¿Qué te gusta? (*What do you like?*)

Paso 1. You will hear a series of questions. For each question, check the appropriate answer. No answers will be given.

The answers you choose should be correct for you.

1. ☐ ¡Sí, me gusta!   ☐ ¡No, no me gusta!
2. ☐ ¡Sí, creo que (*I think*) es fantástico!   ☐ ¡No, no me gusta!
3. ☐ Sí, me gusta.   ☐ No, no me gusta.
4. ☐ Sí, me gusta.   ☐ No, no me gusta.

Paso 2. Interview Professor Morales about his likes and dislikes using the oral cues. Remember to use **¿Le gusta... ?** and to repeat the correct question. You will hear his answer.

MODELO: (*you hear*) la universidad →
(*you say*) ¿Le gusta la universidad?   (*you hear*) Sí, me gusta mucho.

1. ...   2. ...   3. ...   4. ...

B. Gustos y preferencias. You will hear a series of questions. Each will be said twice. You should be able to guess the meaning of the verbs based on context. Answer based on your own experience. You will hear a possible answer. (Remember to repeat the answer.)

MODELO: (*you see*) jugar
(*you hear*) ¿Te gusta jugar al tenis? →
(*you say*) Sí, me gusta jugar al tenis. OR No, no me gusta jugar al tenis.

1. jugar   2. estudiar   3. tocar   4. comer

■■■Los hispanos hablan: ¿Qué tipo de música te gusta más?

In this section of the Laboratory Manual, you will hear authentic passages from Hispanics about a variety of subjects, including their school experiences, food preferences, hobbies, and so on. As you listen, try not to be distracted by unfamiliar vocabulary. Concentrate instead on what you *do* know and understand.*

In addition to the types of music that most young people listen to here in the United States (soft rock, heavy metal, and so on), Hispanic students also listen to music that is typical of their own country or region. Have you heard of **la salsa, el merengue,** or **el tango?** These are all types of music from different regions of Spanish America. Note that the word **conjunto** means *musical group*.

You will hear a passage in which a student tells about her likes and dislikes in music. First, listen to get a general idea of the content. Then, go back and listen again for specific information. Then you will hear a series of statements. Circle **C** (**cierto**) if the statement is true or **F** (**falso**) if it is false.

Habla Teresa: Me gusta más el *rock* en inglés y en español. Mis cantantes favoritos son Sting y Whitney Houston. Mis conjuntos favoritos son Metálica y Hombres G, un conjunto que canta en español. Me gusta la música instrumental y me encanta la música latina por su ritmo y su sabor... y porque es nuestra. Me gustan la salsa y el merengue. Me gusta la música en inglés y español. ¡Amo toda la música!

1. C F   2. C F   3. C F

---

*The listening text for the **Los hispanos hablan** sections will appear in the Laboratory Manual through **Capítulo 2**.

■■■¿Qué hora es?

A. ¿Qué hora es?

Paso 1. You will hear a series of times. Each will be said twice. Circle the letter of the clock face that indicates the time you hear.

   MODELO: (*you hear*) Son las diez de la mañana. → (*you circle the letter a*)

a.

b.

1. a.

   b.

2. a.

   b.

3. a.

   b.

4. a.

   b.

Paso 2. Now when you hear a number, tell the time that you see on the corresponding clock. Repeat the correct answer.

MODELO: (*you see*) 1.

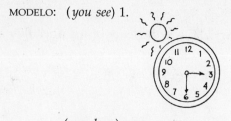

(*you hear*) uno
(*you say*) Son las tres y media de la tarde.

B. **¿A qué hora es... ?** You will hear a series of questions about Marisol's schedule. Answer based on her schedule. (Remember to repeat the correct answer.) First, pause and look at the schedule.

MODELO: (*you hear*) ¿A qué hora es la clase de español? →
(*you say*) Es a las ocho y media de la mañana.

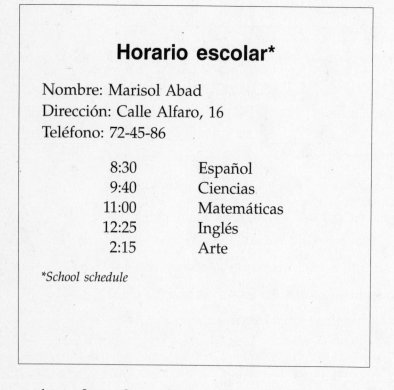

Horario escolar*

Nombre: Marisol Abad
Dirección: Calle Alfaro, 16
Teléfono: 72-45-86

8:30	Español
9:40	Ciencias
11:00	Matemáticas
12:25	Inglés
2:15	Arte

*School schedule

1. ... 2. ... 3. ... 4. ...

UN POCO DE TODO | (Para entregar)*

A. En el periódico (*newspaper*). You will hear a series of headlines from a Spanish newspaper. Each will be said twice. Write the number of the headline next to the section of the newspaper in which it most likely appears. Try not to be distracted by unfamiliar vocabulary; concentrate instead on the key words in the headline. First, listen to the list of sections.

_____ Política

_____ Libros (*Books*)

_____ Espectáculos (*Entertainment*)

_____ Deportes (*Sports*)

_____ Economía

B. *Listening Passage:* **¿Qué idiomas se hablan en Latinoamérica?†**

> The first listening passage, as well as the passages in other chapters of the Laboratory Manual, will be preceded by prelistening exercises (**Antes de escuchar**). They will involve strategies such as predicting and guessing content before you listen, reading the true/false statements before listening, and so on. You should always do the prelistening section *before* you listen to the passage. Don't be distracted by unfamiliar vocabulary. Focus on what you *do* know. In most cases, you will be asked to listen for specific information.

Antes de escuchar (*Before listening*). Before you listen to the passage, pause and do the following prelistening exercises.

Paso 1. Read the true/false statements. As you read them, try to infer the information you will hear in the passage, as well as listen for specific information.

1. Julia es de México.
2. Tegucigalpa es la capital de Honduras.
3. Julia habla guaraní.
4. No se habla portugués en Latinoamérica.
5. Las palabras (*words*) **español** y **castellano** son sinónimas.
6. El español es la única (*only*) lengua que se habla en Latinoamérica.

Paso 2. What can you infer from the true/false statements? Check all that apply.

☐ Julia will probably tell us where she is from and what language she speaks.

☐ There may be more than one word to describe the Spanish language.

☐ It is possible that more than one language is spoken throughout Latin America.

Now resume listening.

---

*No answers are given for **Para entregar** activities.
†The text for the Listening Passages will appear in the Laboratory Manual through **Capítulo 2.**

Listening Passage. Now, you will hear a passage about the Spanish language and where it is spoken. First, listen to get a general idea of the content. Then, go back and listen again for specific information.

¡Hola! Me llamo Julia y soy de Tegucigalpa. ¡Sí! Tegucigalpa. ¿Es un nombre difícil? Tegucigalpa es la capital de Honduras. Honduras está en Centroamérica. En mi país se habla el castellano o español. **Español** y **castellano** son palabras sinónimas para hablar del mismo idioma. El castellano también se habla en España y en toda Latinoamérica. Bueno, no en toda Latinoamérica, porque en el Brasil se habla portugués y en Belice se habla inglés. Además del castellano, en el mundo hispánico se hablan otros idiomas también. Por ejemplo, en el Paraguay hay dos lenguas oficiales, el español y el guaraní. El guaraní es una lengua indígena original de la región. Mi amiga Susana es paraguaya y habla español y guaraní.

El español es una lengua muy importante en el mundo, porque lo hablan muchas personas. ¿Se habla español en tu estado?

Now pause and do the exercises in **Después de escuchar.**

Después de escuchar (*After listening*)

Paso 1. Here are the true/false statements. Circle **C** (**cierto**) if the statement is true or **F** (**falso**) if it is false. Then, correct the statements that are false, according to the passage.

1. C F Julia es de México.

   _____

2. C F Tegucigalpa es la capital de Honduras.

   _____

3. C F Julia habla guaraní.

   _____

4. C F No se habla portugués en Latinoamérica.

   _____

5. C F Las palabras (*words*) **español** y **castellano** son sinónimas.

   _____

6. C F El español es la única (*only*) lengua que se habla en Latinoamérica.

   _____

Paso 2. Go back and listen to the passage again. Then, pause and complete the following sentences with words chosen from the list.

castellano   lengua
español   paraguaya
inglés

1. La palabra **idioma** es sinónimo de _____.

2. Julia es de Honduras: es **hondureña.** Susana es de Paraguay: es _____.

3. Susana habla guaraní y _____ (o _____).

4. En Belice se habla _____.

Now resume listening.

C. Dictado. You will hear a radio announcement that tells the times of this afternoon's programs. Listen carefully and, while listening, write the time of each program next to the name of the program. After you listen to the radio announcement, pause and write the type of program you think each is in English. First, listen to the names of the programs.

HORA	PROGRAMA	TIPO DE PROGRAMA
_____	Radionovela	_____
_____	Informe meteorológico	_____
_____	Visita con el veterinario	_____
_____	Tarde musical	_____
_____	Radionoticias	_____
_____	Programa del Dr. Rodríguez	_____

Now resume listening.

D. Y para terminar... Entrevista. You will hear a series of questions. Each will be said twice. Answer based on your own experience. Pause and write the answers.

1. _____

2. _____

3. _____

4. _____

5. _____

6. _____

7. _____

VIDEOTECA Minidramas*

Paso 1. Saludos y expresiones de cortesía. In the following conversation, Diego González introduces himself to Professor Salazar. Diego's lines will be read with pauses for repetition. But first, listen.

DIEGO: Perdón. ¿Es usted el profesor Salazar?
PROFESOR: Sí, yo soy.
DIEGO: Buenas tardes. Me llamo Diego González. Soy el estudiante de la Universidad de California.
PROFESOR: Ah, sí. El estudiante de Los Ángeles. Mucho gusto.
DIEGO: Igualmente.
PROFESOR: ¡Bienvenido a México! Él es Antonio Sifuentes. Es estudiante posgraduado en la facultad.
ANTONIO: ¿Qué tal, Diego?
DIEGO: Muy bien, gracias. ¿Y tú?
ANTONIO: Muy bien. Mucho gusto.
DIEGO: Igualmente, Antonio.

Paso 2. Aplicación. Now you will participate in a similar conversation, partially printed in your manual, in which you will play the role of Mariana, an exchange student in Mexico. Complete the conversation using the written cues. (Remember to repeat the correct answer. If you wish, pause and write the answers.) Here are the cues for your conversation.

> mucho gusto, Gabriel   muchas gracias   es fantástica

PABLO: Mariana, te presento a (*I'd like to introduce you to*) Gabriel Herrera, un estudiante posgraduado de la facultad.

MARIANA: _____

GABRIEL: El gusto es mío (*mine*). Bienvenida a México, Mariana.

MARIANA: _____

GABRIEL: ¿Qué tal te gusta la universidad?

MARIANA: Pues, ¡creo que (*I think that*) _____!

PRUEBA CORTA

Hablando (*Speaking*) de las clases. You will overhear a conversation between Geraldo and Delia. Listen carefully. Try not to be distracted by unfamiliar vocabulary; concentrate instead on what you do know. Then, you will hear a series of statements. Circle **C** if the statement is true (**cierto**) and **F** if it is false (**falso**).

1. C F   2. C F   3. C F   4. C F   5. C F

---

*This **Minidramas** videoclip is available on the Video on CD to accompany *Puntos de partida* Seventh Edition.

C. Y para terminar... Entrevista. You will hear a series of questions. Each will be said twice. Answer, based on your own experience. Pause and write the answers.

1. _____

2. _____

3. _____

4. _____

5. _____

6. _____

7. _____

8. _____

VIDEOTECA   Minidramas*

Paso 1. La rutina diaria. In this conversation, Diego and Antonio talk about their daily routine. Diego's lines will be read with pauses for repetition. But first, listen.

DIEGO: Dime, Antonio, ¿cómo es el horario de Uds.?

ANTONIO: Normalmente, yo me levanto a las siete y Juan se levanta a las seis y media. ¿A qué horas te levantas tú?

DIEGO: Si tengo clases, me levanto a las siete y media.

ANTONIO: ¡Perfecto! Primero Juan se baña y se afeita, después yo y por último tú.

DIEGO: ¿Y vuelven Uds. a casa para almorzar?

ANTONIO: Bueno, los lunes, miércoles y viernes sí vuelvo a casa para almorzar, porque no tengo clases por la tarde. Pero los martes y jueves almuerzo en la cafetería de la universidad. Juan no vuelve a casa para almorzar. Come en casa de su novia.

DIEGO: Muy bien. Entonces, los lunes, miércoles y viernes podemos almorzar aquí tú y yo. Antonio, creo que sí me va a gustar mucho vivir aquí.

Paso 2. Aplicación. Now you will participate in a similar conversation, partially printed in your manual, in which you play the role of Alfonso. Complete the conversation using the written cues. If you wish, pause and write the correct answers. Here are the cues for your conversation.

      gracias   quién prepara la comida   el viernes por la tarde   especial

MARCOS: Bienvenido a nuestro apartamento, Alfonso.

ALFONSO: _____[1], Marcos.

MARCOS: ¿Tienes alguna pregunta acerca del (*about the*) horario?

ALFONSO: Pues, sí. ¿_____[2] esta noche?

MARCOS: Bueno, Lucas prepara la comida esta noche, yo cocino (*cook*) el jueves y tú vas a cocinar el viernes.

ALFONSO: Perfecto. No tengo clases _____[3] y puedo preparar una

cena (*dinner*) _____[4].

MARCOS: ¡Eso es magnífico!

---

*This **Minidramas** videoclip is available on the Video on CD to accompany *Puntos de partida* Seventh Edition.

PRUEBA CORTA

A. Asociaciones. You will hear a series of statements. Circle the location with which you associate each statement.

1. a. la lámpara   b. el comedor   c. la cocina
2. a. la sala   b. el baño   c. la alcoba
3. a. el sofá   b. el armario   c. el lavabo
4. a. la piscina   b. el almacén   c. el garaje
5. a. la cocina   b. el comedor   c. la sala
6. a. la mesita   b. el plato   c. el sillón
7. a. la cómoda   b. el estante   c. el jardín

B. La rutina diaria. Practice talking about your daily routine, using the written cues. When you hear the corresponding number, form sentences using the words provided in the order given, making any necessary changes or additions.

MODELO: (*you see*) 1. (yo) despertarse y levantarse / 7:00 A.M. (*you hear*) uno →
(*you say*) Me despierto y me levanto a las siete de la mañana.

2. (yo) ducharse / vestirse / y/ peinarse
3. hacer / el desayuno / y / sentarse a comer
4. hacer / la cama / y / salir / de casa / 8:00
5. después de las clases / ir / al gimnasio
6. hacer ejercicio / hasta / 3:30
7. volver a casa / y / poner el televisor
8. empezar / a preparar / comida
9. por fin / acostarse / 11:00 P.M. / y / dormirse

C. Apuntes. You will hear a brief paragraph that tells about a house for sale. Listen carefully and, while listening, write in the information requested. Write all numbers as numerals. First, listen to the new vocabulary and the requested information.

mide	*measures*
el metro	*meter*
por	*by (as in 3 meters by 2 meters)*
el vecindario	*neighborhood*

El número de alcobas: _____

El número de baños: _____

¿Cuántos metros mide la sala? _____

Esta casa está cerca de _____ y enfrente de _____ .

La dirección (*address*) de la casa: _____

UN POCO DE TODO | (Para entregar)

A. En la plaza Santa Ana

Paso 1. ¿Qué pasa? You will hear a series of statements about the following drawing. Each will be said twice. Circle **C** if the statement is true or **F** if it is false. First, pause and look at the drawing.

1. C F   2. C F   3. C F   4. C F   5. C F

Paso 2. Descripción. Now pause and write five sentences that describe the drawing. You can talk about the weather, what the people are doing, how they seem to be feeling, their clothing, and so on. You can also make comparisons.

1. _____
2. _____
3. _____
4. _____
5. _____

Now resume listening.

B. *Listening Passage:* Hablando del clima

Antes de escuchar. Before you listen to the passage, pause and do the following prelistening exercises.

Paso 1. Read the following true/false statements. As you read them, try to infer the information the passage will give you, as well as the specific information for which you need to listen.

1. En las regiones tropicales, por lo general, hay una estación seca (*dry*) y una lluviosa (*rainy*).
2. En Latinoamérica, no hace frío en ninguna (*any*) región.
3. Hay climas muy variados en el mundo hispánico.
4. En Sudamérica, las estaciones del año son opuestas a las (*opposite to those*) de los países del Hemisferio Norte.

Paso 2. You probably do know quite a bit about the climate in most of Latin America. That information will be fairly easy for you to recognize in the listening passage. Read the next set of true/false statements, and try to infer what type of information you need to listen for regarding the person who will narrate the passage.

La persona que habla...

1. es de Vermont.
2. prefiere el frío del invierno.
3. no sabe (*doesn't know how to*) esquiar.
4. quiere vivir en los Andes.

A la persona que habla...

5. no le gustan las estaciones lluviosas en los países tropicales.

Now resume listening.

Listening Passage. Now, you will hear a passage about the climate in different regions of the Hispanic world. This passage is read by Nicanor, a friend of Susana's. The following words appear in the passage.

seca	*dry*
lluviosa	*rainy*
yo lo tengo claro	*it's clear to me*

Después de escuchar. Here is another version of the true/false statements you did in **Antes de escuchar.** Circle **C** if the statement is true or **F** if it is false. Then correct the statements that are false, according to the passage.

1. C F Nicanor es de Vermont.

   _____

2. C F A Nicanor no le gusta el frío.

   _____

3. C F En el mundo hispánico, hay climas muy variados.

   _____

4. C F En Sudamérica no hace frío en ninguna región.

   _____

5. C F A Nicanor le gustaría (*would like*) vivir en los Andes.

   _____

6. C F Cuando es verano en el Hemisferio Norte, también es verano en el Hemisferio Sur.

   _____

Now resume listening.

C. Y para terminar... Entrevista. You will hear a series of questions. Each will be said twice. Answer, based on your own experience. Write out all numbers. Pause and write the answers.

1. _____
2. _____
3. _____
4. _____
5. _____
6. _____

VIDEOTECA — Minidramas*

Paso 1. Hablando por teléfono. In this conversation, Carolina Díaz calls her friend Marta Durán Benítez. Marta's father, Manolo Durán, takes a phone message for his daughter. Carolina's lines will be read with pauses for repetition. But first, listen.

MANOLO: ¿Diga?

CAROLINA: Buenos días. Habla Carolina Díaz. ¿Está Marta?

MANOLO: No, Carolina. Marta no está en este momento. Está en el parque con su tío abuelo. ¿Quieres dejarle un recado?

CAROLINA: Sí, muchas gracias. Me gustaría decirle que si quiere venir esta tarde a jugar conmigo. Hace buen tiempo y podríamos ir a jugar afuera.

MANOLO: Muy bien, Carolina. Yo le doy el recado. Saluda a tus padres de mi parte, por favor.

CAROLINA: Sí. Adiós.

MANOLO: Adiós.

Paso 2. Aplicación. Now you will participate in a similar conversation, partially printed in your manual, in which you play the role of Susanita. Complete the conversation using the written cues. Here are the cues for your conversation. ¡OJO! The cues are not in order.

Habla Susanita Márquez.	Adiós.
Hola.	No, gracias.
¿Está Elena?	Puedo llamar más tarde.
Muchas gracias.	

EDUARDO: ¿Bueno? (*Hello?*)

SUSANITA: _____¹. ¿_____²?

EDUARDO: ¿De parte de quién, por favor? (*Who's calling, please?*)

SUSANITA: _____³.

EDUARDO: Hola, Susanita. Lo siento, pero Elena está en casa de su tía. ¿Quieres dejar un recado?

SUSANITA: _____⁴. _____⁵.

EDUARDO: Está bien. Elena va a regresar dentro de (*within*) una hora.

SUSANITA: _____⁶. _____⁷.

EDUARDO: Adiós.

---

*This **Minidramas** videoclip is available on the Video on CD to accompany *Puntos de partida* Seventh Edition.

A. Comparaciones. You will hear a series of statements about the following chart. Each will be said twice. Circle **C** if the statement is true, or **F** if it is false. First, pause and read the chart.

PAÍS	POBLACIÓN (HABITANTES)	ÁREA (MILLAS CUADRADAS) (SQUARE MILES)	TEMPERATURA COSTAL / TEMPERATURA INTERIOR EN GRADOS FAHRENHEIT	NÚMERO DE PERIÓDICOS DIARIOS (DAILY NEWSPAPERS)
Costa Rica	3.896.092	19.730	90° / 63°	4
Guatemala	13.909.384	42.042	82° / 68°	5
Nicaragua	5.128.517	50.838	77° / 79°	6
México	104.907.991	756.066	120° / 61°	285

Now resume listening.

1. C F   2. C F   3. C F   4. C F   5. C F   6. C F

B. La nueva profesora guatemalteca. Tell about the new professor, using the written cues. When you hear the corresponding number, form sentences using the words provided in the order given, making any necessary changes or additions. You will be given a choice of verbs. Choose the correct one.

> MODELO: *(you see)* 1. la profesora / (ser / estar) / Isabel Darío
> *(you hear)* uno → *(you say)* La profesora es Isabel Darío.

2. la profesora / (ser / estar) / de Puerto Barrios, Guatemala
3. Puerto Barrios / (ser / estar) / lejos de la capital
4. la profesora / (ser / estar) / cansada por el viaje
5. ella / se (ser / estar) / quedando con unos amigos
6. la profesora / (ser / estar) / inteligente y simpática
7. los estudiantes / (ser / estar) / contentos con la nueva profesora

C. Hablando de viajes. Imagine that you will travel to a variety of places this year. Answer the questions you hear about each of your trips using the written cues. ¡OJO! The questions may vary slightly from those in the model. Change your answers accordingly.

> MODELO: *(you see)* 3/30 / fresco
> *(you hear)* ¿Cuándo sales para Detroit? → *(you say)* Salgo el treinta de marzo.
> *(you hear)* ¿Y qué tiempo hace allí? → *(you say)* Hace fresco.

1. 7/15 / calor
2. 12/1 / nevando
3. 1/10 / sol
4. 5/24 / viento

VIDEOTECA   Minidramas*

Paso 1. En el restaurante. In this conversation, Manolo Durán and his wife, Lola Benítez, have dinner in a restaurant. Manolo's lines will be read with pauses for repetition. But first, listen.

CAMARERO: ¿Ya saben lo que desean de comer los señores?

MANOLO: Creo que sí, pero, ¿qué recomienda Ud.?

CAMARERO: Hoy tenemos un plato especial: gambas al limón con arroz, un plato ligero y delicioso. Y también tenemos un salmón buenísimo que acaba de llegar esta tarde.

LOLA: ¡Qué rico! Yo quiero las gambas, por favor.

MANOLO: Eh, para mí, el bistec estilo argentino, poco asado. Y una ensalada mixta para dos.

CAMARERO: ¿Y para empezar? Tenemos una sopa de ajo muy rica.

LOLA: Para mí, una sopa, por favor.

MANOLO: Y para mí también. Y le dice al chef que por favor le ponga un poco de atún a la ensalada.

CAMARERO: Muy bien, señor.

Paso 2. Aplicación. Now you will participate in a similar conversation, partially printed in your manual, in which you play the role of the **cliente** in a restaurant. Complete the conversation using the written cues. Here are the cues for your conversation. ¡OJO! The cues are not in order.

       el flan de naranja   un coctel de camarones

       los tacos de pollo   un vino blanco

CAMARERA: ¿Sabe ya lo que desea de comer?

CLIENTE: Sí. Favor de traerme _____[1].

CAMARERA: Sí, cómo no. ¿Y para empezar? Tenemos una gran variedad de antojitos (*appetizers*) que seguramente le van a gustar.

CLIENTE: Bueno, tráigame _____[2], por favor.

CAMARERA: ¿Algo de postre?

CLIENTE: Sí, quiero _____[3], por favor.

CAMARERA: Muy bien. ¿Y para beber?

CLIENTE: ¿Me puede traer _____[4]?

CAMARERA: Sí. Se lo traigo en seguida (*I'll bring it to you right away*).

_____

*This **Minidramas** videoclip is available on the Video on CD to accompany *Puntos de partida* Seventh Edition.

A. *Los hispanos hablan:* ¿Qué te gusta mucho comer?

In this passage, Clara tells about two dishes typical of Spain: **el cocido** and **el gazpacho.** Then you will hear a series of statements. Circle **C** if the statement is true or **F** if it is false. The following words appear in the passage.

el hueso de codillo	*leg bone (as in ham)*
la morcilla	*blood sausage*
el pepino	*cucumber*
el pimiento	*pepper*
el ajo	*garlic*
el aceite de oliva	*olive oil*
el vinagre	*vinegar*
echarle por encima	*to sprinkle on top of it*
trocitos	*little bits (pieces)*

1. C F   2. C F   3. C F   4. C F

B. Cosas de todos los días. Practice talking about a new restaurant, using the written cues. When you hear the corresponding number, form sentences using the words provided in the order given, making any necessary changes or additions. When you are given a choice between verbs or words, choose the correct one.

> MODELO: (*you see*) 1. ¿(saber / conocer) / tú / un buen restaurante?
> (*you hear*) uno → (*you say*) ¿Conoces un buen restaurante?

2. sí, yo / (saber / conocer) / un buen restaurante
3. ellos / (la / lo) / acabar de / abrir
4. yo / (saber / conocer) / al dueño / (*owner*)
5. ellos / preparar / unos camarones deliciosos
6. ellos / (las / los) / cocinar / en vino blanco
7. no hay / (algo / nada) / malo en el menú
8. yo / (siempre / nunca) / cenar allí

C. ¡Qué maleducados! Mr. Alarcón's children have not been behaving lately, and he is constantly telling them what to do and what not to do. Play the role of Mr. Alarcón, using the oral cues.

> MODELO: (*you hear*) no jugar en la sala → (*you say*) No jueguen en la sala.

1. ...   2. ...   3. ...   4. ...   5. ...

CAPÍTULO **9**

VOCABULARIO Preparación

A. Gustos y preferencias. You will hear a series of descriptions of what people like to do. Each will be said twice. Listen carefully, and circle the letter of the activity or activities that are best suited to each person.

1. a. nadar   b. jugar al ajedrez   c. tomar el sol
2. a. dar fiestas   b. ir al teatro   c. ir a un bar
3. a. ir a un museo   b. hacer *camping*   c. hacer un *picnic*
4. a. pasear en bicicleta b. esquiar   c. correr
5. a. jugar al fútbol b. ir a un museo   c. ir al cine

B. Las actividades y el tiempo. You will hear a series of descriptions of weather and activities. Write the number of the description next to the corresponding picture. ¡OJO! Listen carefully. There is an extra description.

a. _____

b. _____

c. _____

d. _____

C. Mandatos para el nuevo robot. Imagine that your family has been chosen to test a model robot in your home. Tell the robot what to do in each of the following situations, using the oral cues. ¡OJO! You will be using **Ud.** command forms.

MODELO: (*you hear*) 1. (*you see*) →
(*you say*) Lave los platos.

1.

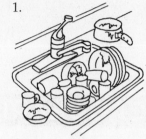

2.

3.

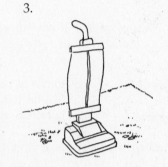

4.

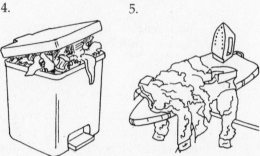

5.

D. ¿Qué están haciendo estas personas? Tell what each person is doing when you hear the corresponding name. Use the present progressive in your answers.

MODELO: (*you hear*) 1. (*you see*) →
(*you say*) Jorge está lavando las ventanas.

1.

2.

3.

4.

5.

■■■Los hispanos hablan: ¿Cuál es tu pasatiempo favorito?

Paso 1. You will hear two answers to this question. Listen carefully and jot down notes about what each person says. The following words appear in the answers.

los aparadores	*display windows*
las sodas	*soda fountains*
los bancos	*benches*

Xiomara

_____

_____

_____

Gabriela

_____

_____

_____

Paso 2. Now, pause and answer these questions. (Check your answers in the Appendix.)

1. ¿Qué actividades tienen en común las dos jóvenes?

   _____

2. ¿Qué pasatiempos no tienen en común Gabriela y Xiomara?

   _____

Now resume listening.

PRONUNCIACIÓN Y ORTOGRAFÍA   *p* and *t*

A. Repeticiones. Like the [k] sound, Spanish **p** and **t** are not aspirated as they are in English. Compare the following pairs of aspirated and nonaspirated English sounds.

pin / spin   pan / span   tan / Stan   top / stop

Repeat the following words, imitating the speaker.

1. pasar   patinar   programa   puerta   esperar
2. tienda   todos   traje   estar   usted

Now, read the following phrases and sentences after you hear the corresponding number. Repeat the correct pronunciation after the speaker.

3. una tía trabajadora
4. unos pantalones pardos
5. Tomás, toma tu té.
6. Pablo paga el periódico.

B. Repaso: [p], [t], [k]. You will hear a series of words. Each will be said twice. Circle the letter of the word you hear.

1. a. pata   b. bata
2. a. van   b. pan
3. a. coma   b. goma

4. a. dos   b. tos
5. a. de   b. té
6. a. callo   b. gallo

C. Dictado. You will hear four sentences. Each will be said twice. Listen carefully and write what you hear.

1. _____

2. _____

3. _____

4. _____

GRAMÁTICA

27. Descriptions and Habitual Actions in the Past • Imperfect of Regular and Irregular Verbs

A. Minidiálogo: Diego habla de los aztecas

Paso 1. Dictado. You will hear the following paragraph in which Diego, a student from California who studied for one year in Mexico City, describes some aspects of Aztec culture. Listen carefully and write the missing words.

Los aztecas construyeron grandes pirámides para sus dioses.

En lo alto de cada pirámide _____ un

templo donde _____ lugar las ceremonias y

se _____ los sacrificios. Las pirámides

_____ muchísimos escalones, y

_____ necesario subirlos todos para llegar

a los templos.

Cerca de muchas pirámides _____ un terreno como el de una cancha de

basquetbol. Allí se _____ partidos que _____ parte de una

ceremonia. Los participantes _____ con una pelota de goma dura, que sólo

_____ mover con las caderas y las rodillas…

Paso 2. ¿Qué recuerda Ud.? Now pause and complete the following sentences with words chosen from the list. (Check the answers in the Appendix.)

ceremonia   dioses   pirámides   religiosa   sacrificios

1. Los aztecas ofrecían _____ a sus _____.

2. El juego de pelota que se jugaba era parte de una _____.

3. Las _____ eran estructuras altas que tenían una función

_____.

Now resume listening.

B. Encuesta: ¿Qué hacía Ud. y cómo era cuando era joven? You will hear a series of statements about what you used to do or what you were like when you were younger. For each statement, check the appropriate answer. No answers will be given. The answers you choose should be correct for you!

1. ☐ Sí   ☐ No   4. ☐ Sí   ☐ No   6. ☐ Sí   ☐ No

2. ☐ Sí   ☐ No   5. ☐ Sí   ☐ No   7. ☐ Sí   ☐ No

3. ☐ Sí   ☐ No

C. En el aeropuerto: Una despedida

Paso 1. You will hear a description of a farewell between parents and their son, who is leaving home to attend medical school. Listen carefully, and indicate the appropriate actions for each person. First, pause and look at the chart.

	ESTAR EN EL AEROPUERTO	IR A SAN JOSÉ	ESTAR MUY NERVIOSO/A	ESTAR PREOCUPADO/A	SENTIRSE TRISTE
Gustavo					
la madre de Gustavo					
el padre de Gustavo					

Paso 2. Now you will hear a series of statements about the passage. Each will be said twice. Circle **C** if the statement is true or **F** if it is false.

1. C F   2. C F   3. C F   4. C F   5. C F

Paso 3. Now answer the questions you hear, based on the information in your chart. Check the answers for **Paso 1** in the Appendix before you begin **Paso 3.** Each question will be said twice. Pause and write the answers.

1. _____

2. _____

3. _____

4. _____

5. _____

D. Describiendo el pasado: En la primaria. Practice telling what you and others used to do in grade school, using the oral and written cues.

MODELO: (*you see*) (yo) (*you hear*) jugar mucho → (*you say*) Jugaba mucho.

1. Rodolfo   2. (tú)   3. todos   4. (nosotros)

28. Expressing Extremes • Superlatives

A. Las opiniones de Margarita

Paso 1. Apuntes. You will hear a brief paragraph in which Margarita gives her opinions about a variety of topics. Listen carefully and write down her opinions. First, listen to the list of topics.

la fiesta más divertida del año: _____

el peor mes del año: _____

la mejor película del mundo: _____

el quehacer doméstico más aburrido: _____

Paso 2. Now pause and express your own opinion about the same topics. No answers will be given. The answers you choose should be correct for you!

En mi opinión...

1. La fiesta más divertida del año es _____

2. El peor mes del año es _____

3. La mejor película del mundo es _____

4. El quehacer doméstico más aburrido es _____

Now resume listening.

B. Sólo lo mejor... Imagine that your friend's **quinceañera** has the best of everything. Answer some questions about it, using the written cues.

MODELO: (*you see and hear*) Los vestidos son elegantes, ¿no? (*you see*) fiesta →
(*you say*) Sí, son los vestidos más elegantes de la fiesta.

1. Antonio es un chico guapo, ¿verdad? / fiesta
2. La música es buena, ¿no? / mundo
3. Y la comida, qué rica, ¿no? / mundo
4. La fiesta es divertida, ¿verdad? / año

29. Getting Information • Summary of Interrogative Words

A. Preguntas y respuestas. You will hear a series of questions. Each will be said twice. Circle the letter of the best answer to each.

1. a. Es de Juan.   b. Es negro.
2. a. Están en México.   b. Son de México.
3. a. Soy alto y delgado.   b. Bien, gracias. ¿Y Ud.?
4. a. Mañana.   b. Tengo cinco.
5. a. Es gris.   b. Tengo frío.
6. a. Con Elvira.   b. Elvira va a la tienda.
7. a. A las nueve.   b. Son las nueve.

VIDEOTECA   Minidramas*

Paso 1. La invitación. In the following conversation, Lupe tells Antonio and Juan about a surprise party for Diego. Listen and read along with the speakers. Pay close attention to how Rocío rejects Lupe's invitation, and how Antonio and Juan accept it.

ANTONIO: ¡Hola, Lupe!

LUPE: Hola, Antonio. Oye, ¿está aquí Diego?

ANTONIO: No, no está. ¿Por qué?

LUPE: Ah, muy bien. Pues, el próximo fin de semana le quiero dar una fiesta sorpresa a Diego. Es su cumpleaños. Quiero invitar a todos Uds. a la fiesta.

ANTONIO: ¡Qué padre! ¿Y cuándo es la fiesta? ¿El viernes? ¿El sábado?

LUPE: El sábado. Rocío, ¿te gustaría venir?

ROCÍO: Ay, Lupe, me gustaría mucho, pero no puedo. Ya tengo planes para el sábado. Mis padres vienen al D.F. a visitarme y vamos a ir al Ballet Folklórico esa noche.

JUAN: ¡Qué pena! Pero yo sí voy.

ANTONIO: Y yo también. Gracias por la invitación. ¿Puedo invitar a Mónica y a José Luis también?

LUPE: ¡Claro que sí! ¡Muy bien! Entonces, ¿por qué no vienen a mi casa a las siete? Y por favor, no le vayan a decir nada a Diego.

JUAN: No te preocupes. Él va a estar muy sorprendido.

Paso 2. Aplicación. Now you will participate in two similar conversations, partially printed in your manual, in which you reject and accept invitations. Complete them using the written cues. Here are the cues for your first conversation. You will need to conjugate the verbs.

        gracias / pero no poder / tener que estudiar

1. TEODORO: Oye, ¿te gustaría ir al cine el viernes? Dan (*They're showing*) una película buenísima.

    UD.: _____¹, _____². _____³.

    TEODORO: ¡Qué lástima! Tal vez podamos ir el próximo viernes.

Here are the cues for your second conversation. You will also need to conjugate the verbs.

        ser una buena idea / a qué hora querer (tú) salir / sí, estar bien

2. CARIDAD: ¿Qué tal si vamos al parque esta tarde y hacemos un *picnic*?

    UD.: ¡_____¹! ¿_____²?

    CARIDAD: A las tres, más o menos. ¿Vale? (*O.K.?, Sp.*)

    UD.: _____³.

---

*This **Minidramas** videoclip is available on the Video on CD to accompany *Puntos de partida* Seventh Edition.

PRUEBA CORTA

A. Recuerdos. You will hear a passage about a person's childhood memories. Then you will hear a series of questions. Circle the letter of the best answer for each.

1. a. Trabajaba en Panamá. b. Vivía en Panamá.
2. a. Hacía calor. b. No hacía calor.
3. a. Jugaba béisbol. b. Patinaba con sus amigos.
4. a. Iba al cine. b. Iba al centro.
5. a. Patinaba con sus padres. b. Patinaba con sus amigos.
6. a. Daba paseos en el parque. b. Daba paseos en el cine.
7. a. Su quehacer favorito era lavar los platos. b. No le gustaba lavar los platos.

B. Cosas de todos los días: una niñez feliz. Practice talking about your imaginary childhood, using the written cues. When you hear the corresponding number, form sentences using the words provided in the order given, making any necessary changes or additions.

MODELO: (*you see*) 1. (yo) / ser / niño muy feliz   (*you hear*) uno →
(*you say*) *Era* un niño muy feliz.

2. cuando / (yo) / ser / niño, / vivir / Colombia
3. mi familia / tener / una casa / bonito / Medellín
4. mi hermana y yo / asistir / escuelas públicas
5. todos los sábados, / mi mamá / ir de compras
6. me / gustar / jugar / con mis amigos
7. los domingos / (nosotros) / reunirse / con / nuestro / abuelos

CAPÍTULO **10**

VOCABULARIO   Preparación

A. Asociaciones. You will hear a series of activities. Each will be said twice. Circle the body part that you associate with each. ¡OJO! There may be more than one answer for each activity.

1. los pies	las piernas	los dientes	la garganta
2. los pulmones	las manos	la nariz	los ojos
3. los pulmones	la boca	las manos	las piernas
4. los dientes	la garganta	el corazón	la boca
5. los ojos	los pulmones	las piernas	el estómago
6. la nariz	los oídos	las orejas	la garganta

B. Algunas partes del cuerpo. Identify the following body parts when you hear the corresponding number. Use **Es...** or **Son...** and the appropriate definite article.

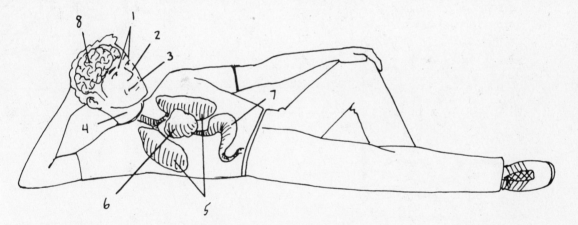

C. Para completar. You will hear a series of incomplete statements. Each will be said twice. Circle the letter of the word or phrase that best completes each statement.

1. a. ponerle una inyección   b. respirar bien
2. a. guardamos cama   b. nos sacan una muela
3. a. una tos   b. un jarabe
4. a. frío   b. un resfriado

D. Descripción: Hablando de problemas de salud

Paso 1. In each of the drawings, a person is suffering from some type of ailment. Pause and write what the ailment is, based on the cues in the drawing. You should also tell where each person might be. The first one is partially done for you. (The small circles are for **Paso 2.** Check your answers to **Paso 1** in the Appendix before you begin **Paso 2.**)

1.

Darío tiene dolor de _____.

(A Darío le duele el _____.)

Él está en _____.

2. _____

_____

3. _____

_____

4. _____

_____

Now resume listening.

Paso 2. Now you will hear a doctor's recommendations. Each will be said twice. Write the letter of the recommendation in the circle of the corresponding drawing.

■■■Los hispanos hablan: ¿Practicas un deporte? ¿Por qué?

Paso 1. You will hear several Hispanic students tell about the sports they play and why. The first time you listen, write the name of the sport or sports played by each student. Then, listen again and jot down each person's reasons for choosing the sport. The following words appear in the passages.

emocionante	*exciting*	habilidad y destreza	*ability and skill*
entretenido	*entertaining, fun*	mantenerse en forma	*to stay in shape*
que uno se engorde	*that one get fat*		

	DEPORTE(S)	RAZÓN POR LA CUAL SE PRACTICA
Clara		
Antonio		
Gabriela		
Patricia		
Teresa		
José		
Xiomara		
Erick		

Paso 2. Now pause and answer these questions, based on the chart. Check your answers to **Paso 1** in the Appendix before you begin **Paso 2**.

1. ¿Qué deporte es más popular entre los estudiantes que contestaron las preguntas?

   _____

2. ¿Cuántas personas mencionaron entre sus razones la salud o los beneficios para el cuerpo?

   _____

Now resume listening.

PRONUNCIACIÓN Y ORTOGRAFÍA   *s, z, ce,* and *ci*

A. El sonido [s]. The [s] sound in Spanish can be spelled several different ways and has several variants, depending on the country or region of origin of the speaker. Listen to the difference between these pronunciations of the [s] sound in two distinct Spanish-speaking areas of the world.*

Spain: Vamos a llamar a Susana este lunes.

Latin America: Vamos a llamar a Susana este lunes.

Spain: Cecilia siempre cena con Alicia.

Latin America: Cecilia siempre cena con Alicia.

(Continued on p. 114)

*The Latin American variant of the [s] sound is used by most speakers in this audio program.

(*Continued from p. 113*)

Spain:	Zaragoza	Zurbarán	zapatería
Latin America:	Zaragoza	Zurbarán	zapatería

Notice also that in some parts of the Hispanic world, in rapid speech, the [s] sound becomes aspirated at the end of a syllable or word. Listen as the speaker pronounces these sentences.

¿Hasta cuándo vas a estar allí?   Les mandamos las cartas.

B. Repeticiones. Repeat the following words, imitating the speaker.

1.	sala	pastel	vaso	años
2.	cerebro	ciencias	piscina	ciudad
3.	corazón	azul	perezoso	zapatos
4.	estación	solución	inyección	situación

Now read the following words, phrases, and sentences after you hear the corresponding number. Repeat the correct pronunciation.

5. los ojos
6. las orejas
7. unas médicas españolas

8. unas soluciones científicas
9. No conozco a Luz Mendoza de Pérez.
10. Los zapatos de Celia son azules.

C. Repaso. You will hear a series of words spelled with **c** or **qu.** Each will be said twice. Circle the letter or letters used to spell each word. ¡ojo! Most of the words will be unfamiliar to you. Concentrate on the sounds you hear.

1. c   qu   2. c   qu   3. c   qu   4. c   qu   5. c   qu   6. c   qu

GRAMÁTICA

30. Narrating in the Past • Using the Preterite and the Imperfect

A. Dictado: Minidiálogo: En el consultorio de la Dra. Méndez. Lola and Manolo's daughter Marta is feeling ill, and Lola takes her to see Dra. Méndez. You will hear the conversation that takes place in the doctor's office. Listen carefully and write the missing words. Then you will hear a series of statements about the dialogue. Circle **C, F,** or **ND (No lo dice).**

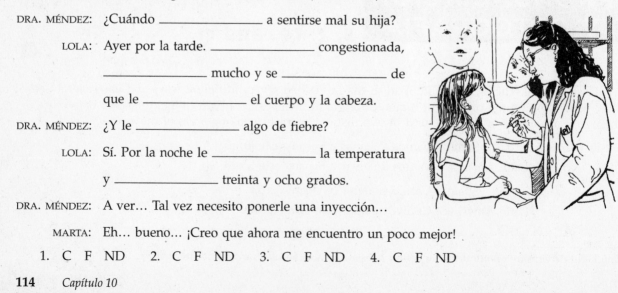

DRA. MÉNDEZ: ¿Cuándo _____ a sentirse mal su hija?

LOLA: Ayer por la tarde. _____ congestionada,

_____ mucho y se _____ de

que le _____ el cuerpo y la cabeza.

DRA. MÉNDEZ: ¿Y le _____ algo de fiebre?

LOLA: Sí. Por la noche le _____ la temperatura

y _____ treinta y ocho grados.

DRA. MÉNDEZ: A ver... Tal vez necesito ponerle una inyección...

MARTA: Eh... bueno... ¡Creo que ahora me encuentro un poco mejor!

1. C F ND   2. C F ND   3. C F ND   4. C F ND

B. Condiciones y acciones: De viaje. You will hear a series of sentences describing conditions. Each will be said twice. Write the number of each condition next to the logical action. First, listen to the list of actions.

a. _____ Por eso llegué tarde al aeropuerto. d. _____ Por eso pedí un vuelo directo.

b. _____ Por eso pedí asiento en la sección de no fumar. e. _____ Por eso compré un boleto de ida y vuelta.

c. _____ Por eso lo facturé.

C. ¿Un sábado típico? You will hear a series of sentences that describe Carlos's usual Saturday routine. Form new sentences using the oral cues to talk about what he did *last* Saturday. Begin each sentence with **El sábado pasado... .**

> MODELO: (*you see and hear*) Todos los sábados, Carlos se despertaba a las siete.
> (*you hear*) ocho → (*you say*) El sábado pasado, se despertó a las ocho.

1. Todos los sábados, iba al centro comercial.   3. Todos los sábados, visitaba a su madre.
2. Todos los sábados, tomaba té por la mañana.   4. Todos los sábados, se acostaba temprano.

D. Descripción. Tell what the following people were doing when you hear the corresponding number. Follow the model. You will hear a possible answer.

> MODELO: (*you hear*) uno   (*you see*) cocinar / mientras / poner la mesa →
> (*you say*) Luis cocinaba mientras Paula ponía la mesa.

1. cocinar / mientras / poner la mesa

2. leer / cuando / entrar

3. cantar / mientras / tocar el piano

4. llorar / mientras / ponerle una inyección

5. jugar / cuando / pegarle

E. Una decisión difícil

Paso 1. You will hear the following sentences about Laura's decision to leave her hometown. Then, when you hear the cue in parentheses, restate the sentences, changing the italicized verbs to the preterite or imperfect, as appropriate. In each case, you will insert the cue at the beginning of the sentence. In this excercise, you will practice narrating in the past.

> MODELO: (*you see and hear*) *Vivimos* en un pequeño pueblo en las montañas.
> (*you hear*) (de niños) →
> (*you say*) De niños, vivíamos en un pequeño pueblo en las montañas.

1. Mi madre *trabaja* en una panadería (*bakery*).   (los martes y los jueves)
2. Mi padre *trabaja* en una tienda de comestibles (*food store*).   (todos los días)
3. *Vamos* a la ciudad y *compramos* cosas que no *podemos* encontrar en nuestro pueblo.   (con frecuencia)
4. *Consigo* trabajo permanente en la ciudad y *decido* dejar mi pueblo para siempre.   (un verano)
5. *Empiezo* a tomar clases de noche en la universidad y *dejo* mi puesto permanente por uno de tiempo parcial.   (al año siguiente)
6. Mis padres *están* tristes porque yo no *vivo* con ellos, pero ahora están contentos con mi decisión.   (antes)

Paso 2. Answer the questions you hear, based on the preceding story. Each question will be said twice.

1. ...   2. ...   3. ...   4. ...

31. Recognizing *que*, *quien(es)*, *lo que* • Relative Pronouns

A. Minidiálogo: La salud es lo que importa.

Paso 1. Dictado. You will hear the following paragraph. Listen carefully and write the missing words.

¿Sabe Ud. _____ debe hacer para ser saludable

emocionalmente? ¿Vive Ud. la vida _____ debe

vivir? Para estar seguro de _____ necesita para la

salud física, consulte con un doctor en _____ confía.

Pero para lograr un estado de bienestar mental, hágase estas

preguntas:

• ¿Hay personas con _____ puedo hablar si tengo problemas?

• ¿Qué métodos uso para combatir el estrés _____ me causan los problemas diarios?

Paso 2. Preguntas personales. Now pause and write answers to the following questions. No answers will be given.

1. ¿Sabe Ud. lo que debe hacer para ser saludable emocionalmente?

_____

2. ¿Vive Ud. la vida que debe vivir?

_____

3. ¿Hay personas con quienes puede hablar si tiene problemas?

_____

4. ¿Qué métodos usa para combatir el estrés que le causan los problemas diarios?

_____

Now resume listening.

B. En el consultorio

Paso 1. Una visita con la doctora. You will hear a brief paragraph describing a visit to the doctor's office. Listen carefully and take notes on a separate sheet of paper, if you wish.

Paso 2. ¿Qué recuerda Ud.? Now pause and provide the following information based on the paragraph. (Check your answers in the Appendix.)

1. lo que tenía la narradora: _____

2. la persona con quien quería hablar: _____

3. lo que le dijo la recepcionista: _____

4. la persona a quien va a llamar la próxima vez que se enferme: _____

Now resume listening.

32. Expressing *each other* • Reciprocal Actions with Reflexive Pronouns

A. Minidiálogo: Rosa y Casandra. You will hear a brief passage about Rosa and Casandra. Then you will hear a series of statements. Circle **C** if the statement is true or **F** if it is false. If the information in the statement is not contained in the passage, circle **ND** (**No lo dice.**)

1. C   F   ND

2. C   F   ND

3. C   F   ND

4. C   F   ND

B. Descripción: ¿Qué hacen estas personas? Using the written cues, tell what the following pairs of people are doing when you hear the corresponding number. You will be describing reciprocal actions.

1. quererse mucho
2. escribirse con frecuencia
3. darse la mano (*to shake hands*)
4. hablarse por teléfono

UN POCO DE TODO | (Para entregar)

A. En el periódico: La salud

Paso 1. You will hear the following ads from Hispanic newspapers. Listen to them and circle the Spanish words or phrases that express the following. First, pause and scan the list of English words.

DEJE DE FUMAR

1. killers
2. medical treatment
3. a vice

LENTES DE CONTACTO

4. a replacement pair
5. immediate replacement
6. soft or flexible

Paso 2. Now you will hear a series of statements about the ads. Each will be said twice. Circle **C, F,** or **ND** (**No lo dice**), according to the ads.

1. C F ND   3. C F ND

2. C F ND   4. C F ND

B. *Listening Passage:* **El sistema médico en los países hispánicos**

Antes de escuchar. Pause and do the following prelistening exercise. Read the following statements about medical systems. Check those that you think apply only to the United States.

1. ☐ El sistema médico está controlado por el gobierno (*government*).

2. ☐ Hay una gran cantidad de compañías de seguro (*insurance companies*).

3. ☐ Hay menos compañías de seguro.

4. ☐ Cada persona paga los gastos médicos de acuerdo con (*according to*) su salario y no de acuerdo con el tipo de seguro que tiene.

5. ☐ Cualquier (*Any*) persona tiene derecho (*right*) al mejor tratamiento médico posible.

6. ☐ Hay muchas personas que no tienen acceso al tratamiento médico, ya sea (*be it*) por falta de dinero o porque no tienen seguro.

7. ☐ A veces, es necesario esperar mucho tiempo para ver al médico.

8. ☐ A veces hay mucha demanda, pero hay pocos servicios y personal disponibles (*available personnel*).

Now resume listening.

Listening Passage. Now you will hear a passage about the medical systems in most of the Hispanic world. The following words and phrases appear in the passage.

proveen	*they provide*
la cobertura	*coverage*
innegables	*undeniable*
la capacidad económica	*economic ability (to pay)*
el impuesto	*tax*
imprescindible	*indispensable*
tiende a disminuir	*tends to diminish or reduce*
el quebradero de cabeza	*problem, something that requires great thought*

Después de escuchar. Indicate whether the following statements are true or false, according to the passage. Correct the false statements.

1. C F El sistema médico más común en los países hispanos es el privado.

_____

2. C F El gobierno controla el sistema médico en los Estados Unidos.

_____

3. C F En un sistema de medicina socializada, todos tienen derecho a recibir tratamiento médico.

_____

4. C F Una desventaja de la medicina socializada, especialmente en países menos ricos, es que a veces no hay suficientes servicios médicos o suficientes doctores.

_____

5. C F El sistema de medicina socializada no diferencia entre los que pagan más y los que pagan menos.

_____

Now resume listening.

C. Y para terminar... Entrevista. You will hear a series of questions. Each will be said twice. Answer, based on your own experience. Pause and write the answers.

Hablando de la última vez que estuviste enfermo o enferma

1. _____

2. _____

3. _____

Hablando de la salud en general

4. _____

5. _____

6. _____

VIDEOTECA Minidramas*

Paso 1. En el consultorio de la Dra. Méndez. In the following conversation, Marta is sick and is being examined by Dra. Méndez. Listen and read along with the speakers.

DRA. MÉNDEZ: ¿Así que no te sientes bien, Marta? Dime lo que te pasa.

MARTA: Anoche me dolió mucho el estómago. Y también la garganta.

LOLA: Sí, y ayer por la tarde estaba muy congestionada.

DRA. MÉNDEZ: ¿Sí? ¿Y cuándo comenzó a sentir estos síntomas?

LOLA: Fue unos días después de que se reunió con su amiga Carolina, quien ya estaba enferma.

DRA. MÉNDEZ: Ajá. Marta, saca la lengua, por favor. Di «ahhh».

MARTA: Ahhh…

DRA. MÉNDEZ: A ver… Respira. Más fuerte. Otra vez.

LOLA: ¿Qué pasa, doctora? ¿Es grave?

DRA. MÉNDEZ: No, no se preocupe. No es nada grave. Lo que tiene es un resfriado. Marta, debes guardar cama durante unos días y tomar muchos líquidos. Sra. Durán, voy a darle dos recetas. Las pastillas son para quitarle la congestión. Y el jarabe se lo puede dar cuando ella tosa.

LOLA: Muy bien, doctora.

DRA. MÉNDEZ: Y debe quedarse en casa algunos días.

MARTA: ¡Estupendo!

LOLA: Marta, por favor…

Paso 2. Aplicación. Now you will participate in a similar conversation, partially printed in your manual, in which you play the role of a patient. Complete the dialogue using the written cues. You will need to conjugate the verbs. Here are the cues for your conversation. **¡OJO!** The cues are not in order.

el lunes pasado

estar muy cansado/a

no tener fiebre

tener dolor de cabeza

DOCTORA: Siéntese, por favor. ¿Qué le ocurre?

UD.: Bueno, _____[1] y

_____.[2]

DOCTORA: ¿Cuándo empezó a tener estos síntomas?

UD.: _____.[3]

DOCTORA: Bueno, le voy a tomar la temperatura. Si tiene fiebre, le voy a recomendar que guarde cama por uno o dos días y que tome un antibiótico.

UD.: Y, ¿si _____[4]?

DOCTORA: Entonces le voy a recomendar que tenga paciencia. Es posible que sólo sea un resfriado.

---

*This **Minidramas** videoclip is available on the Video on CD to accompany *Puntos de partida* Seventh Edition.

A. Consejos para la buena salud. Imagine that you are a doctor and that you are giving advice to one of your patients. Use formal commands based on the oral cues.

MODELO: (*you hear*) hacer ejercicios aeróbicos → (*you say*) Haga ejercicios aeróbicos.

1. ...   2. ...   3. ...   4. ...   5. ...

B. Cosas de todos los días: Una enfermedad muy grave. Practice talking about an event that took place in the past, using the written cues. When you hear the corresponding number, form sentences using the words provided in the order given, making any necessary changes or additions. You will hear the correct answer. ¡OJO! You will be using the preterite or the imperfect forms of the verbs.

MODELO: (*you see*) 1. el mes pasado / (yo) / enfermarse / gravemente   (*you hear*) uno →
(*you say*) El mes pasado *me enfermé* gravemente.

2. estar / en el trabajo / cuando / de repente / (yo) / sentirse muy mal
3. estar / mareado / y / tener / fiebre / muy alta
4. mi jefe (*boss*) / llamar / hospital / inmediatamente
5. ambulancia / llevarme / en seguida / sala de emergencia
6. enfermero / tomarme / temperatura / cuando / entrar / médica
7. tener que / pasar / cuatro días / en el hospital

CAPÍTULO **11**

VOCABULARIO Preparación

A. Descripción: ¡Qué día más terrible! You will hear a series of sentences. Each will be said twice. Write the letter of each sentence next to the appropriate drawing. First, pause and look at the drawings.

1. _____

2. _____

3. _____

4. _____

5. _____

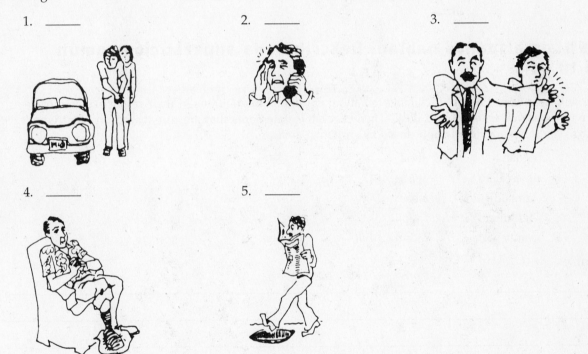

B. Más partes del cuerpo. Identify the following body parts when you hear the corresponding number. Begin each sentence with **Es...** or **Son...** and the appropriate definite article.

C. Presiones de los estudios. Imagine that you have been under a lot of pressure at school and it is affecting your judgment as well as other aspects of your life. Describe what has happened to you, using the oral and written cues.

> MODELO: (*you hear*) no pagar (*you see*) mis cuentas → (*you say*) No pagué mis cuentas.

1. el informe escrito
2. las escaleras
3. el escritorio

4. la pierna
5. un examen

D. Preguntas personales. You will hear a series of questions about how you do certain things. Answer, using the written cues or your own information. You will hear a possible answer. First, listen to the cues.

hablar español	hacer cola	salir con mis amigos
jugar al béisbol	escuchar el estéreo	limpiar la estufa
faltar a clase	tocar el piano	

1. ... 2. ... 3. ... 4. ...

■■■Los hispanos hablan: Describe una superstición común en tu país

You will hear three Hispanic students tell about common superstitions in their respective countries. Take notes as you listen, if you wish. Then check the statements that are true, based on what you heard. The following words appear in the students' answers.

evitan	*avoid*
la escalera	*ladder*
la maldición	*curse*
derramar	*to spill*
campanadas	*tolls (of a bell)*

Apuntes

_____

_____

_____

_____

_____

1. ☐ En los tres países, el gato juega un papel (*plays a role*) en las supersticiones.

2. ☐ En Colombia, es buena suerte derramar sal para el Año Nuevo.

3. ☐ El martes trece es un día de mala suerte en uno de los países mencionados.

4. ☐ Muchas de estas supersticiones son semejantes (*similar*) a las supersticiones estadounidenses.

Now resume listening.

PRONUNCIACIÓN Y ORTOGRAFÍA
ñ and *ch*

A. La letra *ñ*: Repeticiones. The pronunciation of the letter **ñ** is similar to the sound [ny] in the English words *canyon* and *union*. However, in Spanish it is pronounced as one single sound.

Repeat the following words, imitating the speaker.

1. cana / caña   sonar / soñar   mono / moño   tino / tiño   cena / seña
2. año   señora   cañón   español   pequeña   compañero

Now read the following sentences when you hear the corresponding number. Repeat the correct pronunciation.

3. El señor Muñoz es de España.
4. Los niños pequeños no enseñan español.
5. La señorita Ordóñez tiene veinte años.
6. El cumpleaños de la señora Yáñez es mañana.

B. A escoger. You will hear a series of words. Each will be said twice. Circle the letter of the word you hear.

1. a. pena   b. peña
2. a. una   b. uña
3. a. lena   b. leña
4. a. suena   b. sueña
5. a. mono   b. moño

C. El sonido *ch*: Repeticiones. In Spanish, when the letters **c** and **h** are combined, they are pronounced like the English *ch* in *church*. Read the following words when you hear the corresponding number, then repeat the correct pronunciation.

1. mucho
2. muchacho
3. Conchita
4. Chile
5. mochila
6. hache

D. Dictado. You will hear five sentences. Each will be said twice. Write what you hear.

1. _____

2. _____

3. _____

4. _____

5. _____

GRAMÁTICA

33. Telling How Long Something Has Been Happening or How Long Ago Something Happened • *Hace... que:* Another Use of *hacer*

A. **¿Cuánto tiempo hace... ?** Each of the following drawings shows how long something has been going on. Pause and look at the drawings. Then answer the questions. Each will be said twice.

1. ...

2. ...

3. ...

4. ...

B. **¡Felicidades, Arturo y Matilde!** You will hear a series of questions about a couple celebrating their 50th wedding anniversary. Answer, using the written cues.

1. 55 años
2. 50 años
3. 48 años
4. 10 años

34. Expressing Unplanned or Unexpected Events • Another Use of *se*

A. Encuesta: ¿Cómo era Ud. en la escuela primaria? You will hear a series of questions about what you were like when you were in grade school. For each question, check the appropriate answer. No answers will be given. The answers you choose should be correct for you!

1. ☐ Sí ☐ No

2. ☐ Sí ☐ No

3. ☐ Sí ☐ No

4. ☐ Sí ☐ No

5. ☐ Sí ☐ No

6. ☐ Sí ☐ No

B. ¡Qué distraído! You will hear a description of Luis, followed by a series of statements about what he forgot to do this morning. Place the number of each statement next to its logical result. First, listen to the results.

a. _____ Va a llegar tarde al trabajo.

b. _____ No va a poder arrancar (*start*) el coche.

c. _____ Es posible que se le queme (*burn down*) el apartamento.

d. _____ Le van a robar la computadora.

e. _____ Lo van a echar (*evict*) de su apartamento.

C. Dictado. You will hear the following sentences. Each will be said twice. Listen carefully and write the missing words.

1. A ellos _____ _____ _____ el número de teléfono de Beatriz.

2. A Juan _____ _____ _____ las gafas.

3. Durante nuestro último viaje _____ _____ _____ el equipaje en la estación del tren.

4. A los niños _____ _____ _____ los juguetes (*toys*).

35. *¿Por o para?* • A Summary of Their Uses

A. ¿Qué hacen estas personas? Using **por,** tell what the following people are doing when you hear the corresponding number.

> MODELO: *(you hear)* uno *(you see)* 1. hablar / teléfono →
> *(you say)* Marcos habla por teléfono.

1. hablar / teléfono

2. viajar / barco

3. caminar / playa

4. correr / parque

5. pagar / 15 dólares / bolígrafos

6. nadar / mañana

B. ¿Para qué están Uds. aquí? Using the oral and written cues, tell why the people mentioned are in the locations you hear. Each question will be said twice. First, listen to the list of reasons.

       celebrar nuestro aniversario

       descansar y divertirse

       hablar con el médico

       hacer reservaciones para un viaje a Acapulco

       preparar la comida

      MODELO: (*you see*) Armando: Está allí…
               (*you hear*) ¿Para qué está Armando en la cocina? →
               (*you say*) Está allí para preparar la comida.

1. Diana: Está allí…
2. el Sr. Guerra: Está allí…
3. mi esposo/a y yo: Estamos aquí…
4. la familia Aragón: Está allí…

C. La vida diaria. You will hear the following sentences followed by an oral cue. Extend each sentence, using **por** or **para,** as appropriate.

      MODELO: (*you see and hear*) Tengo que mandar los cheques.
               (*you hear*) el miércoles →
               (*you say*) Tengo que mandar los cheques para el miércoles.

1. Salen el próximo mes.
2. Fueron al cine.
3. Estuvo en Honduras.
4. Habla muy bien el inglés.
5. A las ocho vamos a salir.
6. Vendieron su coche viejo.

UN POCO DE TODO (Para entregar)

A. Situaciones delicadas. You will hear four situations. Choose the best response to each.

1. a. ¡Ay, me hice daño en la mano!
   b. ¡Qué mala suerte, Sr. Ramos! ¿Tiene otro vaso?
   c. Lo siento muchísimo, Sr. Ramos. Fue sin querer. ¿Puedo comprarle otro?
2. a. No me importa que no te guste el menú. Vamos a comer aquí.
   b. Lo siento mucho, pero pensé que te gustaría este restaurante. ¿Quieres ir a otro?
   c. Bueno, yo me quedo aquí, pero si tú quieres irte (*to leave*) a mí no me importa.
3. a. Lo siento, viejo, pero no tengo ganas de trabajar más hoy.
   b. Bueno, si Ud. insiste, me quedo a trabajar.
   c. Solamente voy a trabajar tarde si me da un aumento de sueldo.
4. a. No se preocupe. Estoy bien.
   b. Mire, señor, si sus niños no dejan de hacer tanto ruido, voy a llamar a la policía.
   c. Por favor, señor, dígales a sus niños que no hagan tanto ruido... ¡Tengo un dolor de cabeza tremendo!

B. *Listening Passage:* Un accidente. You will hear a conversation between a person who has just had an accident and a person who was on the scene. First, listen to get a general idea of the content. Then go back and listen again for specific information.

Después de escuchar. You will hear a series of questions. Each will be said twice. Not all the questions are based on details of the conversation; some will ask for your opinion. Pause and write the answers. The following words and expressions appear in the questions.

perdió el conocimiento	*became unconscious*
el accidentado	la víctima del accidente
deprimido	*depressed*

1. _____
2. _____
3. _____
4. _____
5. _____

C. Y para terminar... Entrevista. You will hear a series of questions. Each will be said twice. Answer, based on your own experience. Pause and write the answers.

1. _____
2. _____
3. _____
4. _____
5. _____
6. _____

VIDEOTECA   Minidramas*

Paso 1. Un día fatal. In the following conversation, José Miguel, his mother, and his grandmother are in the dining room. Listen and read along with the speakers.

JOSÉ MIGUEL: Bueno, mamá, aquí están las compras del mercado.

ELISA: ¡Ay! ¡José Miguel! ¡Se te cayó todo!

JOSÉ MIGUEL: Lo siento, mamá. ¡Fue sin querer!

ELISA: Debes tener más cuidado, hijo.

JOSÉ MIGUEL: Perdóname. Parece que me levanté con el pie izquierdo hoy. ¡Qué lata!

ELISA: Ay, no vale la pena molestarte.

MARÍA: Bueno, pero hay algo bueno en todo esto...

ELISA: ¿Qué es?

MARÍA: ¡Que no llevamos una vida aburrida!

Paso 2. Aplicación. Now you will participate in two conversations, partially printed in your manual, in which you play the role of **Ud.** Complete each conversation using the written cues. Remember to repeat the correct answer. Here are the cues for your conversations. ¡OJO! The cues are not in order.

> Discúlpeme.
>
> No se preocupe.
>
> ¡Lo siento! Fue sin querer.

1. En la farmacia: Ud. se da con una señora y a ella se la cae el frasco (*jar*) de medicina que llevaba.

   SRA.: ¡Ay, no!... ¡el frasco!

   UD.: _____[1].

   SRA.: ¿Qué voy a hacer? Era una medicina para mi hijito, que está enfermo.

   UD.: _____[2]. Yo le compro otro frasco.

2. En el avión: Ud. se equivoca y toma el asiento de otro pasajero. Cuando la persona vuelve, quiere que Ud. le dé su puesto.

   SR.: Perdón, pero ese es mi asiento.

   UD.: _____[3]. Aquí lo tiene.

   SR.: Muchas gracias.

---

*This **Minidramas** videoclip is available on the Video on CD to accompany *Puntos de partida* Seventh Edition.

PRUEBA CORTA

A. ¿Cuánto tiempo hace que... ? You will hear a series of questions. Each will be said twice. Answer based on the following chart. ¡ojo! Assume that the current year is 2004. First, pause and look at the chart.

PERSONA(S)	ACTIVIDAD	AÑO EN QUE EMPEZÓ (EMPEZARON) LA ACTIVIDAD
Silvia	trabajar para la universidad	2002
Ernesto	vivir en California	1980
Samuel y Ana	casarse	1992
Laura y su hermana	hacer ejercicios aeróbicos	1998
el Sr. Alvarado	llegar a los Estados Unidos	1999

1. ...   2. ...   3. ...   4. ...   5. ...

B. Cosas de todos los días: Recuerdos. Practice talking about your friend Benito, using the written cues. When you hear the corresponding number, form sentences using the words provided in the order given, making any necessary changes or additions. ¡ojo! You will be using the preterite or the imperfect forms of the verbs.

> MODELO: (*you see*) 1. de niño / Benito / ser / muy torpe   (*you hear*) uno →
> (*you say*) De niño, Benito *era* muy torpe.

2. (él) lastimarse / con frecuencia
3. Benito / también / ser / muy distraído
4. frecuentemente / (él) olvidarse de / poner / despertador
5. casi siempre / quedársele / en casa / tarea
6. muchas veces / perdérsele / llaves
7. una vez / (él) caerse / y / romperse / brazo
8. el médico / ponerle / yeso (*cast*)

CAPÍTULO **12**

VOCABULARIO Preparación

A. Hablando de «cositas» (*"a few small things"*). You will hear a brief dialogue between two friends, Lidia and Daniel. Listen carefully and circle the items that are mentioned in their conversation. Don't be distracted by unfamiliar vocabulary. First, pause and look at the drawing.

B. Definiciones. You will hear a series of statements. Each will be said twice. Circle the letter of the word that is defined by each.

1. a. la videocasetera   b. el Walkman
2. a. el inquilino   b. el alquiler
3. a. la vecindad   b. la vecina
4. a. la jefa   b. el sueldo
5. a. el contestador automático   b. la motocicleta
6. a. el control remoto   b. la grabadora
7. a. el primer piso   b. la planta baja

C. Identificaciones. Identify the following items when you hear the corresponding number. Begin each sentence with **Es un…** or **Es una…** .

1. …   2. …   3. …   4. …   5. …

■■■Los hispanos hablan: Quiero...

Paso 1. Listen to Diana, José, and Karen describe what they want. As you listen to their descriptions, check the appropriate boxes. First, listen to the list of objects.

	DIANA	JOSÉ	KAREN		DIANA	JOSÉ	KAREN
ropa	☐	☐	☐	un radio portátil	☐	☐	☐
un estéreo	☐	☐	☐	un gran trabajo	☐	☐	☐
cosméticos	☐	☐	☐	un boleto de avión	☐	☐	☐
discos compactos	☐	☐	☐	una grabadora	☐	☐	☐
una guitarra	☐	☐	☐	una batería (*drum set*)	☐	☐	☐
aretes	☐	☐	☐	un ordenador	☐	☐	☐
un auto	☐	☐	☐	una bicicleta	☐	☐	☐

Paso 2. Now, pause and answer the following questions about the descriptions and the chart you completed in **Paso 1.** Check your answers to **Paso 1** in the Appendix before you begin **Paso 2.**

1. De las tres personas, ¿quién quiere más cosas?

   _____

2. De las tres personas, ¿quién quiere viajar?

   _____

3. ¿Qué cosas desea más de una persona?

   _____

Now resume listening.

PRONUNCIACIÓN Y ORTOGRAFÍA *y and ll*

A. El sonido [y]. At the beginning of a word or syllable, the Spanish sound [y] is pronounced somewhat like the letter *y* in English *yo-yo* or *papaya*. However, there is no exact English equivalent for this sound. In addition, there are variants of the sound, depending on the country of origin of the speaker.

Listen to these diferences.

el Caribe:	Yolanda lleva una blusa amarilla. Yo no.
España:	Yolanda lleva una blusa amarilla. Yo no.
la Argentina:	Yolanda lleva una blusa amarilla. Yo no.

B. El sonido [ly]. Although **y** and **ll** are pronounced exactly the same by most Spanish speakers, in some regions of Spain **ll** is pronounced like the [ly] sound in *million*, except that it is one single sound.

Listen to these differences.

España: Guillermo es de Castilla.

Sudamérica: Guillermo es de Castilla.

C. Repeticiones. Repeat the following words, imitating the speaker.

1. llamo llueve yogurt yate (*yacht*) yanqui yoga
2. ellas tortilla millón mayo destruyo (*I destroy*) tuyo (*yours*)

D. ¿Ll o l? You will hear a series of words. Each will be said twice. Circle the letter used to spell each.

1. ll l 2. ll l 3. ll l 4. ll l 5. ll l 6. ll l

E. Repaso: ñ, l, ll, y: Dictado. You will hear three sentences. Each will be said twice. Write what you hear.

1. _____
2. _____
3. _____

GRAMÁTICA

36. Influencing Others • *Tú* Commands

A. Minidiálogo: «¡Marta, tu cuarto es un desastre!» You will hear a brief paragraph in which Manolo complains to his daughter Marta about her room. Then you will hear a series of statements. Circle the letter of the person who might have made each statement.

1. a. Manolo b. Marta
2. a. Manolo b. Marta
3. a. Manolo b. Marta
4. a. Manolo b. Marta

B. Encuesta: ¿Qué le decían sus padres? You will hear a series of commands that your parents may or may not have given to you when you were a child. For each command, check the appropriate answer. No answers will be given. The answers you choose should be correct for you!

Mandatos afirmativos

1. ☐ Sí ☐ No   3. ☐ Sí ☐ No

2. ☐ Sí ☐ No   4. ☐ Sí ☐ No

Mandatos negativos

5. ☐ Sí ☐ No   7. ☐ Sí ☐ No

6. ☐ Sí ☐ No   8. ☐ Sí ☐ No

C. La vida doméstica de la Cenicienta (*Cinderella*). Play the role of the stepmother and tell Cinderella what she has to do before she can go to the ball. Use affirmative informal commands for the infinitives you will hear.

1. ... 2. ... 3. ... 4. ... 5. ...

D. ¡No lo hagas! Imagine that you are a parent of the child depicted in the drawings. When you hear the corresponding number, tell her *not* to do the things she is doing in each drawing. Use negative informal commands. You will hear a possible answer.

MODELO: (*you hear*) uno   (*you see*) 1. pegar / Isabel →
(*you say*) No le pegues a Isabel.

1. pegar / Isabel

2. saltar (*to jump*) / cama

3. poner / mesa

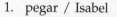

4. pasear / calle

5. jugar / tantos videojuegos

6. escribir / pared

37. Expressing Subjective Actions or States • Present Subjunctive: An Introduction

A. Minidiálogo: Una decisión importante. You will hear a dialogue in which José Miguel asks Gustavo for advice on purchasing a computer. Then you will hear a series of statements about the dialogue. Circle **C, F,** or **ND** (**No lo dice**).

1. C F ND

2. C F ND

3. C F ND

4. C F ND

5. C F ND

B. Encuesta: Hablando de la tecnología. You will hear a series of statements about technology. For each statement, check the appropriate answer. No answers will be given. The answers you choose should be correct for you!

1. ☐ Sí   ☐ No   ☐ No tengo opinión.

2. ☐ Sí   ☐ No   ☐ No tengo opinión.

3. ☐ Sí   ☐ No   ☐ No tengo opinión.

4. ☐ Sí   ☐ No   ☐ No tengo opinión.

5. ☐ Sí   ☐ No   ☐ No tengo opinión.

6. ☐ Sí   ☐ No   ☐ No tengo opinión.

C. ¿Qué quiere Arturo?

Paso 1. You will hear Arturo talk about what he wants his siblings to do. Listen to what he says, and complete the following chart by checking the thing he wants each sibling to do or not to do.

PERSONA	NO JUGAR «NINTENDO»	NO USAR SU COCHE	PRESTARLE SU CÁMARA	BAJAR EL VOLUMEN DEL ESTÉREO
su hermana				
su hermano menor				
sus hermanitos				

Paso 2. Now answer the questions you hear, based on the completed chart. Each question will be said twice. Check the answers to **Paso 1** in the Appendix before you begin **Paso 2.**

1. ...   2. ...   3. ...   4. ...

D. ¿Qué quieren? Answer the following questions using the oral cues.

1. ¿Qué quiere la jefa?

   MODELO: (*you hear*) Sara → (*you say*) Quiere que Sara llegue a tiempo.

   a. ...   b. ...   c. ...   d. ...

2. ¿Qué quieres que haga Juan?

   MODELO: (*you hear*) comer ahora → (*you say*) Quiero que Juan coma ahora.

   a. ...   b. ...   c. ...   d. ...

38. Expressing Desires and Requests • Use of the Subjunctive: Influence

A. Presiones de la vida moderna

Paso 1. You will hear a brief paragraph in which Margarita describes her job and what she doesn't like about it. Listen carefully and take notes on a separate sheet of paper.

Paso 2. ¿Qué recuerda Ud.? Now pause and complete the following sentences based on the passage and your notes. Use phrases from the list. Be sure to use the correct present subjunctive form of the verbs. (Check your answers in the Appendix.)

equivocarse	tener teléfono celular
ser más flexible	trabajar los fines de semana
solucionar sus problemas	

1. Los clientes quieren que Margarita _____ técnicos.

2. Su jefa no quiere que ella _____.

3. Margarita quiere que su horario _____.

4. A veces, es necesario que Margarita _____.

5. Margarita prefiere que su coche no _____.

Now resume listening.

B. ¿Qué recomienda el nuevo jefe? Imagine that you have a new boss in your office, and he is determined to make some changes. When you hear the corresponding numbers, tell what he recommends, using the written cues.

MODELO: (*you hear*) uno   (*you see*) 1. El jefe recomienda... Ud. / buscar otro trabajo →
(*you say*) El jefe recomienda que Ud. busque otro trabajo.

2. El jefe recomienda... yo / copiar el contrato
3. El jefe insiste en... todos / trabajar hasta muy tarde
4. El jefe prohíbe... Federico / dormir en la oficina
5. El jefe sugiere... tú / aprender a manejar tu computadora

C. Antes del viaje: ¿Qué quiere Ud. que hagan estas personas? Imagine that you are a tour leader traveling with a large group of students. Using the oral and written cues, tell each person what you want him or her to do. Begin each sentence with **Quiero que...**, as in the model.

MODELO: (*you hear*) hacer las maletas   (*you see*) Uds. →
(*you say*) Quiero que Uds. hagan las maletas.

1. Toño   2. (tú)   3. Ana y Teresa   4. todos   5. todos

UN POCO DE TODO | (Para entregar)

A. Descripción: Una familia de la era de la tecnología

Paso 1. You will hear five brief descriptions. Write the letter of each description next to the drawing that it describes. ¡OJO! Not all the drawings will be described. First, pause and look at the drawings.

1. _____   2. _____   3. _____

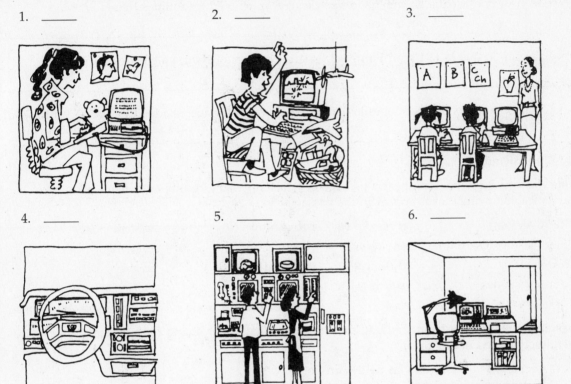

4. _____   5. _____   6. _____

Paso 2. Now pause and write a description of the drawing for which there was no match.

_____

_____

_____

_____

_____

Now resume listening.

B. *Listening Passage:* **Recuerdos de España**

Antes de escuchar. Pause and do the following prelistening exercises.

Answer these questions about Spain to see how much you already know about this European country.

1. ¿Cómo piensa Ud. que es el nivel de vida (*standard of living*) en España?

    _____

2. ¿Cree Ud. que España ha cambiado (*has changed*) mucho en los últimos treinta años?

    _____

3. ¿Sabe Ud. lo que es la Unión Europea? España pertenece (*belongs*) a ella desde 1986.

    _____

4. ¿Cuántas semanas de vacaciones le dan al año si trabaja en los Estados Unidos? ¿Y en España?

    _____

Now resume listening.

Listening Passage. Now you will hear a passage in which a person from Spain tells us about his homeland. The following words appear in the passage.

a finales de	*at the end of*	occidental	*western*
en vías de desarrollo	*developing*	con eficacia	*efficiently*
a nivel	*at the level*	los medios	*means*
las cuestiones	*matters*	el ascenso	*promotion*
incluso	*even*	me he americanizado	*I have become Americanized*

Después de escuchar. Pause and check all the statements that, according to the speaker of the passage, describe present-day Spain.

1. ☐ España es un país en vías de desarrollo.

2. ☐ El nivel de vida en las ciudades grandes es bueno.

3. ☐ A los españoles no les gusta trabajar.

4. ☐ Es normal que los españoles tengan cuatro semanas de vacaciones al año.

5. ☐ Las universidades españolas tienen un mejor sistema de bibliotecas que las norteamericanas.

6. ☐ España es un país moderno y desarrollado.

7. ☐ La Unión Europea ha beneficiado (*has benefitted*) a España.

Now resume listening.

C. Y para terminar… Entrevista. You will hear a series of questions. Each will be said twice. Answer, based on your own experience. Pause and write the answers.

1. _____

2. _____

3. _____

4. _____

5. _____

6. _____

VIDEOTECA   Minidramas*

Paso 1. Buscando una computadora. In the following conversation, José Miguel and Gustavo talk to a salesperson about computers. Listen and read along with the speakers.

VENDEDORA: Buenas tardes. ¿En qué les puedo atender?

JOSÉ MIGUEL: Buenas tardes. Leímos su anuncio en el periódico. Quisiéramos ver las computadoras.

VENDEDORA: ¿Qué modelo buscan? Tenemos varios aquí. Este es nuevo. Viene con monitor, ratón ergonómico y un módem interno.

JOSÉ MIGUEL: Pero, no tiene lector de CD-ROM interno, ¿verdad? Prefiero uno que lo tenga.

VENDEDORA: Ese modelo allí tiene lector de CD-ROM interno. Venga. Esta es la mejor de las que tienen CD-ROM.

JOSÉ MIGUEL: ¿Qué te parece, Gustavo?

GUSTAVO: No está mal… ¿Tiene suficiente memoria para navegar por el *Internet*?

VENDEDORA: Sí.

GUSTAVO: ¿Y se puede utilizar también un *browser* de páginas o programas de multimedia?

VENDEDORA: Este modelo es ideal para multimedia. Y lleva incluidos los programas necesarios para navegar la red.

JOSÉ MIGUEL: Ah, muy bien, porque pienso utilizar el *Internet* para ayudarme con mis trabajos en la universidad…

---

*This **Minidramas** videoclip is available on the Video on CD to accompany *Puntos de partida* Seventh Edition.

Paso 2. Aplicación. In the preceding conversation, José Miguel and Gustavo were shopping for a computer. It is also important to know how to arrange for repairs once you've bought one! Complete the following dialogue using the written cues. You will play the role of the client. Here are the cues for your conversation. ¡OJO! The cues are not in order.

> va a estar lista (*ready*)
>
> muy buenas
>
> mi computadora no funciona
>
> es una marca (*brand*) nacional

DEPENDIENTE: Buenas tardes. ¿En qué puedo servirle?

CLIENTE: _____¹. _____².

DEPENDIENTE: ¿La compró Ud. aquí?

CLIENTE: No, pero _____³.

DEPENDIENTE: En ese caso no hay problema. Se la arreglamos en seguida.

CLIENTE: Muchas gracias. ¿Cuándo _____⁴?

DEPENDIENTE: Dentro de (*Within*) dos días.

PRUEBA CORTA

A. Una oficina con problemas. You are the boss of a large office with an unruly staff that is on the verge of a strike. You will hear what they do not want to do. Tell them what you would like them to do, using the written and oral cues.

> MODELO: (*you hear*) No queremos mandar los documentos.   (*you see*) querer →
> (*you say*) Pues, yo quiero que Uds. los manden.

1. recomendar
2. sugerir
3. querer
4. querer
5. mandar

B. Los mandatos de la niñera (*baby-sitter*). Imagine that you are Tito's baby-sitter. Tell him what to do or what not to do, using the oral cues. ¡OJO! You will be using **tú** commands in your sentences.

> MODELO: (*you hear*) sentarse en el sofá → (*you say*) Tito, siéntate en el sofá.

1. …   2. …   3. …   4. …   5. …   6. …

CAPÍTULO **13**

VOCABULARIO Preparación

A. Encuesta. You will hear a series of questions. Check the appropriate boxes. No answers will be given. The answers you choose should be correct for you!

1. ☐ Sí ☐ No 5. ☐ Sí ☐ No

2. ☐ Sí ☐ No 6. ☐ Sí ☐ No

3. ☐ Sí ☐ No 7. ☐ Sí ☐ No

4. ☐ Sí ☐ No 8. ☐ Sí ☐ No

B. Identificaciones. You will hear a series of words. Write the number of each word next to the item the word describes. First, pause and look at the drawings.

C. Definiciones. You will hear a series of definitions. Each will be said twice. Circle the letter of the word that is defined by each.

1. a. el bailarín   b. el cantante   4. a. la escultora   b. el dramaturgo
2. a. la arquitecta   b. la aficionada   5. a. la compositora   b. el guía
3. a. el músico   b. la ópera   6. a. el poeta   b. el artista

D. Descripción: ¿En qué piso? You will be asked to tell on what floor a number of families live or on which floor businesses are located. Each question will be said twice. Answer, based on the following drawing. First, pause and look at the drawing.

1. ...
2. ...
3. ...
4. ...
5. ...

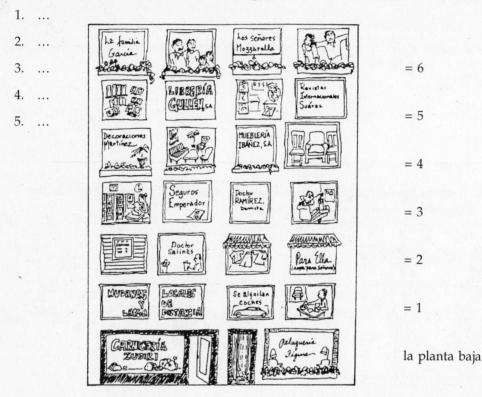

= 6

= 5

= 4

= 3

= 2

= 1

la planta baja

E. Poniendo las cosas en orden

Paso 1. You will hear a series of questions. Each will be said twice. Circle the correct answer.

1. febrero   enero   junio   abril

2. julio   agosto   octubre   diciembre

3. lunes   jueves   sábado   martes

4. Michael Jordan   Rosie O'Donnell   Neil Armstrong   Antonio Banderas

Paso 2. Now pause and write a sentence, using ordinal numbers, about each of the answers you circled. Number four is done for you.

1. _____

2. _____

3. _____

4.   *La primera persona que caminó en la luna fue Neil Armstrong.* _____

Now resume listening.

■■■Los hispanos hablan: Dinos algo acerca de la ciudad donde vives

Paso 1. First, pause and check the statements that are true for the city or town in which you live. ·

1. ☐ Muchas personas viven en el centro de la ciudad.

2. ☐ Hay muchas partes antiguas (*old*).

3. ☐ La mayoría de los teatros, museos, tiendas, etcétera, se encuentran en el centro.

4. ☐ Es normal que la gente esté en las calles hasta muy tarde.

5. ☐ Hay metro (*subway*).

6. ☐ Hay mucha vida cultural.

7. ☐ Es normal que la gente camine en vez de (*instead of*) usar el coche.

Now resume listening.

Paso 2. Pause and check the statements that are true, according to the passage.

1. ☐ Clara nació en Madrid.

2. ☐ Madrid es una ciudad cosmopolita.

3. ☐ Si uno vive en Madrid, es absolutamente necesario tener coche.

4. ☐ En Madrid, es normal que la gente esté en las calles hasta muy tarde.

5. ☐ Es común que mucha gente viva en el centro de la ciudad.

6. ☐ La mayoría de las actividades culturales se encuentran en el centro.

Now resume listening.

PRONUNCIACIÓN Y ORTOGRAFÍA *x* and *n*

A. La letra *x*. The letter **x** is usually pronounced [ks], as in English. Before a consonant, however, it is often pronounced [s]. Repeat the following words, imitating the speaker.

1. [ks]   léxico   sexo   axial   existen   examen
2. [s]   explican   extraordinario   extremo   sexto   extraterrestre

Read the following sentences when you hear the corresponding numbers. Repeat the correct pronunciation.

3. ¿Piensas que existen los extraterrestres?
4. ¡Nos explican que es algo extraordinario!
5. No me gustan las temperaturas extremas.
6. La medicina no es una ciencia exacta.

B. La letra *n*. Before the letters **p, b, v,** and **m,** the letter **n** is pronounced [m]. Before the sounds [k], [g], and [x], **n** is pronounced like the [ng] sound in the English word *sing.* In all other positions, **n** is pronounced as it is in English. Repeat the following words and phrases, imitating the speaker.

1. [m]   convence   un beso   un peso   con Manuel   con Pablo
           en Venezuela

2. [ng]   encontrar   conjugar   son generosos   en Quito   en Granada
           con Juan

Read the following phrases and sentences when you hear the corresponding numbers. Repeat the correct pronunciation.

3. en Perú
4. son jóvenes
5. con Gloria
6. en México
7. En general, sus poemas son buenos.
8. Los museos están en Caracas.

GRAMÁTICA

39. Expressing Feelings • Use of the Subjunctive: Emotion

A. Minidiálogo: Diego y Lupe escuchan un grupo de mariachis.
You will hear a dialogue in which Diego and Lupe discuss mariachi music. Then you will hear a series of statements. Circle the letter of the person who might have made each statement.

1. a. Lupe   b. Diego   3. a. Lupe   b. Diego
2. a. Lupe   b. Diego   4. a. Lupe   b. Diego

B. El día de la función (*show*). Tell how the following people feel, using the oral and written cues.

> MODELO: (*you hear*) el director (*you see*) temer que / los actores / olvidar sus líneas →
> (*you say*) El director teme que los actores olviden sus líneas.

1. esperar que / los actores / no enfermarse
2. temer que / la actriz / estar muy nerviosa
3. temer que / los otros actores / no llegar a tiempo
4. esperar que / la obra / ser buena
5. tener miedo de que / la obra / ser muy larga

C. Descripción: Esperanzas (*Hopes*) **y temores** (*fears*). You will hear two questions about each drawing. Answer, based on the drawings and the written cues.

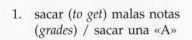

1. sacar (*to get*) malas notas (*grades*) / sacar una «A»

2. funcionar su computadora / no funcionar su computadora

3. haber regalos para él / no haber nada para él

40. Expressing Uncertainty • Use of the Subjunctive: Doubt and Denial

A. ¿Cierto o falso?

Paso 1. Encuesta. You will hear a series of statements. Tell whether each statement is true or false. Answer, based on your own experience. No answers will be given. The answers you give should be correct for you!

1. ☐ No es cierto que me encante.   ☐ Es cierto que me encanta.

2. ☐ No es cierto que lo tenga.   ☐ Es cierto que lo tengo.

3. ☐ No es cierto que lo prefiera.   ☐ Es cierto que lo prefiero.

4. ☐ No es cierto que conozca a uno.   ☐ Es cierto que conozco a uno.

5. ☐ No es cierto que sea aficionado/a.   ☐ Es cierto que soy aficionado/a.

Paso 2. Para completar. Now pause and complete the following sentences based on your own preferences.

1. Es cierto que me encanta(n) _____.

2. No es cierto que me encante(n) _____.

3. Es cierto que tengo _____.

4. No es cierto que tenga _____.

5. Es cierto que soy aficionado/a al / a la _____.

6. No es cierto que sea aficionado/a al / a la _____.

Now resume listening.

B. ¿Qué piensa Ud.? Imagine that your friend Josefina has made a series of statements. Respond to each, using the written cues. You will hear each one twice. ¡OJO! You will have to use the indicative in some cases.

> MODELO: (*you hear*) Anita va al teatro esta noche.   (*you see*) No creo que… →
> (*you say*) No creo que Anita vaya al teatro esta noche.

1. No creo que…
2. Dudo que…
3. Es imposible que…
4. Es verdad que…
5. Estoy seguro/a de que…

C. Observaciones. You will hear a series of statements about the following drawings. Each will be said twice. React to each statement, according to the model. Begin each answer with **Es verdad que…** or **No es verdad que… .**

> MODELO: (*you hear*) Amalia tiene un auto nuevo. →
> (*you say*) No es verdad que Amalia tenga un auto nuevo.

1.

2.

3.

4.

5.

41. Expressing Influence, Emotion, Doubt, and Denial • The Subjunctive: A Summary

A. Minidiálogo: Lola Benítez les habla a sus estudiantes norteamericanos. You will hear a brief paragraph in which Lola Benítez asks her students to write a composition about the art of Sevilla. Then you will hear a series of statements about the passage. Circle **C, F,** or **ND** (**No lo dice**).

1. C F ND

2. C F ND

3. C F ND

4. C F ND

5. C F ND

B. Se venden coches nuevos y usados. You will hear three ads for automobiles. Listen and complete the following sentences by writing the number of the ad in the appropriate space. First, pause and read the incomplete statements.

a. Dudo que el coche del anuncio número _____ sea una ganga.

b. El auto del anuncio número _____ es un auto pequeño y económico.

c. Es probable que el coche del anuncio número _____ gaste mucha gasolina.

Now resume listening.

C. ¿Qué quiere Ud. que hagan estas personas? You will hear a series of questions. Answer, using an appropriate written cue.

MODELO: (*you hear*) ¿Qué quiere Ud. que haga el profesor? →
(*you say*) Quiero que no nos dé un examen.

explicarme las obras de arte

mostrarme el lector de DVD

no darnos un examen

tomarme la temperatura

traerme la ensalada

1. ...   2. ...   3. ...   4. ...

A. En un museo. You will hear a dialogue in which a museum guide explains Pablo Picasso's famous painting, *Guernica,* to some visitors. You will also hear two of the visitors' reactions to the painting. Then you will hear a series of statements. Circle **C, F,** or **ND** (**No lo dice**).

1. C F ND   2. C F ND   3. C F ND   4. C F ND

B. *Listening Passage:* **Primeras impresiones**

Antes de escuchar. You will hear a passage in which a person who is now living in this country tells about her first impressions of people in the United States. The following words and phrases appear in the passage.

las amistades	los amigos	echo de menos	*I miss*
aumentó	*increased*	el pueblo	*people*
judía	*Jewish*	demuestra	*shows*
para que yo pudiera	*so that I could*	nos besamos	*we kiss each other*
maravillosa	*marvelous, wonderful*	(nos) abrazamos	*we hug (each other)*
para que yo tuviera	*so that I would have*		

Listening Passage. Here is the passage. First, listen to it to get a general idea of the content. Then go back and listen again for specific information.

Después de escuchar. Circle the best answer to each of the following questions. ¡OJO! There may be more than one answer for some items.

1. Es probable que la persona que habla sea de…
   a. España.   b. los Estados Unidos.   c. Latinoamérica.   d. Nueva York.
2. Al principio (*beginning*), esta persona pensaba que los estadounidenses eran…
   a. abiertos.   b. perezosos.   c. fríos.   d. contentos.
3. La amiga que invitó a esta persona a su casa era…
   a. protestante.   b. judía.   c. ateísta.   d. católica.
4. Antes de visitar a la familia de Abi, la narradora…
   a. no conocía Nueva York.
   b. compró regalos.
   c. pasaba la Navidad con su familia.
   d. no sabía mucho de las tradiciones judías.
5. La familia de Abi no entendía…
   a. español.
   b. la tradición de Navidad.
   c. por qué se dan regalos el seis de enero.
   d. por qué la narradora no tenía muchos amigos.
6. Ahora, la estudiante hispánica piensa que…
   a. los estadounidenses son gente fría.
   b. los estadounidenses no se besan lo suficiente.
   c. los estadounidenses no saben nada de las tradiciones hispánicas.
   d. los estadounidenses demuestran el cariño de una manera distinta de la de los hispanos.

Now resume listening.

C. Y para terminar... Entrevista. You will hear a series of questions. Each will be said twice. Answer, based on your own experience. Pause and write the answers.

1. _____

2. _____

3. _____

4. _____

5. _____

6. _____

VIDEOTECA   Minidramas*

Paso 1. Hablando del arte. In this conversation, Diego and Lupe are talking about art preferences. Listen and read along with the speakers.

DIEGO: ¿Ya sabes sobre qué vas a escribir tu trabajo para la clase de arte?

LUPE: Creo que sí. Me interesan mucho el arte y la vida de Frida Kahlo, así que voy a escribir algo sobre ella.

DIEGO: Kahlo pintó muchos autorretratos, ¿no?

LUPE: Sí, y sus autorretratos siempre tienen elementos simbólicos que representan sus emociones y su estado de ánimo. Sus cuadros me gustan muchísimo. Su esposo fue Diego Rivera, uno de los muralistas más famosos de México. Mira. Aquí ves uno de sus cuadros.

DIEGO: Conozco varios murales de Rivera. Los vi en el Palacio Nacional. Pero a mí me impresionan más los murales de José Clemente Orozco.

LUPE: Sí, Orozco fue un muralista excelente. Mira. Aquí ves uno de sus cuadros.

DIEGO: Así que vas a escribir sobre Frida Kahlo. ¿Qué más te interesa sobre ella?

LUPE: Bueno, me interesa mucho su arte, claro. Pero también me interesa porque llevó una vida muy difícil. Sufrió mucho, pero nunca dejó de apreciar la belleza de vivir...

Paso 2. Aplicación. Now you will participate in a similar conversation, partially printed in your manual, in which you play the role of **Ud.** Complete it using the written cues. You will need to conjugate the verbs. Here are the cues for your conversation. ¡OJO! The cues are not in order.

> haber entradas
>
> ir (nosotros) a un concierto de música clásica
>
> ser más emocionante

SU AMIGA: ¿Qué tal si vamos a un concierto este fin de semana? Hace tiempo que no vamos.

UD.: Está bien, pero esta vez prefiero que _____.[1]

SU AMIGA: Bueno, si insistes. Pero, ¿por qué te gusta tanto ese tipo de música?

UD.: Me gusta porque creo que _____.[2]

SU AMIGA: Bueno, hay un concierto de Beethoven el sábado a las ocho. ¿Qué te parece?

UD.: ¡Perfecto! Ojalá que todavía _____.[3]

---

*This **Minidramas** video clip is available on the Video on CD to accompany *Puntos de partida* Seventh Edition.

A. Apuntes. You will hear a brief paragraph that tells about a new museum that is opening soon. Listen carefully and, while listening, write the information requested. Write all numbers as numerals. First, listen to the requested information. (Check your answers in the Appendix.)

El nombre del museo: _____

El tipo de arte que se va a exhibir: _____

La fecha en que se va a abrir el museo: _____

El nombre del director del museo: _____

La hora de la recepción: _____

¿Es necesario hacer reservaciones? _____

¿Va a ser posible hablar con algunos de los artistas? _____

B. Cosas de todos los días: Se buscan bailarines. Practice talking about dance director Joaquín Cortés's search for new dancers for his dance troupe, using the written cues. When you hear the corresponding number, form sentences using the words provided in the order given, making any necessary changes or additions. ¡OJO! You will need to make changes to adjectives and add articles, if appropriate.

> MODELO: (*you see*) 1. Joaquín / insitir en / que / bailarines (*dancers*) / tener / mucho / experiencia
> (*you hear*) uno →
> (*you say*) Joaquín *insiste* en que *los* bailarines *tengan mucha* experiencia.

2. él / querer / que / bailarines / ser / atlético
3. también / ser/ necesario / que / (ellos) saber / cantar / música / flamenco
4. es cierto / que / Joaquín / ser / muy / exigente
5. Joaquín / temer / que / no / poder / encontrarlos / pronto
6. ¡ojalá / que / bailarines / desempeñar / bien / papeles!

CAPÍTULO **14**

VOCABULARIO Preparación

A. ¿Qué opina sobre el medio ambiente? You will hear a series of statements about environmental concerns. Express your opinion about the issues by checking the appropriate boxes. No answers will be given. The answers you choose should be correct for you!

	SÍ ENFÁTICO	SÍ	NO TENGO OPINIÓN	NO	NO ENFÁTICO
1.	☐	☐	☐	☐	☐
2.	☐	☐	☐	☐	☐
3.	☐	☐	☐	☐	☐
4.	☐	☐	☐	☐	☐
5.	☐	☐	☐	☐	☐
6.	☐	☐	☐	☐	☐

B. Los animales

Paso 1. Descripción. Identify the following animals when you hear the corresponding number. Begin each sentence with **Es un...**, **Es una...**, or **Son...** .

1.

2.

3.

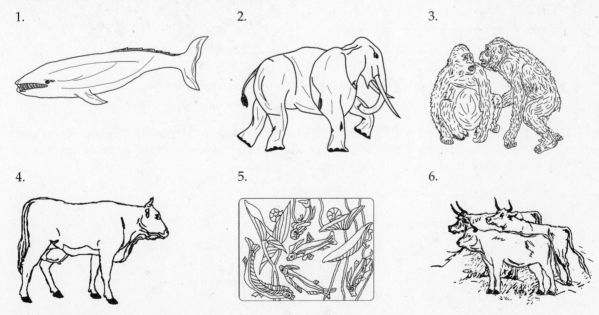

4.

5.

6.

Paso 2. Preguntas. You will hear a series of questions. Each will be said twice. Answer using the animals depicted in the drawings in **Paso 1.**

1. ... 2. ... 3. ... 4. ...

C. Definiciones: Hablando de coches. You will hear a series of statements. Each will be said twice. Circle the letter of the word that is best defined by each.

1. a. la batería   b. la gasolina   c. la licencia

2. a. la licencia   b. el camino   c. el taller

3. a. el parabrisas   b. los frenos   c. el semáforo

4. a. la esquina   b. la carretera   c. la llanta

5. a. el accidente   b. el aceite   c. el taller

D. Un accidente

Paso 1. Identify the following items when you hear the corresponding number. Begin each sentence with **Es un...**, **Es una...**, or **Son...**.

Paso 2. Now you will hear a series of statements about the preceding drawing. Circle **C** or **F**.

1. C F   2. C F   3. C F   4. C F   5. C F   6. C F

E. Gustos y preferencias. You will hear descriptions of two people, Nicolás and Susana. Then you will hear a series of statements. Write the number of each statement next to the name of the person who might have made it.

Nicolás: _____

Susana: _____

■■■Los hispanos hablan: En tu opinión, ¿cuáles son las semejanzas y diferencias más grandes entre las ciudades hispánicas y las norteamericanas?

You will hear excerpts from several answers to this question. After you listen, pause and check the appropriate boxes to describe Hispanic and U.S. cities. The following words and phrases appear in the answers.

recorrer un gran trecho	*to travel a great distance*
no hace falta	*no es necesario*
las fuentes	*fountains*
como no sea	*unless it is* (*unless we are talking about*)
a la par de	*al lado de*
seguro	*safe*

	LAS CIUDADES HISPÁNICAS	LAS CIUDADES NORTEAMERICANAS
1. Son muy grandes.	☐	☐
2. Están contaminadas.	☐	☐
3. Tienen más vida.	☐	☐
4. Son menos seguras.	☐	☐
5. La gente vive en la ciudad misma (*proper*).	☐	☐
6. Las tiendas están en las vecindades.	☐	☐
7. Hay más árboles, vegetación y parques.	☐	☐

Now resume listening.

PRONUNCIACIÓN Y ORTOGRAFÍA   More Cognate Practice

A. Repeticiones. You were introduced to cognates in the **Ante todo** sections of *Puntos de partida*. As you know, English and Spanish cognates do not always share the same pronunciation or spelling. Listen to the following pairs of cognates, paying close attention to the differences in spelling and pronunciation.

chemical / químico   affirm / afirmar   national / nacional

Read the following cognates when you hear the corresponding number. Remember to repeat the correct pronunciation.

1. correcto
2. anual
3. teoría
4. alianza

5. físico
6. teléfono
7. patético
8. intención

B. Dictado. You will hear the following words. Each will be said twice. Listen carefully and write the missing letters.

1. _____os_____ato

2. a_____ención

3. a_____oníaco

4. _____eología

5. o_____osición

6. _____otogra_____ía

7. co_____e_____ión

8. ar_____itecta

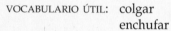

GRAMÁTICA

42. Más descripciones • Past Participle Used as an Adjective

A. Descripción. Which picture is best described by the sentences you hear? You will hear each sentence twice.

VOCABULARIO ÚTIL: colgar   *to hang up*
enchufar   *to plug in*

1. a.   b.

2. a.   b.

3. a.   b.

4. a.

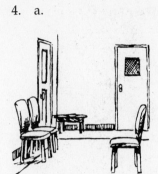

b.

5. a.

b.

6. a.

b.

B. Definiciones. You will hear a series of definitions. Each will be said twice. Circle the answer that best matches each definition. ¡OJO! There may be more than one answer for some items.

1. a. el agua   b. el aire   c. la batería

2. a. Stephen King   b. Descartes   c. John Grisham

3. a. la mano   b. los ojos   c. la ventana

4. a. el papel   b. el pie   c. la computadora

C. Consecuencias lógicas. You will hear a series of sentences that describe actions. Respond to each sentence, telling the probable outcome of the action.

MODELO: (*you hear*) Escribí la composición. → (*you say*) Ahora la composición está escrita.

1. ...   2. ...   3. ...   4. ...   5. ...

43. ¿Qué has hecho? • Perfect Forms: Present Perfect Indicative and Present Perfect Subjunctive

A. Minidiálogo: Una llanta desinflada. You will hear a dialogue in which Lola and Manolo experience car trouble. Then you will hear a series of statements. Circle **C**, **F**, or **ND** (**No lo dice**).

1. C F ND

2. C F ND

3. C F ND

4. C F ND

5. C F ND

B. ¿Qué ha pasado ya? You will hear a series of sentences. Each will be said twice. Circle the letter of the subject of the verb in each sentence.

1. a. yo   b. ella

2. a. él   b. nosotros

3. a. nosotros   b. tú

4. a. nosotros   b. yo

5. a. ellos   b. él

C. ¿Qué hemos hecho hoy? Form new sentences, using the oral and written cues. Use the present perfect indicative of the verbs.

1. despertarse
2. hacer las camas
3. vestirse
4. desayunar
5. salir para la oficina
6. llevar el auto a la gasolinera

D. ¿Te puedo ayudar? Imagine that you have a lot to do before a dinner party, and your friend Ernesto wants to know if he can help. You appreciate his offer, but you have already done the things he asks about. You will hear each of his questions twice. Answer them according to the model.

> MODELO: (*you hear*) ¿Quieres que llame a los Sres. Moreno? →
> (*you say*) No, gracias, ya los he llamado.

1. ... 2. ... 3. ... 4. ... 5. ...

E. Un caso de contaminación ambiental. Imagine that a case of environmental pollution was discovered earlier this year in your community. Using the oral and written cues, form sentences that express what the residents have said about the incident. Follow the model.

> MODELO: (*you see*) ya estudiar el problema (*you hear*) es probable →
> (*you say*) Es probable que ya hayan estudiado el problema.

1. todavía no avisar (*to notify*) a todos los habitantes de la ciudad
2. ya consultar con los expertos
3. encontrar la solución todavía
4. proteger los animales de la zona

UN POCO DE TODO | (Para entregar)

A. Descripciones. You will hear a series of descriptions. Each will be said twice. Write the number of each description next to the drawing described. ¡OJO! There is one extra drawing. First, pause and look at the drawings.

a. _____

b. _____

c. _____

d. _____

e. _____

B. *Listening Passage:* **Los coches**

Antes de escuchar. You will hear a passage about the types of cars driven in the Hispanic world. The following words appear in the passage.

la molestia	*bother*
la ayuda	*something helpful*
la clase media-baja	*lower middle class*

Listening Passage. Here is the passage. First, listen to it to get a general idea of the content. Then go back and listen again for specific information.

Después de escuchar. Read the following statements. Circle **C** or **F.** Correct the statements that are false, according to the passage.

1. C   F   Las personas que viven en los países hispanos no están acostumbradas a conducir.

   _____

2. C   F   Hay muchos autos japoneses y estadounidenses en España.

   _____

3. C   F   No se venden marcas europeas en Latinoamérica.

   _____

4. C   F   El precio de la gasolina es comparable en España y en los Estados Unidos.

   _____

5. C   F   En México, es posible encontrar marcas que ya no se fabrican en otras partes del mundo.

   _____

Now resume listening.

C. Y para terminar... Entrevista. You will hear a series of questions. Each will be said twice. Answer, based on your own experience. Pause and write the answers.

1. _____
2. _____
3. _____
4. _____
5. _____
6. _____
7. _____
8. _____

VIDEOTECA   Minidramas*

Paso 1. En busca de un taller. In the following conversation, Elisa and José Miguel help out a motorist in trouble. Listen and read along with the speakers.

CONDUCTORA: Buenos días. Disculpe, señora. ¿Podría decirme a cuánto queda el pueblo más cercano?

ELISA: Bueno, hay un pueblo no muy lejos de aquí, como a unos diez minutos. Pero es muy pequeño. ¿Qué busca?

CONDUCTORA: Es el carro. Temo que tenga algo serio. Ha comenzado a hacer un ruido muy extraño, y quiero que lo revise un mecánico. ¿Sabe Ud. si hay un taller en el pueblo?

ELISA: Ay, lo dudo mucho. Pero hay otro pueblo más grande no muy lejos, y es muy posible que haya un taller allí. Siga todo derecho unos cinco kilómetros, y luego doble a la izquierda en la carretera para Quito. ¿Sabe? Se me ocurre algo. Nosotros vamos en esa dirección. La podemos acompañar. No me gusta que se quede sola en este camino con un carro que no arranca.

CONDUCTORA: Eso es muy amable de su parte, pero no se molesten.

JOSÉ MIGUEL: De veras, no es ninguna molestia. Necesitamos encontrar una gasolinera. Tenemos que llenar el tanque.

CONDUCTORA: Muchas gracias. Uds. me han ayudado muchísimo.

ELISA: No hay de qué. ¿Vamos?

Paso 2. Aplicación. Now you will participate in a conversation, partially printed in your manual, in which you play the role of a motorist (**conductor**) who needs help. You are now at the repair shop. Complete it using the written cues. You will need to conjugate the verbs. Here are the cues for your conversation. ¡OJO! The cues are not in order.

muchísimas gracias	ser el motor	ser un auto nuevo
revisarle las llantas y los frenos	tener algo serio	haber comenzado

CONDUCTOR: Temo que mi auto _____.^{1} _____^{2} a hacer un ruido extraño.

MECÁNICO: Es posible que sea el motor.

CONDUCTOR: Dudo que _____^{3}... _____.^{4}

MECÁNICO: En ese caso, le recomiendo que lo deje aquí para poder revisarlo con cuidado.

CONDUCTOR: Está bien. También quiero que _____.^{5}

MECÁNICO: Por supuesto. Eso es parte de nuestro servicio normal. Puede venir a buscar su auto dentro de tres horas.

CONDUCTOR: _____.^{6}

---

*This **Minidramas** video clip is available on the Video on CD to accompany *Puntos de partida* Seventh Edition.

PRUEBA CORTA

A. **¿Por qué no... ?** The speaker will ask you why you don't do certain things. Answer her questions, following the model.

> MODELO: (*you hear*) ¿Por qué no resuelve Ud. ese problema? →
> (*you say*) Porque ya está resuelto.

1. ...   2. ...   3. ...   4. ...   5. ...

B. **Cosas de todos los días: El medioambiente.** Practice talking about what has happened recently, using the written cues. When you hear the corresponding number, form sentences using the words provided in the order given, making any necessary changes or additions. ¡OJO! You will need to make changes to adjectives and add articles, if appropriate.

> MODELO: (*you see*) 1. gobierno / construir / mucha / carreteras / nuevo   (*you hear*) uno →
> (*you say*) *El* gobierno *ha construido* muchas carreteras nuevas.

2. gobierno / tratar de / proteger / naturaleza
3. gobierno / no / resolver / problema / de / tránsito
4. alguno / compañías / desarrollar / energía / hidráulico
5. otro / compañías / descubrir / petróleo
6. público / no / conservar / energía

CAPÍTULO

15

VOCABULARIO Preparación

A. Encuesta: Hablando de las relaciones sentimentales. You will hear a series of statements about personal relationships. Express your opinion by checking the appropriate box. No answers will be given. The answers you choose should be correct for you!

1. ☐ Sí ☐ No
2. ☐ Sí ☐ No
3. ☐ Sí ☐ No
4. ☐ Sí ☐ No
5. ☐ Sí ☐ No

6. ☐ Sí ☐ No
7. ☐ Sí ☐ No
8. ☐ Sí ☐ No
9. ☐ Sí ☐ No
10. ☐ Sí ☐ No

B. Definiciones. You will hear a series of definitions. Each will be said twice. Circle the letter of the word defined. ¡OJO! There is more than one answer for some items.

1. a. la amistad
   b. el corazón
   c. el amor

2. a. una separación
   b. el divorcio
   c. una visita al consejero matrimonial

3. a. la luna de miel
   b. la cita
   c. la pareja

4. a. el noviazgo
   b. la boda
   c. la cita

5. a. la dueña
   b. la consejera
   c. la novia

C. Asociaciones. You will hear a series of phrases. Each will be said twice. Circle the letter of the word that you associate with each.

1. a. la infancia
   b. la niñez
   c. la adolescencia

2. a. la vejez
   b. la juventud
   c. el nacimiento

3. a. la madurez
   b. la adolescencia
   c. la infancia

4. a. la infancia
   b. la vejez
   c. la juventud

■■■Los hispanos hablan: Las relaciones sociales

As you might expect, social relations differ from country to country. You will hear Eduardo's impressions of the differences in social relations between the United States and his native country, Uruguay. The passage has been divided into two parts. Remember to concentrate on the vocabulary you know. Don't be distracted by unfamiliar vocabulary.

Paso 1. Before you listen to the passage, pause and indicate if the following statements are true for you. There are no right or wrong answers.

1. ☐ Sí   ☐ No   Me gusta que mis amigos vengan a visitarme sin avisar (*without letting me know ahead of time*).

2. ☐ Sí   ☐ No   Por lo general, mi vida social es espontánea; es decir, generalmente, no planeo todas mis actividades.

3. ☐ Sí   ☐ No   Participo en actividades sociales en las cuales (*in which*) hay personas de varias generaciones (niños, jóvenes, personas de mi edad, personas mayores o viejas).

4. ☐ Sí   ☐ No   Para mí, la vida privada (*privacy*) es algo importante.

5. ☐ Sí   ☐ No   Todavía vivo con mi familia.

Now resume listening.

La vida social: Parte 1. The following words appear in the first part of the passage.

extrañan	*they miss*
se dedica	*spend a lot of time on (something)*
sin avisar	*without letting one know ahead of time*
mal visto	*not looked upon favorably*

La vida social: Parte 2. The following words appear in the second part of the passage.

la vida privada	*privacy*
insólito	*unusual*

Paso 2. Now, pause and write a brief paragraph that summarizes how Eduardo feels about social relations in the United States. It may help to look back at the statements you read before listening to the passage.

Eduardo piensa que... _____

_____

_____

_____

_____

_____

_____

_____

Now resume listening.

PRONUNCIACIÓN Y ORTOGRAFÍA
More Cognate Practice

A. Amigos falsos. Unlike true cognates, false cognates do not have the same meaning in English as they do in Spanish. Repeat the following words, some of which you have already seen and used actively, paying close attention to their pronunciation and true meaning in Spanish.

la carta (*letter*)

dime (*tell me*)

emocionante (*thrilling*)

asistir (*to attend*)

el pan (*bread*)

el éxito (*success*)

sin (*without*)

el pie (*foot*)

actual (*current, present-day*)

actualmente (*nowadays*)

embarazada (*pregnant*)

el pariente (*relative*)

dice (*he/she says*)

dice (*he/she says*)

la red (*net*)

B. Un satélite español. You will hear the following paragraphs from an article in a Spanish newspaper. Pay close attention to the pronunciation of the indicated cognates. Then you will practice reading the paragraphs.

El *ministro* de *Transportes* y *Comunicaciones*, Abel Caballero, ha *declarado* que el Gobierno está dando los primeros pasos para la *construcción* de un *satélite* español de *telecomunicaciones* que, de tomarse la *decisión final*, *comenzará* a ser *operativo* el año que viene.

Muchos de los *componentes* del *satélite* tendrían que ser *importados*, pero al menos el treinta y seis por ciento los podría construir la *industria* española.

Now, pause and read the paragraphs. You may also wish to go back and read along with the speaker.

Now resume listening.

GRAMÁTICA

44. ¿Hay alguien que... ? ¿Hay un lugar donde... ? • Subjunctive after Nonexistent and Indefinite Antecedents

A. Minidiálogo: La persona ideal. You will hear a dialogue followed by a series of statements. Each will be said twice. Circle **C**, **F**, or **ND** (**No lo dice**).

1. C   F   ND

2. C   F   ND

3. C   F   ND

4. C   F   ND

5. C   F   ND

B. En busca de una nueva casa. Form new sentences, using the oral cues.

1. (*you see and hear*) ¿Qué tipo de casa buscan Uds.?   (*you hear*) estar en el campo →
   (*you say*) Buscamos una casa que esté en el campo.

   a. ...   b. ...   c. ...

2. (*you see and hear*) ¿Y cómo quieren Uds. que sean los vecinos?   (*you hear*) jugar a las cartas
   (*you say*) Queremos vecinos que jueguen a las cartas.

   a. ...   b. ...   c. ...

C. Escenas de la vida. You will hear a series of statements. Each will be said twice. Respond to each statement, using the written cues.

> MODELO: (*you hear*) Necesitamos un secretario que hable español.
>   (*you see*) Pues, yo conozco... →
>   (*you say*) Pues, yo conozco a un secretario que habla español.

1. Yo te puedo recomendar...
2. Lo siento, pero no hay nadie aquí...
3. Pues yo busco...
4. Pues yo también quiero...
5. Ellos van a ofrecerte un puesto...

D. ¿Qué quieren estas personas? You will hear what these people already have. Say what they want, using the written cues. If you prefer, pause and write the answers.

MODELO: (*you see*) es viejo / ser nuevo →
(*you hear*) Arturo tiene un auto que es viejo.
(*you say*) Quiere un auto que sea nuevo.

1. no tiene vista / tener vista

_____

_____

2. es perezoso / ser trabajador

_____

_____

3. es muy grande / ser pequeño

_____

_____

4. hacen mucho ruido / no hacer tanto ruido

_____

_____

45. *Lo hago para que tú...* • Subjunctive after Conjunctions of Contingency and Purpose

A. Minidiálogo: Antes del viaje. You will hear a dialogue between Francisco and Araceli about their upcoming trip. Then you will hear a series of statements. Circle **C, F,** or **ND** (**No lo dice**).

1. C F ND

2. C F ND

3. C F ND

4. C F ND

5. C F ND

B. Un viaje. You will hear the following pairs of sentences. Then you will hear a conjunction. Join each pair of sentences, using the conjunction and making any necessary changes.

> MODELO: (*you see and hear*) Hacemos el viaje. No cuesta mucho. (*you hear*) con tal que →
> (*you say*) Hacemos el viaje con tal que no cueste mucho.

1. Tenemos que salir. Empieza a llover.
2. No queremos ir. Hace sol.
3. Pon las maletas en el coche. Podemos salir pronto.
4. Trae el mapa. Nos perdemos.

C. ¿Quién lo dijo? When you hear the number, read aloud each of the following statements, giving the present subjunctive form of the verb in parentheses. You will hear the correct answer. Then you will hear the names of two different people. Circle the letter of the person who might have made each statement.

1. a b No les doy los paquetes a los clientes antes de que me (*pagar*).

2. a b Voy a revisar las llantas en caso de que (*necesitar*) aire.

3. a b No compro esa computadora a menos que (*ser*) fácil de manejar.

4. a b Voy a tomarle la temperatura al paciente antes de que lo (*ver*) la doctora.

UN POCO DE TODO | (Para entregar)

A. Identificaciones. You will hear six sentences. Each will be said twice. Write the number of each sentence next to the drawing that is described. ¡OJO! There are two extra drawings. First, pause and look at the drawings.

a. _____

b. _____

c. _____

d. _____

e. _____

f. _____

g. _____

h. _____

B. *Listening Passage:* **Semejanzas y diferencias**

Antes de escuchar. You will hear a conversation, already in progress, between two students: one is from Spain and the other is from the United States. They are talking about the similarities and differences between people of their age group in the United States and Spain. Notice that the student from Spain uses the **vosotros** forms of verbs, pronouns, and possessive adjectives instead of the **Uds.** forms. Although the **vosotros** forms are not frequently used in *Puntos de partida*, you should be able to recognize them.

Listening Passage. The following words and phrases appear in the conversation.

nos independizamos	*we become independent*
me di cuenta que	*I realized*
no se ve tan mal	*it is not looked down upon (considered odd, viewed as bad)*
dura	*lasts*
los préstamos	*loans*
las becas	*scholarships, grants*
los ingresos	*earnings, assets*
estatales	*state run (adj.)*

Después de escuchar. Indicate the country to which the following sentences refer, based on the conversation that you just heard.

	ESPAÑA	LOS ESTADOS UNIDOS
1. La mayoría de las universidades son estatales.	☐	☐
2. Es normal obtener un préstamo para asistir a la universidad.	☐	☐
3. Es normal que una persona mayor de 18 años viva con sus padres.	☐	☐
4. Se ve mal que los hijos vivan con la familia después de cumplir los dieciocho años.	☐	☐
5. La universidad dura cinco años, generalmente.	☐	☐
6. A los jóvenes les gusta la música *rock* y llevar *jeans*.	☐	☐

Now resume listening.

C. Y para terminar... Entrevista. You will hear a series of questions. Each will be said twice. Answer, based on your own experience. Pause and write the answers. Write out all numbers as words.

1. _____

2. _____

3. _____

4. _____

5. _____

6. _____

VIDEOTECA   Minidramas*

Paso 1. Una invitación. In this conversation, Lola and her friend Eva make plans for the weekend. Listen and read along with the speakers.

LOLA: ¡Por fin es viernes! Qué semana más larga, ¿eh?

EVA: ¿Qué vais a hacer este fin de semana?

LOLA: Pues, nos vamos a pasar el día con mi hermano en Cádiz. Es el cumpleaños de mi sobrino. Y el domingo no tenemos planes. Y vosotros, ¿qué hacéis?

EVA: El domingo vamos a una boda aquí en Sevilla. Se casa una prima mía. ¿Tenéis planes para esta noche?

LOLA: Creo que no, a menos que Manolo haya hecho planes.

EVA: ¿Y por qué no salimos todos juntos? ¡Hace tanto tiempo que no lo hacemos!

LOLA: Por mí, encantada. Podemos ir a cenar o al cine. Hay dos o tres películas interesantes que a Manolo y a mí nos gustaría ver. También podemos llevar a las niñas. ¡Carolina y Marta ya son como hermanas! Se lo voy a preguntar a Manolo y te llamo después.

EVA: Muy bien. Yo también hablo con Jesús. Hablamos luego y entonces decidimos qué hacer, ¿vale?

LOLA: Estupendo.

Paso 2. Aplicación. Now you will participate in a similar conversation, partially printed in your manual, in which you play the role of **Ud.** Complete it using the written cues. You will need to conjugate the verbs. Here are the cues for your conversation. ¡OJO! Use the cues in the order given.

> estar libre / esta tarde
>
> venir conmigo / tomar un café

UD.: ¡Hola, Yolanda! ¡Hace tiempo que no te veo! ¿_____[1]?

YOLANDA: ¡Qué coincidencia! Te iba a llamar anoche. Resulta que no tengo que trabajar esta tarde.

UD.: ¡Magnífico! ¿Quieres _____[2]?

YOLANDA: Pues, ¡claro! Tengo un montón (*lot*) que contarte…

---

*This **Minidramas** video clip is available on the Video on CD to accompany *Puntos de partida* Seventh Edition.

A. En busca de los amigos perfectos. Practice talking about ideal friends. When you hear the corresponding number, form sentences using the written cues. Begin each sentence with **Quiero...** . Make any necessary changes or additions.

> MODELO: (*you see*) 1. amigo / ser / simpático → (*you hear*) uno
> (*you say*) Quiero *un* amigo *que sea simpático.*

2. amiga / ser / amable
3. amigos / ser / flexible
4. amigas / vivir / cerca de mí
5. amigo / tener / coche
6. amiga / saber / mucho de computadoras

B. Cosas de todos los días: La boda de Mireya y Alonso. Practice talking about Mireya and Alonso's upcoming wedding, using the written cues. When you hear the corresponding number, form sentences using the words provided in the order given, making any necessary changes or additions. ¡OJO! You will need to make changes to adjectives and add articles, if appropriate.

> MODELO: (*you see*) 1. padre de Mireya / pensar / que / (ellos) no deber / casarse /
> a menos que / (ellos) / llevarse bien   (*you hear*) uno →
> (*you say*) *El* padre de Mireya *piensa* que no *deben casarse* a menos que *se lleven* bien.

2. padres de Alonso / pensar / que / (ellos) deber / casarse / con tal que / (ellos) estar / enamorado
3. Mireya / pensar / confirmar / fecha / antes de que / su / padres / mandar / invitaciones
4. padres de Mireya / ir / alquilar / sala / grande / en caso de que / venir / mucho / invitados
5. (ellos) pensar / regalarles / dinero / para que / novios / empezar / ahorrar
6. Mireya y Alonso / ir / pasar / luna de miel / en Cancún / con tal que / poder / encontrar / hotel / barato

CAPÍTULO 16

VOCABULARIO Preparación

A. ¿A quién necesitan en estas situaciones? You will hear a series of situations. Each will be said twice. Circle the letter of the person or professional who would best be able to help.

1. a. un arquitecto   b. un analista de sistemas
2. a. una dentista   b. una enfermera
3. a. una consejera matrimonial   b. un policía
4. a. una fotógrafa   b. un bibliotecario
5. a. un plomero   b. una electricista

B. ¿Quiénes son? Using the list of professions below, identify these people after you hear the corresponding number. Begin each sentence with **Es un...** or **Es una...** . First, listen to the list of professions.

obrero/a   cocinero/a
peluquero/a   fotógrafo/a
periodista   plomero/a
veterinario/a   hombre o mujer de negocios

1.   2.   3.   4.   5.   6.   7.   8.

C. En busca de un puesto

Paso 1. Imagine that you are looking for a new job in a large corporation. Tell how you will go about getting the job, using phrases from the following list. First, listen to the list, then pause and put the remaining items in order, from 3 to 6.

_____ tratar de caerle bien al entrevistador

_____ aceptar el puesto y renunciar a mi puesto actual

__2__ pedirle una solicitud de empleo

_____ ir a la entrevista

_____ llenar la solicitud

__1__ llamar a la directora de personal

Now resume listening.

Paso 2. Now tell what you will do to look for a job when you hear the numbers. Follow the model.

MODELO: (*you hear*) uno   (*you see*) llamar a la directora de personal →
(*you say*) Llamo a la directora de personal.

D. Descripción. You will hear a series of questions. Each will be said twice. Answer, based on the drawing. If you prefer, pause and write the answers.

1. _____

2. _____

3. _____

4. _____

5. _____

■■■Los hispanos hablan: ¿Cuáles son las profesiones de más prestigio (*prestige*) en su país? ¿Qué profesión es menos apreciada?

You will hear two answers to these questions. Then, after each answer, you will hear a series of statements about the answer. Circle **C** or **F**. The following words appear in the answers.

el agente de bolsa *stockbroker*

la remuneración el pago (el sueldo)

sea cual sea su profesión no importa la profesión que tenga

la enseñanza *teaching*

remuneradas pagadas

Habla Tomás, un arquitecto español.　　　　Habla Francisco, un científico español.

　1. C　F　　2. C　F　　3. C　F　　　　　　1. C　F　　2. C　F　　3. C　F

PRONUNCIACIÓN Y ORTOGRAFÍA　More on Stress and the Written Accent

A. El acento escrito y los verbos. You have probably noticed that the written accent is an important factor in the spelling of some verbs. You know that in the case of the preterite, for example, a missing accent can change the meaning of the verb. Listen to the following pairs of words.

habló　(*he, she, or you spoke*)　/ hablo　(*I am speaking or I speak*)

hablé　(*I spoke*)　　　　　　　/ hable　(*that he, she, you, or I may speak—present subjunctive; speak [formal command]*)

When you hear the corresponding number, read the following pairs of words. Then repeat the correct pronunciation, imitating the speaker.

　1.　tomo / tomó
　2.　ahorro / ahorró
　3.　limpie / limpié

B. El acento escrito. The written accent also is important in maintaining the original stress of a word to which syllables have been added. In the word **jóvenes,** for example, the written accent maintains the stress of the singular word **joven,** even though another syllable has been added. Sometimes, the reverse will be true. A word that has a written accent will lose the accent when a syllable is added. Compare **inglés** and **ingleses.** This happens because the new word receives the stress naturally; that is, it follows the rules of stress.

When you hear the corresponding number, read the following groups of words. Then repeat the correct pronunciation, imitating the speaker.

　1.　dígame / dígamelo
　2.　póngase / póngaselo
　3.　escriba / escríbanos

　4.　depositen / depositenlos
　5.　almacén / almacenes
　6.　nación / naciones

C. Dictado. You will hear the following words. Each will be said twice. Write in an accent mark, if necessary.

1. cobro
2. cobro
3. toque
4. toque
5. describe
6. describemela
7. levantate
8. levanta
9. franceses
10. frances

D. El acento diacrítico. You have probably noticed that when a pair of words is written the same but has different meanings, one of the words is accented. This accent is called a *diacritical* accent.

Listen to and repeat the following words, paying close attention to the meaning of each.

1. mi (*my*) / mí (*me*)
2. tu (*your*) / tú (*you*)
3. el (*the*) / él (*he*)
4. si (*if*) / sí (*yes*)
5. se (*oneself*) / sé (*I know; be* [informal command])
6. de (*of, from*) / dé (*give* [formal command]; *give* [present subjunctive])
7. te (*you, yourself*) / té (*tea*)
8. solo (*alone, sole* [adjective]) / sólo (*only* [adverb])
9. que (*that, which*) / ¿qué? (*what?*)

E. Dictado. Listen to the following sentences. Determine by context whether or not the meaning of the italicized words requires a written accent. If so, write it in. Each sentence will be said twice.

1. Creo *que* ese regalo es para *mi.*
2. Aquí *esta tu te.* ¿*Que* más quieres?
3. *El* dijo *que te* iba a llamar a las ocho.
4. *Si, mi* amigo *se* llama Antonio.

GRAMÁTICA

46. Talking About the Future • Future Verb Forms

A. Un futuro perfecto

Paso 1. You will hear a brief paragraph in which Angélica talks about her future. Then you will hear a series of statements. Circle **C, F,** or **ND.**

1. C F ND
2. C F ND
3. C F ND

4. C F ND
5. C F ND

Paso 2. Now pause and complete the following statements according to your own preferences. No answers will be given.

1. Cuando yo me gradúe, _____.

2. Trabajaré para _____.

3. Viviré en _____.

4. Mi casa será _____.

5. Tendré un auto _____.

6. Pasaré mis vacaciones en _____.

7. Mi vida será _____.

Now resume listening.

B. El viernes por la tarde. Using the oral and written cues, tell what the following people will do with their paychecks.

1. Bernardo
2. Adela y yo

3. tú... ¿verdad?
4. yo

C. El cumpleaños de Jaime. Jaime's birthday is next week. Answer the questions about his birthday, using the written cues. Each question will be said twice.

> MODELO: (*you hear*) ¿Cuántos años va a *cumplir* Jaime?   (*you see*) dieciocho →
> (*you say*) Cumplirá dieciocho años.

1. sus amigos y sus parientes
2. una videocasetera
3. un pastel de chocolate

4. discos compactos
5. ¡Feliz cumpleaños!

47. Expressing Future or Pending Actions • Subjunctive and Indicative after Conjunctions of Time

A. Minidiálogo: Antes de la entrevista. You will hear a dialogue in which Tomás' mother, Mrs. López, gives him advice about a job interview. Then you will hear a series of statements. Circle the letter of the person who might have made each statement.

1. a. Tomás
   b. la Sra. López
2. a. Tomás
   b. la Sra. López
3. a. Tomás
   b. la Sra. López
4. a. Tomás
   b. la Sra. López
5. a. Tomás
   b. la Sra. López

B. Escenas de la vida cotidiana. You will hear the following pairs of sentences. Combine them to form one complete sentence, using the oral cues.

MODELO: (*you see and hear*) Voy a decidirlo. Hablo con él. (*you hear*) después de que →
(*you say*) Voy a decidirlo después de que hable con él.

1. Amalia va a viajar. Consigue un poco de dinero.
2. No estaré contenta. Recibo un aumento.
3. Podrán ahorrar más. Sus hijos terminan sus estudios.
4. Tito, devuélveme el dinero. Se te olvida.

C. Asuntos económicos. You will hear a series of incomplete sentences. Circle the letter of the correct ending for each, then repeat the completed sentence. ¡OJO! In this exercise, you will be choosing between the present subjunctive and the present indicative.

MODELO: (*you hear*) Voy a depositar mi cheque cuando…   a. lo reciba   b. lo recibo →
(*you say*)   a. Voy a depositar mi cheque cuando lo reciba.

1. a. las reciba
   b. las recibo
2. a. tenga más dinero
   b. tengo más dinero
3. a. consiga otro puesto
   b. consigo otro puesto
4. a. lo firme
   b. lo firmo

UN POCO DE TODO (Para entregar)

A. **¿Qué cree Ud. que van a hacer estas personas?** You will hear three situations. Each will be said twice. Choose the most logical solution for each and repeat it.

1. a. Teresa comprará un coche barato y económico.
   b. Comprará un coche de lujo (*luxury*).
   c. No comprará ningún coche.
2. a. Basilio tendrá que conseguir otro trabajo para pagar el nuevo alquiler.
   b. Robará un banco.
   c. Compartirá (*He will share*) su apartamento con cuatro amigos.
3. a. Luisa empezará a poner el dinero que gasta en diversiones en su cuenta de ahorros.
   b. Ella comprará el regalo la próxima semana.
   c. Insistirá en que su jefe le dé un aumento de sueldo inmediatamente.

B. *Listening Passage:* **El sistema universitario hispánico**

Antes de escuchar. You will hear a passage about the differences between the university system in most of the Hispanic world and that of the United States. The following words appear in the passage.

la etapa	*stage*	una vez que	*once*
suele durar	*usually lasts*	el requisito	*requirement*
se matricula	*enrolls*	la profundidad	*depth*
por lo tanto	*therefore*		

Listening Passage. Here is the passage. First, listen to it to get a general idea of the content. Then go back and listen again for specific information.

Después de escuchar. Indicate whether the following statements refer to the Hispanic world or to the United States, according to the information in the passage.

	EL MUNDO HISPÁNICO	LOS ESTADOS UNIDOS
1. La mayoría de las carreras duran menos de cinco años.	☐	☐
2. Al entrar (*Upon entering*) en la universidad, un estudiante se matricula directamente en el área de su especialización.	☐	☐
	☐	☐
3. El estudiante tiene pocas opciones una vez que empieza sus estudios.	☐	☐
4. Hay requisitos «generales» como ciencias naturales, ciencias sociales o humanidades.	☐	☐
5. El currículum es bastante estricto.	☐	☐
6. Los estudios que se hacen para una licenciatura son bastante profundos y variados.	☐	☐
7. Por lo general, la especialización no se «declara» el primer año de estudios universitarios.	☐	☐

Now resume listening.

C. En el periódico: Empleos. The following ads for jobs appeared in a Mexican newspaper. Choose the ad you are most interested in, based on the profession, and scan it. Then, after you hear each question, answer it based on the ad. If the information requested is not in the ad, write **No lo dice.** First, pause and look at the ads. Pause to write the answers.

1. _____

2. _____

3. _____

4. _____

5. _____

IMPORTANTE EMPRESA FARMACEUTICA, REQUIERE

QUIMICO ANALISTA

(QBP, QSB, QFI o equivalente)

REQUISITOS:
- Ambos sexos
- Edad de 25 a 45 años
- Experiencia un año en el área de microbiología
- Antecedentes de estabilidad de trabajos anteriores

OFRECEMOS:
- ★ Sueldo y prestaciones muy atractivas

Interesados presentarse o concertar cita con el Lic. FERNANDO MARTINEZ en AVENIDA 1o. DE MAYO No. 130. Naucalpan de Juárez, Edo. de México. Tel. 576-00-44.

IMPORTANTE EMPRESA TEXTIL, SOLICITA:

SECRETARIAS

Requisitos: Experiencia de 1 a 3 años, excelente presentación

AUXILIAR DE CONTABILIDAD

Requisitos: Escolaridad mínima 5o. semestre de la carrera de C.P., con o sin experiencia

Ofrecemos: Sueldo según aptitudes, prestaciones superiores a las de la ley, magnífico ambiente de trabajo

Interesados presentarse en: AV. VIA MORELOS No. 68, XALOSTOC, EDO. DE MEXICO. Tel. 569-29-00.

At'n. Departamento de Personal.

SOLICITA:

ANALISTA DE SISTEMAS

REQUISITOS:
- Dos años de experiencia mínima en VSE/SP o VM, DOS, JCL, VSAM, CICS, COBOL deseable
- Conocimientos de SQL, CSP

PROGRAMADOR

- Dos años de experiencia mínima en alguno de los siguientes lenguajes: COBOL (preferentemente), RPG, EDL, deseable
- Conocimientos de: DBASE III, LOTUS, DISPLAY-WRITE

Todos los candidatos deberán tener estudios profesionales (preferentemente), de 25 a 35 años de edad y excelente presentación.

Por nuestra parte ofrecemos:
- ★ Una compensación económica bastante competitiva, un paquete de prestaciones muy superiores a las de ley y amplias posibilidades de desarrollo

Interesados concertar cita al 541-30-60 y 541-61-00. Atención licenciado HERNANDEZ.

IMPORTANTE EMPRESA SOLICITA

EJECUTIVA DE VENTAS

Para Agencias de Viajes

REQUISITOS:
- Egresada de la carrera en Administración de Empresas Turísticas
- Excelente presentación
- Edad de 20 a 30 años
- Disponibilidad inmediata

OFRECEMOS:
- Sueldo según aptitudes
- Prestaciones de ley
- Agradable ambiente de trabajo

Interesados presentarse de lunes a viernes en horas hábiles en PLATEROS 31, San José Insurgentes.

IMPORTANTE GRUPO INDUSTRIAL EN NAUCALPAN, SOLICITA:

CONTRALOR CORPORATIVO

REQUISITOS:
- Contador Público ● Mayor de 35 años ● Sexo masculino ● Experiencia 5 años en manejo de empresas Holding, Planeación Fiscal, Consolidación, Trato con Consultores y Sistemas de Información ● Casado ● Sin problemas de horario.

Interesados, enviar curriculum vitae, mencionando pretensiones, al APARTADO POSTAL 150-A, Centro Cívico, C.P. 53100, Ciudad Satélite, Estado de México. U R G E N T E

D. Y para terminar... Entrevista. You will hear a series of questions. Each will be said twice. Answer, based on your own experience. Pause and write the answers. Note that in number six, you will need to write a longer answer.

1. _____

2. _____

3. _____

4. _____

5. _____

6. _____

_____

_____

_____

_____

VIDEOTECA   Minidramas*

Paso 1. Lupe solicita un puesto. In the following conversation, Lupe is being interviewed for a position as a receptionist in a bank. Read the conversation along with the speakers.

SRA. IBÁÑEZ: He hablado con varios aspirantes para el puesto de recepcionista, pero Ud. tiene el currículum más interesante. Veo que ha trabajado como recepcionista en la oficina de un abogado. ¿Por qué renunció a ese trabajo?

LUPE: Bueno, soy estudiante en la universidad. Me gustaba mucho el trabajo en la oficina del abogado, pero querían que trabajara la jornada completa. Desafortunadamente, no me era posible.

SRA. IBÁÑEZ: Y cuando trabajaba para el abogado, ¿cuáles eran sus responsabilidades?

LUPE: Contestaba el teléfono, hacía las citas con los clientes, organizaba el archivo... también le llevaba sus cuentas y pagaba los gastos básicos de la oficina. Eran las típicas responabilidades de una recepcionista.

SRA. IBÁÑEZ: Ajá, entiendo. Srta. Carrasco, buscamos una persona que sea amable, que aprenda rápidamente, que sepa escribir a máquina y utilizar una computadora y que tenga paciencia con los clientes. Parece que Ud. cumple con estos requisitos. ¿Podrá asistir a un entrenamiento de seis horas la semana que viene?

LUPE: Sí, Sra. Ibáñez.

SRA. IBÁÑEZ: ¿Y podrá trabajar de vez en cuando en las otras sucursales del banco?

LUPE: ¡Claro que sí! No hay problema.

SRA. IBÁÑEZ: Muy bien.

*This **Minidramas** video clip is available on the Video on CD to accompany *Puntos de partida* Seventh Edition.

Paso 2. Aplicación. Now you will participate in a similar conversation, partially printed in your manual, in which you play the role of **Ud.** and answer questions about your imaginary job. Complete it using the written cues. Here are the cues for your conversation. ¡OJO! The cues are not in order.

es muy amable ya encontraste trabajo

fantástico tres semanas

AMIGA: ¡Hola! Hace tiempo que no te veo. ¿Qué tal te va en tu nuevo trabajo?

UD.: ¡_____[1]! Es un puesto estupendo.

AMIGA: Y tu jefa, ¿cómo es?

UD.: _____.[2] Nos llevamos muy bien.

AMIGA: Espero que te den vacaciones este año.

UD.: Sí, sí… Fíjate que me dan _____.[3] Y tú,

¿_____[4]?

AMIGA: ¡Qué va! Todavía ando buscando…

PRUEBA CORTA

A. ¿Cuándo? You will hear a series of statements about what your friends plan to do. Ask them when they plan to do these things, using the future tense. Follow the model.

MODELO: (*you hear*) Voy a pagar mis cuentas → (*you say*) ¿Cuándo *las pagarás*?
(*you hear*) Las pagaré la próxima semana.

1. … 2. … 3. … 4. … 5. …

B. Cosas de todos los días: Empleos diversos. Practice talking about what people in various jobs do or will do, using the written cues. When you hear the corresponding number, form sentences using the words provided in the order given, making any necessary changes or additions. Use the indicative or the subjunctive, as appropriate. ¡OJO! You will need to make changes to adjectives and add articles and prepositions, if appropriate.

MODELO: (*you see*) 1. técnica / arreglar (*future*) / computadoras / cuando / llegar / oficina
(*you hear*) uno →
(*you see*) La técnica *arreglará las* computadoras cuando *llegue a la* oficina.

2. periodista (*m.*) / entrevistar (*future*) / empleados / antes de que / publicarse / artículo
3. vendedora / siempre / depositar (*present*) / cheques / después de que / recibirlos
4. ingeniera / viajar (*future*) / Acapulco / cuando / jubilarse
5. veterinario / mudarse (*future*) / tan pronto como / encontrar / nuevo / oficina
6. traductora / siempre / hacer (*present*) / traducción / en cuanto / leer / documentos
7. obreros / no / trabajar (*future*) / hasta que / recibir / bueno / aumento de sueldo

CAPÍTULO **17**

VOCABULARIO Preparación

A. Encuesta: ¿Con qué frecuencia... ? You will hear a series of statements about different ways of learning about what goes on in the world. For each statement, check the appropriate answer. No answers will be given. The answers you choose should be correct for you!

	TODOS LOS DÍAS	DE VEZ EN CUANDO	CASI NUNCA
1.	☐	☐	☐
2.	☐	☐	☐
3.	☐	☐	☐
4.	☐	☐	☐
5.	☐	☐	☐
6.	☐	☐	☐
7.	☐	☐	☐
8.	☐	☐	☐

B. El noticiero del Canal 10. You will hear a brief "newsbreak" from a television station. Then you will hear a series of statements about the newscast. Circle **C, F,** or **ND**.

1. C F ND   3. C F ND   5. C F ND

2. C F ND   4. C F ND

C. Definiciones. You will hear a series of statements. Each will be said twice. Place the number of the statements next to the word that is best defined by each. First, listen to the list of words.

_____ una guerra   _____ la testigo

_____ la prensa   _____ el reportero

_____ un dictador   _____ la huelga

_____ los terroristas   _____ el noticiero

D. Opiniones. You will hear a series of statements. Each will be said twice. React to each statement, using expressions chosen from the list. Be sure to express your own opinion. You will hear a possible answer. If you prefer, pause and write the answers.

Dudo que...   Es verdad que...

Es cierto que...   No es cierto que...

1. _____

2. _____

3. _____

4. _____

5. _____

6. _____

■■■Los hispanos hablan: Más sobre las ciudades hispánicas

When asked about some of the differences between U.S. cities and the Hispanic city in which she lives, Cecilia mentioned that some of the laws were different. As you listen to her answer, write down the effect she thinks each law or situation has on the population.

LEY O SITUACIÓN	RESULTADO
1. Un horario para volver a casa	_____
	_____
2. Una edad permitida para tomar bebidas alcohólicas	_____
	_____
3. Los chicos mayores de dieciocho años están en la universidad	_____

PRONUNCIACIÓN Y ORTOGRAFÍA — Intonation, Punctuation, and Rhythm (Review of Linking)

A. La entonación. As you have probably noticed throughout the audio program and from listening to your instructor in class, intonation plays an important role in Spanish. The meaning of a sentence can change according to its intonation and punctuation. Listen to the following sentences. The arrows indicate a falling or rising intonation.

        ↘

Los reporteros están aquí. (*statement*)

        ↗

¿Los reporteros están aquí? (*question*)

        ↗

¡Los reporteros están aquí! (*exclamation*)

B. Repeticiones. Repeat the following sentences, paying particular attention to punctuation, intonation, and rhythm.

1. ↗
   ¿Ya destruyeron el edificio?

2. ↗
   ¡Es imposible que construyan eso en la ciudad!

3. ↗
   ¿Ya hablaste con la consejera?

4. ↘ ↗ ↘ ↗
   Prepararon la cena, ¿verdad? Espero que ya esté lista (*ready*) porque ¡tengo mucha hambre!

5. ↘
   Ojalá que no perdamos el vuelo… Tenemos que estar en Los Ángeles antes de las ocho de
   ↘
   la noche.

C. La entonación. When you hear the corresponding number, read the following sentences. Then repeat them, imitating the speaker. Write in arrows to indicate rising or falling intonation. Be sure to check your answers in the Appendix.

1. Enero es el primer mes del año.
2. ¡No entiendo lo que me estás diciendo!
3. ¿Trabajaba en una tienda?
4. No olvides el diccionario la próxima vez, ¿eh?
5. Nació el catorce de abril de mil novecientos sesenta y uno.
6. ¿Adónde crees que vas a ir a estas horas de la noche?

D. Dictado. You will hear the following sentences. Each will be said twice. Listen carefully for intonation. Repeat what you hear, then punctuate each sentence.

1. Cuál es tu profesión   Te pagan bien
2. Tú no la conoces verdad
3. Prefiere Ud. que le sirva la comida en el patio
4. Qué ejercicio más fácil
5. No sé dónde viven pero sí sé su número de teléfono

GRAMÁTICA

48. ¡No queríamos que fuera así! • Past Subjunctive

A. Minidiálogo: ¡Qué pena que no nos lleváramos bien! You will hear a dialogue in which Elisa talks about her childhood and her mother. Then you will hear a series of statements. Circle **C, F,** or **ND.**

1. C F ND   4. C F ND

2. C F ND   5. C F ND

3. C F ND

B. Encuesta: Hablando de la escuela secundaria. You will hear a series of statements about what your life was like in high school. For each statement, circle **C** or **F.** No answers will be given. The answers you choose should be correct for you!

1. C F   4. C F   7. C F

2. C F   5. C F   8. C F

3. C F   6. C F   9. C F

C. ¿Qué esperaba? Answer the following questions using the oral cues.

1. ¿Qué esperaba Ud. que hiciera el robot antes de la fiesta?

   MODELO: (*you hear*) lavar las ventanas → (*you say*) Esperaba que lavara las ventanas.

   a. ... b. ... c. ... d. ...

2. ¿Qué esperaba Ud. que hicieran los invitados durante la fiesta?

   MODELO: (*you hear*) bailar → (*you say*) Esperaba que bailaran.

   a. ... b. ... c. ... d. ...

D. Recuerdos de un viaje. Imagine that you have recently returned from a trip abroad, and your friends want to know all the details. Tell them about some of the things you had to do, using the oral cues. Begin each sentence with **Fue necesario que... .** ¡OJO! You will be using the past subjunctive in your answers.

   1. ... 2. ... 3. ... 4. ...

E. ¿Qué quería Ud.? Imagine that you are never happy with your family's plans. What would you rather have done? Use the oral cues to tell what you preferred. Begin each sentence with **Yo quería que... .**

   MODELO: (*you see and hear*) Ayer cenamos en un restaurante. (*You hear*) en casa →
           (*you say*) Yo quería que cenáramos en casa.

1. Ayer vimos una película.
2. El mes pasado fuimos a la playa.
3. Anoche miramos un programa de televisión.
4. Para mi cumpleaños, me regalaron un estéreo.
5. Esta noche mi madre sirvió patatas en la cena.

49. More about Expressing Possession • Stressed Possessives

A. Lo mío y lo tuyo

Paso 1. You will hear a brief conversation between Beto and Anita who are arguing about their bikes. Then you will hear a series of statements. Circle **C, F,** or **ND.**

1. C F ND   3. C F ND

2. C F ND   4. C F ND

Paso 2. Your friend will make a series of statements about things that she has or about members of her family. Each will be said twice. React to each statement using the written cues. You will need to conjugate the verbs.

> MODELO: (*you hear*) Mi auto es nuevo y económico.
> (*you see*) ser viejo y gasta mucha gasolina →
> (*you say*) Pues el mío es viejo y gasta mucha gasolina.

1. tener poca memoria   3. ser arquitecta   5. estar escritas a máquina (*typed*)
2. vivir en el campo   4. no funcionar

B. En el departamento de artículos perdidos y encontrados. You will hear a series of questions. Each will be said twice. Answer in the negative.

> MODELO: (*you hear*) ¿Es de Ud. esta maleta? → (*you say*) No, no es mía.

1. ... 2. ... 3. ... 4. ... 5. ...

UN POCO DE TODO | (Para entregar)

A. En el periódico. You will hear a series of headlines from a Hispanic newspaper. Each will be said twice. Listen and write the number of each headline next to the section of the newspaper to which it belongs. First, listen to the list of sections.

_____ Sociales   _____ Política   _____ Clasificados

_____ Deportes   _____ Negocios   _____ Espectáculos
                                                (*Entertainment*)

B. *Listening Passage:* Resumen de las noticias

Antes de escuchar. You will hear a news brief on the radio, just as it would be if you were listening to it in a Hispanic country. After you listen to the passage, you will be asked to complete the following statements about it. Pause and scan them now to get a general idea of the information to look for.

Noticia 1: Fuerte maremoto en _____, de más de _____ puntos en la escala Richter.

Noticia 2: Tema: _____   Mes: _____

Noticia 3: Visita de Juan Carlos I, _____ de _____. Duración de la visita: _____

Noticia 4: Propuesta del partido de oposición para _____ el precio de la

_____ , el _____ y el _____ , el

primero en un _____ por ciento y los dos últimos en

un _____ por ciento. El próximo noticiero de amplio reportaje será a

las _____ .

Now resume listening.

Listening Passage. The following words and phrases appear in the passage.

el mediodía	*noon*	el paro	*unemployment*
la redacción	*editorial desk*	la propuesta	*proposal*
el maremoto	*seaquake*	el apoyo	*support*
sin hogar	*homeless*	nos sintonicen	*you tune in to us (our broadcast)*

Después de escuchar. Now complete the statements in **Antes de escuchar.**

C. Descripción: Escenas actuales. You will hear the following cartoon caption. Then you will hear a series of questions. Each will be said twice. Answer, based on the cartoon and your own experience. Pause and write the answers.

1. _____

_____

2. _____

_____

3. _____

_____

4. _____

_____

Bob Schroeter

—Lo bueno de las campañas políticas
es que no te las pueden repetir.

D. Y para terminar... Entrevista. You will hear a series of questions. Each will be said twice. Answer, based on your own experience. Pause and write the answers.

1. _____

2. _____

3. _____

4. _____

5. _____

6. _____

VIDEOTECA   Minidramas*

Paso 1. La tertulia. In the following conversation, Manolo, Maricarmen, and Paco get together for a **tertulia,** an informal discussion of various topics. Today they are discussing politics. Read the conversation along with the speakers.

MANOLO: Muy bien, ¿de qué hablamos hoy?

MARICARMEN: Hablamos del partido político de Paco. Y este, como siempre, cree que los líderes políticos de su partido tienen el derecho de dictar cómo viven los demás. Y yo, claro, no estoy de acuerdo.

PACO: Maricarmen, te equivocas. Es todo lo contrario. Mira. Mi partido ofrece soluciones razonables a los problemas más graves de hoy.

MANOLO: Hasta cierto punto, estoy de acuerdo con Maricarmen. ¿Viste las noticias del Canal 2 anoche? Paco, tu querido partido quería votar cuanto antes la nueva legislación, para que nadie más pudiera protestar.

PACO: ¡No, señor! No es así. ¿Siempre crees todo lo que dicen la prensa y la televisión? ¡Ojalá el asunto fuera tan sencillo!

MARICARMEN: Pero Paco, no me parecen razonables las soluciones propuestas por tu partido. Es verdad que necesitamos nuevas leyes laborales, pero estas no resuelven nada.

PACO: ¡Al contrario! Maricarmen, el anterior presidente no había hecho nada en los últimos años. Mira las noticias. Hay huelgas, desempleo, desastres económicos...

MANOLO: ¡Paco! ¿Tú siempre crees todo lo que dicen la prensa y la televisión?

PACO: Pues, ¡parece que lo único en que estamos de acuerdo es en que *no* estamos de acuerdo!

---

*This **Minidramas** video clip is available on the Video on CD to accompany *Puntos de partida* Seventh Edition.

Paso 2. Aplicación. Now you will participate in a similar conversation, partially printed in your manual, in which you will express your own opinions. Use the following phrases to begin your statements. Pause and write the answers. Answer, based on your own opinions. No answers will be given. First, listen to the phrases.

Bueno, pero yo (no) creo que...   Lo siento, pero yo pienso que...

Eso suena (*sounds*) bien, pero...   Sí, pero...

Estoy de acuerdo...

PERSONA 1: Creo que el actual presidente no ha hecho nada para mejorar las condiciones económicas del país.

UD.: _____ 1

PERSONA 2: ¿Y qué tal su política exterior (*foreign policy*)? Creo que es un desastre.

UD.: _____ 2

PERSONA 3: Pues yo pienso que es el mejor presidente que hemos tenido en varios años. El problema es el Congreso. Siempre se opone a las reformas que propone el presidente.

UD.: _____ 3

PRUEBA CORTA

A. Apuntes. You will hear a brief paragraph that tells about a political campaign. Listen carefully and, while listening, write the information requested. Write all numbers as numerals. First, listen to the requested information.

el nombre de la candidata que perdió las elecciones: _____

el nombre del candidato que ganó las elecciones: _____

el porcentaje (*percentage*) de ciudadanos que votó por la candidata que perdió: _____

la cuestión (*issue*) principal de la campaña: _____

B. Cosas de todos los días: Comentarios sobre la política y los acontecimientos. Practice talking about politics, using the written cues. When you hear the corresponding number, form sentences using the words provided in the order given, making any necessary changes or additions. Use the indicative or the subjunctive, as appropriate. ¡OJO! You will need to make changes to adjectives and add articles and prepositions, if appropriate.

MODELO: (*you see*) 1. ciudadanos / insistían en / que / gobierno / gobernar / responsablemente (*you hear*) uno →
(*you say*) *Los* ciudadanos insistían en que *el* gobierno *gobernara* responsablemente.

2. queríamos / que / reporteros / informarnos / acontecimientos
3. candidatos / esperaban / que / público / apoyarlos
4. todos / insistían en / que / gobierno / castigar / criminales
5. dudaban / que / gobierno / poder / economizar
6. nadie / quería / que / haber / huelga
7. a / políticos / les sorprendió / que / huelga / durar / tanto / meses
8. era increíble / que / empleados / pedir / aumento / tan / grande

CAPÍTULO **18**

VOCABULARIO Preparación

A. Encuesta: ¿Qué hizo Ud. en su último viaje? You will hear a series of questions about what you did on your last trip. For each question, check the appropriate answer. No answers will be given. The answers you choose should be correct for you!

1. ☐ Sí ☐ No   6. ☐ Sí ☐ No

2. ☐ Sí ☐ No   7. ☐ Sí ☐ No

3. ☐ Sí ☐ No   8. ☐ Sí ☐ No

4. ☐ Sí ☐ No   9. ☐ Sí ☐ No

5. ☐ Sí ☐ No   10. ☐ Sí ☐ No

B. Definiciones. You will hear a series of definitions. Each will be said twice. Write the number of the definition next to the word or phrase that is best defined by each. First, listen to the list of words and phrases.

_____ viajar a otro país   _____ el huésped

_____ el formulario de inmigración   _____ la frontera

_____ la nacionalidad   _____ el pasaporte

C. Descripción. Identify the following items when you hear the corresponding number. Begin each sentence with **Es un...** , **Es una...** , or **Son...** .

1. ...   2. ...   3. ...   4. ...   5. ...   6. ...   7. ...   8. ...

D. Descripción. Describe what these people are doing, using the written cues and the verbs you will hear for each segment of the drawing. Use present progressive forms (**estar + -ndo**).

1. los pasajeros   2. los turistas   3. el turista   4. el inspector   5. el turista

■■■Los hispanos hablan: Una aventura en el extranjero

You will hear Clara's story of a trip to the city of Fez, which is in Morocco (**Marruecos**). The story is divided into two parts. The first time you listen to the story, try to get the gist of the narration. Then listen again, or as many times as necessary, for specific information. After you hear each part of the story, pause and answer the true/false items.

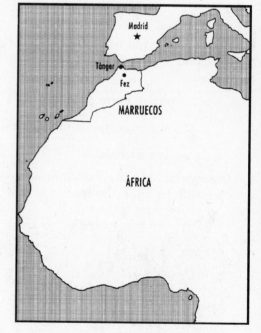

Parte 1. The following words and phrases appear in the first part of the story.

hacer transbordo	*to change planes*
Tánger	*Tangiers*
la plaza	el asiento
el croquis	*sketch*

1. C F Clara viajó a Marruecos para estudiar árabe.

2. C F Clara tomó un vuelo directo de Madrid a Fez.

3. C F El vuelo de Madrid a Tánger fue fácil.

4. C F El aeropuerto de Tánger era muy moderno.

Now resume listening.

Parte 2. The following words and phrases appear in the second part of the story.

el destino	*destination*	chapurreado	*poor*
se levantasen	*they got up*	el sello	*official stamp*
las hélices	*propellers*	a punto de estallar	*about to explode*

1. C F Clara usó el color de su tarjeta de embarque para saber qué vuelo tomar.

2. C F Todo —el avión, el aeropuerto, el pasajero que se sentó con ella— tenía aspecto de película.

3. C F Cuando llegó a Fez, Clara ya había pasado por la aduana.

4. C F El padre de Clara ya estaba en el aeropuerto de Fez cuando el avión de su hija aterrizó (*landed*).

Now resume listening.

PRONUNCIACIÓN Y ORTOGRAFÍA   Nationalities

A. Repeticiones. Repeat the following names of countries and the nationalities of those who were born there.

1. Nicaragua, nicaragüense
    el Canadá, canadiense
    los Estados Unidos, estadounidense
    Costa Rica, costarricense
2. la Argentina, argentino
    el Perú, peruana
    Colombia, colombiano
    Bolivia, boliviana
3. el Uruguay, uruguayo
    el Paraguay, paraguaya
4. Honduras, hondureño
    Panamá, panameña
    el Brasil, brasileño
5. Guatemala, guatemalteca
    Portugal, portugués
    Inglaterra, inglesa

B. Los países y las nacionalidad. Now you will hear a series of nationalities. Each will be said twice. Repeat each and write the number of the nationality next to the country of origin. First, listen to the list of countries.

_____ Chile   _____ el Ecuador

_____ El Salvador   _____ Venezuela

_____ Puerto Rico   _____ Israel

C. Repaso general: Refranes

Paso 1. Pause and match the number of the Hispanic proverb with its English equivalent. ¡OJO! There is no equivalent English proverb in some cases, just a literal translation.

a. _____ He who sleeps gets swept away.

b. _____ There is an exception to every rule.

c. _____ Every cloud has a silver lining.

d. _____ Everything has a purpose.

e. _____ Nothing is impossible.

f. _____ The early bird catches the worm.

g. _____ Tell it like it is.

1. Llamar al pan, pan y al vino, vino.
2. El agua para bañarse, el vino para beberse.
3. Quien mucho duerme, poco aprende.
4. No hay mal que por bien no venga.
5. No hay regla sin excepción.
6. No hay montaña tan alta que un asno cargado de oro no la suba.
7. Camarón que se duerme, se lo lleva la corriente.

Now resume listening.

Paso 2. When you hear the corresponding number, read the proverbs. Then listen to the correct pronunciation and repeat it.

1. Llamar al pan, pan y al vino, vino.
2. El agua para bañarse, el vino para beberse.
3. Quien mucho duerme, poco aprende.
4. No hay mal que por bien no venga.
5. No hay regla sin excepción.
6. No hay montaña tan alta que un asno cargado de oro no la suba.
7. Camarón que se duerme, se lo lleva la corriente.

D. Dictado.
You will hear a series of sentences. Each will be said twice. Write what you hear. Pay close attention to punctuation.

1. _____

2. _____

3. _____

   _____

4. _____

   _____

5. _____

GRAMÁTICA

50. Expressing What You Would Do • Conditional Verb Forms

A. Minidiálogo: La fantasía de Yolanda Torres-Luján. You will hear Yolanda, a very busy business-woman, describe what she would do with some time off. Then you will hear a series of statements. Circle the number of the statement that best summarizes her description.

1.   2.   3.

B. ¿Qué harían para mejorar las condiciones? Using the oral and written cues, tell what the following people would like to do to improve the world.

MODELO: (*you hear*) Gema   (*you see*) eliminar las guerras →
(*you say*) Gema eliminaría las guerras.

1. desarrollar otros tipos de energía
2. construir viviendas para todos
3. resolver los problemas domésticos
4. eliminar el hambre y las desigualdades sociales
5. protestar por el uso de las armas atómicas

C. ¿Qué haría Ud. en Madrid? When you hear the corresponding number, tell what you would do in Madrid. Use the written cues.

MODELO: (*you hear*) uno   (*you see*) quedarse en un buen hotel →
(*you say*) Me quedaría en un buen hotel.

2. comunicarse en español
3. ir al Museo del Prado
4. conocer la ciudad
5. comer paella

D. ¡Entendiste mal! Make statements about your plans, using the written cues when you hear the corresponding numbers. Make any necessary changes or additions. When your friend Alicia misunderstands your statements, correct her. Follow the model.

MODELO: (*you see*) llegar / trece / junio →
(*you say*) UD.: Llegaré el trece de junio.
(*you hear*) ALICIA: ¿No dijiste que llegarías el tres?
(*you say*) UD.: No, te dije que llegaría el trece. Entendiste mal.

1. estar / bar / doce
2. estudiar / Juan
3. ir / vacaciones / junio
4. verte / casa

51. Hypothetical Situations: *What if . . . ?* • *Si* Clause Sentences

A. Los deseos de los amigos hispánicos

Paso 1. You will hear a series of statements that your Hispanic friends made regarding what they would like to do if certain conditions were true. Write the number of the statement below the appropriate drawing. ¡OJO! There is an extra statement.

a. _____   b. _____   c. _____

Paso 2. ¿Qué haría Ud.? Now pause and complete the following sentences according to your own preferences. You will be using the conditional tense. No answers will be given.

1. Si tuviera dinero, _____

2. Si pudiera, _____

3. Si me dieran un aumento de sueldo, _____

4. Si viviera en México, _____

5. Si tuviera más tiempo, _____

Now resume listening.

B. Situaciones. You will hear three brief situations. Circle the letter of the best reaction to each.

1. a. ...regresaría a casa en autobús.
   b. ...llamaría a la policía.

2. a. ...escribiría un cheque.
   b. ...me ofrecería a lavar los platos.

3. a. ...trataría de negociar con el líder del sindicato (*union*) laboral.
   b. ...despediría (*I would fire*) a todos los empleados.

C. Descripción: ¿Qué haría Ud.? You will hear a series of statements. Each will be said twice. Write the number of each statement next to the appropriate drawing. First, pause and look at the drawings.

a. _____   b. _____

c. _____   d. _____

e. _____   f. _____

D. Consejos. Imagine that your friend Pablo has a problem with his roommates. What would you do in his place? Answer, using the oral cues.

> MODELO: (*you hear*) llamar a mis padres → (*you say*) Si yo fuera Pablo, llamaría a mis padres.

1. ...   2. ...   3. ...   4. ...

E. Las finanzas. You will hear the following sentences. Restate each, using the conditional.

> MODELO: (*you see and hear*) No le ofrecerán el puesto a menos que tenga buenas
> recomendaciones. →
> (*you say*) Le ofrecerían el puesto si tuviera buenas recomendaciones.

1. No le harán el préstamo a menos que esté trabajando.
2. No ahorraré más dinero a menos que controle mis gastos.
3. No pagaré las cuentas antes de que reciba el cheque semanal.
4. No te cobrarán el cheque hasta que lo firmes.

A. De vacaciones en el extranjero. You will hear a brief paragraph describing a series of actions and events. Number the actions listed below from one to ten in the order in which they occur in the paragraph.

First, listen to the list of actions.

_____ aterrizar (*to land*) en Madrid

_____ hacer las maletas

_____ recoger los boletos

_____ despegar (*to take off*) otra vez

__9__ pasar por la aduana

__1__ visitar la agencia de viajes

_____ ir al hotel

_____ sentarse en la sección de fumar

_____ bajar del avión

__5__ hacer escala en Londres (*London*)

Now resume listening.

B. *Listening Passage:* La vida de los exiliados

Antes de escuchar. Pause and do the following prelistening exercise.

Entre las personas de diferentes nacionalidades hispánicas que viven en los Estados Unidos, los cubanos forman un grupo importante. Conteste las siguientes preguntas sobre la comunidad cubanoamericana.

1. ¿Dónde viven los cubanoamericanos, principalmente?

   _____

2. Muchos cubanos llegaron a los Estados Unidos dentro de un corto período de tiempo. ¿Por qué emigraron?

   _____

3. ¿Qué tipo de gobierno existe en Cuba hoy día? ¿Cómo se llama la persona que gobierna Cuba actualmente?

   _____

4. ¿Pueden los ciudadanos norteamericanos viajar libremente a Cuba?

   _____

Now resume listening.

Listening Passage. Now you will hear a passage about the immigration of a Cuban family to the United States. The following words appear in the passage.

por si fuera poco	*as if that were not bad enough*
el internado	*internship, residency*
el comercio	*business*
echamos de menos	*we miss, long for*
que en paz descanse	*may she rest in peace*

Después de escuchar. Circle the letter of the phrase that best completes each statement, based on the listening passage.

1. Esta familia, como muchas otras familias cubanas, llegó a los Estados Unidos...
   a. a principio de los años ochenta.
   b. hace poco.
   c. a principio de los años sesenta.
2. Emigraron porque...
   a. no estaban de acuerdo con el gobierno.
   b. no tenían trabajo.
   c. tenían problemas con la discriminación.
3. Al llegar a Florida...
   a. todo fue fácil para ellos.
   b. el esposo pudo encontrar trabajo como médico.
   c. fue necesario que el esposo tuviera dos trabajos.
4. Los padres todavía...
   a. echan de menos su país.
   b. quisieran vivir en la Cuba de Fidel Castro.
   c. piensan que fue un error salir de Cuba.

Now resume listening.

C. En el periódico: Viajes. The following ad appeared in a Mexican newspaper. You will hear a series of statements about the ad. Circle **C** or **F**. First, pause and scan the ad.

1. C F   2. C F   3. C F   4. C F

D. Y para terminar… Entrevista. You will hear a series of questions. Each will be said twice. Answer, based on your own experience. Pause and write the answers.

1. _____

2. _____

3. _____

4. _____

5. _____

6. _____

VIDEOTECA — Minidramas*

Paso 1. En la agencia de viajes. In this conversation, Lupe and Diego visit a travel agency. Read the conversation along with the speakers.

AGENTE: ¿Ya tienen alojamiento en Mérida?

LUPE: No, todavía no. Buscamos un hotel que sea decente, pero que tampoco sea muy caro. No tenemos el dinero para pagar un hotel de lujo.

AGENTE: Entiendo. Muy pocos estudiantes tienen mucho dinero. Bueno, les puedo ofrecer habitaciones en varios hoteles a precios muy razonables. A ver… ¿Cuándo piensan hacer el viaje?

DIEGO: La última semana de mayo.

AGENTE: Ajá… Eso va a estar un poco difícil. Casi todos los hoteles estarán completamente ocupados durante esa semana. Si viajaran una semana más tarde, encontrarían más habitaciones desocupadas.

LUPE: Bueno, está bien. Entonces, la primera semana de junio.

AGENTE: Excelente. Les puedo ofrecer dos habitaciones individuales con baño privado en el hotel Estrella del Mar. No es un hotel de lujo, pero es bueno y muy lindo. El precio por cada habitación es de 150 pesos por noche.

LUPE: Perfecto.

AGENTE: Y, ¿cuántos días piensan quedarse?

DIEGO: Unos cuatros o cinco días, nada más. Yo soy de California, y debo regresar pronto.

AGENTE: Muy bien. Tienen habitaciones reservadas para la primera semana de junio. ¿Sus nombres, por favor?

DIEGO: Sí, cómo no. Yo me llamo Diego González y la señorita es Guadalupe Carrasco.

AGENTE: Muy bien.

DIEGO: Gracias.

---

*This **Minidramas** video clip is available on the Video on CD to accompany *Puntos de partida* Seventh Edition.

Paso 2. Aplicación. Now you will hear a similar conversation, partially printed in your manual, in which you play the role of the **viajero.** Complete the conversation using the written cues. Pause and write the answers. Write out all numbers. First, listen to the cues for your conversation. ¡OJO! The cues are not in order.

        muchas gracias

        556

        la pensión María Cristina

        uno o dos meses

        aquí lo tiene

AGENTE: Pasaporte, por favor.

VIAJERO: _____.[1]

AGENTE: ¿En qué vuelo llegó?

VIAJERO: En el _____.[2]

AGENTE: Y, ¿cuánto tiempo piensa permanecer (*to remain*) en el país?

VIAJERO: Pienso quedarme _____.[3]

AGENTE: ¿Tiene una dirección aquí en la que se le pueda localizar?

VIAJERO: Sí, cómo no. Estaré en _____,[4] la Calle del Prado, número 27.

AGENTE: Está bien. Puede pasar.

VIAJERO: _____.[5]

PRUEBA CORTA

A. ¿Qué haría Ud. si... ? You will hear a series of questions. Answer, using cues chosen from the following list. First listen to the list. ¡OJO! There is an extra cue.

> confirmar las reservaciones
>
> declarar mis compras
>
> conseguir un pasaporte
>
> ir a la pastelería
>
> alojarme en un hotel de lujo
>
> ir a la oficina de correos

1. ...   2. ...   3. ...   4. ...   5. ...

B. Descripción: ¿Unos discos estupendos? You will hear a series of questions. Each will be said twice. Answer, based on the cartoon on page 203. Pause and write the answers. As you look at the cartoon and listen to the questions, keep in mind that the tourist in the drawing wants to go to Kiland, an imaginary country where Kiland is spoken. First, pause and look at the cartoon.

1. _____
2. _____
3. _____
4. _____
5. _____
6. _____

© Quino/Quipos

C. Y para terminar... Entrevista final. You will hear a series of questions, or situations followed by questions. Each will be said twice. Answer, based on your own experience. Model answers will be given for the last two questions. Pause and write the answers.

1. _____

2. _____

3. _____

4. _____

5. _____

_____

_____

_____

6. _____

_____

_____

_____

ANSWER KEY

CAPÍTULO 13

Vocabulario: Preparación

E. Poniendo las cosas en orden. Paso 2 *Possible answers:* 1. Junio es el sexto mes del año. (El sexto mes del año es junio.) 2. Agosto es el octavo mes del año. (El octavo mes del año es agosto.) 3. El primer día de la semana en el calendario hispánico es el lunes. (El lunes es el primer día de la semana en el calendario hispánico.)

Gramática

41 B. Se venden coches nuevos y usados a. 3 b. 2 c. 1.

Prueba corta

A. Apuntes *el nombre del museo:* el Museo del Pueblo; *el tipo de arte que se va a exhibir:* tejidos y objetos de cerámica auténticos; *la fecha en que se va a abrir el museo:* el lunes, 31 de julio; *el nombre del director del museo:* Arturo Rosa; *la hora de la recepción:* las 6 de la tarde; *¿Es necesario hacer reservaciones?:* no; *¿Va a ser posible hablar con algunos de los artistas?:* sí

CAPÍTULO 14

Pronunciación y ortografía

B. Dictado 1. *fosfato* 2. *atención* 3. *amoníaco* 4. *teología* 5. *oposición* 6. *fotografía* 7. *colección* 8. *arquitecta*

CAPÍTULO 15

Los hispanos hablan: Las relaciones sociales

Paso 2 *Here is a transcript of Eduardo's answer. Compare it to the summary that you wrote.*

Creo que una de las cosas más difíciles de aceptar al principio fue la falta de vida social. Generalmente, los latinoamericanos y los españoles dicen que extrañan el contacto social que hay en nuestros países. Aquí la gente se dedica mucho a su trabajo y usa el tiempo libre para estudiar o dedicarse a algún pasatiempo. Esto, naturalmente, casi no les deja tiempo libre para los amigos. Generalmente, la vida social en los países hispanos es más espontánea. Por ejemplo, es muy común que los amigos visiten sin avisar, lo cual aquí es mal visto por mucha gente.

Una diferencia grande que veo es la falta de contacto entre las generaciones. Generalmente, creo que hay mucha más interacción entre las diferentes generaciones en el mundo hispano. Por ejemplo, los niños participan en las actividades de la gente grande y van a todos lados, así también como los viejos.

También la necesidad de la vida privada de los estadounidenses es un concepto un poco incomprensible para nosotros. Cuando alguien de la familia de mi esposa viene a visitarnos de Europa, a veces se queda mucho tiempo en nuestra casa. A muchos amigos de los Estados Unidos, les parece insólito que no nos molesten estas largas visitas. En contraste, a nosotros los hispanos, nos parece insólito que estos amigos, a veces, pongan a sus propios padres en un hotel cuando estos los vienen a visitar.

Creo que, generalizando un poco, se puede decir que los estadounidenses son educados para ser independientes desde jóvenes. En contraste, los hispanos se mantienen más cerca de sus familias. Por ejemplo, no es nada raro que un hijo soltero de treinta años todavía viva con sus padres. Aquí en los Estados Unidos sólo conozco a una persona en esta situación.

CAPÍTULO 16

Vocabulario: Preparación

C. En busca de un puesto. Paso 1 *5:* tratar de caerle bien al entrevistador; *6:* aceptar el puesto y renunciar a mi puesto actual; *2:* pedirle una solicitud de empleo; *4:* ir a la entrevista; *3:* llenar la solicitud; *1:* llamar a la directora de personal

Pronunciación y ortografía

C. Dictado *The following words require a written accent:* 1. cobró 4. toqué 6. descríbemela 7. levántate 10. francés

E. Dictado 1. Creo *que* ese regalo es para *mí.* 2. Aquí *está tu té.* ¿*Qué* más quieres? 3. *Él* dijo *que te* iba a llamar a las ocho. 4. *Sí, mi* amigo *se* llama Antonio.

CAPÍTULO 17

Los hispanos hablan: Más sobre las ciudades hispanas

1. Hace que por la noche no haya nadie en las calles. 2. Hace que los adolescentes tomen más alcohol. 3. Por eso en las ciudades sólo hay menores de 18 años y mayores de 27.

Pronunciación y ortografía

C. La entonación. 1. Enero es el primer mes del año. 2. ¡No entiendo lo que me estás diciendo! 3. ¿Trabajaba en una tienda? 4. No olvides el diccionario la próxima vez, ¿eh? 5. Nació el catorce de abril de mil novecientos sesenta y uno. 6. ¿Adónde crees que vas a ir a estas horas de la noche?

D. Dictado 1. ¿Cuál es tu profesión? ¿Te pagan bien? 2. Tú no la conoces, ¿verdad? 3. ¿Prefiere Ud. que le sirva la comida en el patio? 4. ¡Qué ejercicio más fácil! 5. No sé dónde viven, pero sí sé su número de teléfono.

Prueba corta

A. Apuntes *el nombre de la candidata que perdió las elecciones:* Quejada; *el nombre del candidato que ganó las elecciones:* Sánchez; *el porcentaje de ciudadanos que votó por la candidata que perdió:* treinta (30) por ciento; *la cuestión principal de la campaña:* el medio ambiente

CAPÍTULO 18

Pronunciación y ortografía

D. Dictado 1. Cuando viajes a Madrid, no olvides tu cámara. 2. Mandaré la carta en cuanto compre sellos y un sobre. 3. Perdón, señora, ¿pudiera decirme dónde está la estación del metro? 4. ¡Dios mío! ¡No sabía que iba a costar tanto para hablar con un abogado! 5. Oye, Julia, ¿oíste las últimas noticias?

About the Author

María Sabló-Yates is a native of Panama. She holds a B.A. and an M.A. from the University of Washington (Seattle). She has taught at the University of Washington and Central Michigan University (Mt. Pleasant, Michigan), and is currently a lecturer at Delta College (University Center, Michigan). She is the author of previous editions of the *Puntos de partida* Laboratory Manual, of the first through sixth editions of the Laboratory Manual to accompany *¿Qué tal? An Introductory Course,* and of the *Puntos en breve* Laboratory Manual.